T0257960

Encyclopedia of Robust Control: Advanced Topics

Volume V

Encyclopedia of Robust Control: Advanced Topics
Volume V

Edited by **Zac Fredericks**

LANRYE
INTERNATIONAL

New Jersey

Published by Clanrye International,
55 Van Reypen Street,
Jersey City, NJ 07306, USA
www.clanryeinternational.com

Encyclopedia of Robust Control: Advanced Topics
Volume V
Edited by Zac Fredericks

International Standard Book Number: 978-1-63240-204-2 (Hardback)

Printed in the United States of America.

Contents

Preface

This book presents an elaborative account of the advancements made in robust control system. The purpose of this book is to provide exemplary models and significant challenges faced in the domain of robust control design and applications. It comprises of research and discussion on some breakthrough applications in this domain such as sliding mode, robust PID, H-infinity, etc. These techniques have given new dimension to this genre of science and broadened the application spectra to even non-engineering systems. The book comprises of research chapters grouped under three sections; namely, "Distillation and Food Industry Applications", "Power Plant and Power System Control" and "New Trends in Robust Control Applications".

Significant researches are present in this book. Intensive efforts have been employed by authors to make this book an outstanding discourse. This book contains the enlightening chapters which have been written on the basis of significant researches done by the experts.

Finally, I would also like to thank all the members involved in this book for being a team and meeting all the deadlines for the submission of their respective works. I would also like to thank my friends and family for being supportive in my efforts.

Editor

Part 1

Distillation Process Control and Food Industry Applications

Loop Transfer Recovery for the Grape Juice Concentration Process

Nelson Aros Oñate[1] and Graciela Suarez Segali[2]
[1]Departamento de Ingeniería Eléctrica, Facultad de Ingeniería,
Universidad de La Frontera, Temuco,
[2]Departamento de Ingeniería Química, Facultad de Ingeniería,
Universidad Nacional de San Juan, San Juan,
[1]Chile
[2]Argentina

1. Introduction

It is necessary to ensure the quality of concentrated, because it is highly used in the food industry in juices, drinks, sweets, etc. Its application is in full development because it can compete with any other constituent, it is a natural product, and considering that is a very important regional industry, marketing greatly affects the regional economy. Because of this, that it is extremely important to ensure quality and quantity concentrate.

Argentina is one of the principal producers and exporters of concentrated clear grape juices in the world. They are produced mainly in the provinces of San Juan and Mendoza (Argentine Republic) from virgin grape juice and in the major part from sulfited grape juices. The province of San Juan's legislation establishes that a portion of the grapes must be used for making concentrated clear grape juices. This product has reached a high level of penetration in the export market and constitutes an important and growing productive alternative.

An adequate manufacturing process, a correct design of the concentrate plants and an appropriate evaluation of their performance will facilitate optimization of the concentrated juices quality parameters. The plant efficiency is obtained from knowledge of the physics properties of the raw material and products. These properties are fundamental parameters that are used in the designing and calculations on all the equipment used and also in the control process.

The multi-step evaporation (M-SE) is the most important unit operation used in the food industry to concentrate juices of grapes and apples. Even when the main objective of this process is to produce a concentrated product, it should also possess certain organoleptic properties that are critical with respect to its quality and acceptance grade by the customers.

Product requirements and the complex characteristics of the process such as non-linear behavior, input and output constraints, time delays and loop interactions justify the use of an advanced control system.

The rheological behavior influences directly the heat transfer coefficient (Pilati, 1998; Rubio, 1998) and therefore its knowledge is essential together with the influence of temperature on its value. The juices (concentrate and intermediate products) physical properties, such as density, viscosity, boiling point elevation, specific heat and coefficient of thermal expansion, are affected by their solid content and their temperature. For this reason, it is necessary to know the physical properties values, as a function of the temperature and the solids content, during the manufacture process.

The principal solids constituents of clear grape juices are sugars and its concentration affects directly the density, viscosity and refraction index. Tables were developed to relate reducing sugar contents, refractometric values and density of pure solutions, at 20°C, for concentrate ranges from 0% to 85% w/w and sucrose solutions for different range concentrations 0% to 70% and a temperature range from 0 to 100°C (AOAC, 1995).

Barbieri (1980) worked with white concentrated clear grape juice in a falling film multiple effect evaporators. They obtained 18.2, 27.3, 38.6, 48.6 and 64.6°Brix samples. They measured density, viscosity and boiling point elevation as a function of soluble solids concentration and temperature. They presented the results in plots with predictive equations for the properties which were studied.

Di Leo (1988) published density, refraction index and viscosity data for a rectified concentrated grape juice and an aqueous solution of a 1:1 glucose/levulose mixture, for a soluble solids concentrate range from 60 to 71% (in increments of 0.1%) and 20°C.

Pandolfi, (1991) studied physical and chemical characteristics of grape juices produced in Mendoza and San Juan provinces, Argentina. They determined density at 20°C in sulfited grape juices of 20–22°Bx and concentrated grape juices of 68–72 °Bx. They obtained no information on intermediate concentrations or other temperatures.

In general, the clarified juice concentrates have a Newtonian behavior (Ibarz 1993; Rao 1984; Saenz, 1986; Saravacos, 1970), although some authors have found a small pseudoplasticity in the flow of grape concentrates, from the variety Concord (Vitis labrusca) for concentrations above 55°Bx. It has been attributed to the presence of some soluble solids, mostly pectins and tartrates (Moressi, 1984; Saravacos, 1970). Other authors consider the juice concentrates as Newtonian, even at high soluble solids concentrations of 60–70°Bx (Barbieri, 1980; Di Leo, 1988; Rao, 1984; Schwartz, 1986).

If we analyze the temperature influence on this product's viscosity, it seems which is directly related with soluble solids concentration; the higher the concentration, the higher is the variation of the viscosity with temperature (Rao, 1984; Saravacos, 1970; Bayindirli, 1992; Crapiste, 1988; Constela, 1989).

Schwartz (1986) determined clear grape juice viscosity at 20, 30, 40 and 50°C, for 30, 40, 50, 60 and 66% soluble solids concentration, but did not publish the experimental data. These authors presented the correlation constants values of the Arrhenius equation for temperature, a potential and an exponential model between viscosity and solids concentration for each temperature studied.

The physical property that represents density change in a material, due to an increase in its temperature at constant pressure, is called the coefficient of thermal expansion. The importance of this parameter can be seen in the effect that density change in the product can have over heat transfer during the process. There is not publish data on the coefficient of the thermal expansion for grape juices and their concentrates. The existing information did not cover all the temperature and concentration ranges that are used in the evaporation process, or else cover to pure sugar solutions, or grape juices of other varieties and/ or originating in other geographical zones.

On the other hand, sensitivity theory, originally developed by Bode (Bode, 1945), has regained considerable importance, due to the recent work developed by many researchers. This research effort has made evident the fundamental role played by sensitivity theory to highlight design tradeoffs and to analyze, qualitatively, control system performance. One of the fields of active research is the analysis of different design strategies from to point of view of sensibility properties. From this perspective one of the richest strategies is the optimal linear quadratic regulator (LQR). It is well known that the sensitivity of a LQR Loop is always less than one (Anderson, 1971). However, it is also known that when the state is not directly fed back but reconstructed through an observer this property is normally lost. In fact, the situation more general, since the recovery problem appears every time a control design based on state feedback design is implemented through observers.

It has been shown that when the plant is minimum-phase, a properly design Kalman filter provides complete recovery of the input sensitivity achieved by LQR will full state feedback (Doyle, 1979). Either full or partial-order filter may be used. On the other hand it is also known that it is generally impossible to obtain LTR if we use observers for a plant with unstable zeros. An exception to this rule arises in MIMO Systems when input directions are orthogonal to non-minimum phase zero directions (Zhang, 1990).

On the other hand, it is known that the only way to obtain full recovery for a general non-minimum-phase plant is to increase the number of independent measurements. This idea has been suggested in conjunction with the use of reduced-order Kalman filters (Friedland, 1989).

The additional independent measurements are used to modify the structure of the open loop transfer function. The standard LTR procedure is applied and it is the implemented combining the resulting full-order Kalman filter with the additional measurements optimally weighted. The idea is obviously to feed back only a subset of the state, for that reason we speak of 'partial' state feedback. The basic approach assumes that all states are available for measurement. However in this paper, it is also shown how to do L_2 - optimization on the amount of recovery of the input sensitivity when a given set of measurements is available. This situation is important since in many additional situations there are limitations regarding which variables can be measured and how many additional sensors can be used. This connects the recovery theory with the issue of additional measurements raised in the context of practical ideas for control design, as illustrated in the control of the inverted pendulum; see (Middleton, 1990). The theory supporting the proposal is built on some import technical results which allow for computing the amount of recovery, as a function of frequency (Zhang, 1990).

2. Process description

Figure 1 show the input and output streams in a vertical generic effect evaporator with long tubes. The solution to be concentrated circulates inside the tubes, while the steam, used to heat the solution, circulates inside the shell around the tubes. The evaporator operates in parallel mode. The solution to be concentrated and the steam are fed to the first effect by the bottom and by the upper section of the shell, respectively. Later on, the concentrated solution from the first effect is pumped to the bottom of the second effect, and so on until the fourth effect. On the other hand, the vaporized solvent from each effect serve as heater in the next one. Each effect has a baffle in the upper section that serves as a drops splitter for the solution dragged by the vapor. The vapor from the fourth effect is sent to a condenser and leaves the process as a liquid. Finally, the solution leaving the fourth effect attains the desired concentration and the solution is sent to a storage tank.

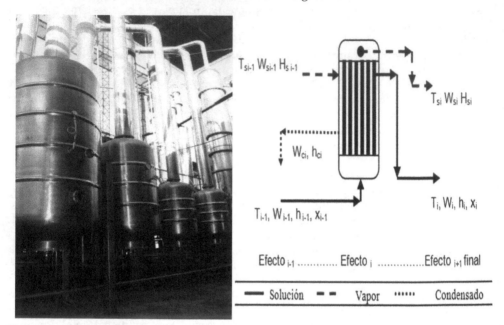

Fig. 1. Photo of evaporator and scheme of effect i in the four-stage evaporator flow sheet. $i = 1, \cdots, 4$.

3. Phenomenological model

Stefanov (2005) has developed a rigorous model with distributed parameters based on partial differential equations for a falling-film evaporator, in which the open-loop stability of the model to disturbances is verified. On the other hand, various methods have been proposed in order to obtain reduced-order models to solve such problems (Armaou, 2002; Camacho, 1999; El-Farra, 2003; Zheng, 2002). However, there is not a general framework yet, which assure an effective implementation of a control strategy in a multiple effect evaporator.

In practice, due to a lack of measurements to characterize the distributed nature of the process and actuators to implement such a solution, the control of systems represented by PDE in the grape juice evaporator, is carried out neglecting the spatial variation of parameters and applying lumped systems methods. However, a distributed parameters model must be developed in order to be used as a real plant to test advance control strategies by simulation.

The mathematical model of the evaporator is obtained by application of the mass and energy balances to each effect:

a. Global mass balances in each effect:

$$\frac{dM_i}{dt} = W_{i-1} - W_{si} - W_i \tag{1}$$

in this equations W_i, $i = 1, \cdots, 4$, are the solution mass flow rates leaving the effects 1 to 4, respectively. W_0 is the input mass flow rate that is fed to the equipment. W_{si}, $i = 1, \cdots, 4$, are the vapor mass flow rates coming from effects 1 to 4, respectively. dM_i/dt, $i = 1, \cdots, 4$, represent the solution mass variation with the time for each effect.

b.   Solute mass balances for each effect:

$$\frac{d(M_i X_i)}{dt} = W_{i-1} X_{i-1} - W_i X_i \qquad (2)$$

where, X_i, $i = 1, \cdots, 4$, are the concentrations of the solutions that leave the effects 1 to 4, respectively. X_0 is the concentration of the fed solution.

c.   Energy balances:

$$\frac{d(M_i h_i)}{dt} = W_{i-1} h_{i-1} - W_i h_i - W_{si} H_{si} + A_i U_i (T_{si-1} - T_i) \qquad (3)$$

where, h_i, $i = 1, \cdots, 4$, are the liquid stream enthalpies that leave the corresponding effects, h_0 is the feed solution enthalpy, and H_{si}, $i = 1, \cdots, 4$, are the vapor stream enthalpies that leave the corresponding effects and, A_i represents the heat transfer area in each effect. The model also includes algebraic equations. The vapor flow rates for each effect are calculated neglecting the following terms: energy accumulation and the heat conduction across the tubes. Therefore:

$$W_{si} = \frac{U_i A_i (T_{si-1} - T_i)}{H_{si-1} - h_{ci}} \qquad (4)$$

For each effect, the enthalpy can be estimated as a function of temperatures and concentrations (Perry, 1997), where:

$$H_{si} = 2509.2888 + 1.6747 \cdot T_{si} \qquad (5)$$

$$h_{ci} = 4.1868 \cdot T_{si} \qquad (6)$$

$$C_{pi} = 0.80839 - 4.3416 \cdot 10^{-3} \cdot X_i + 5.6063 \cdot 10^{-4} \cdot T_i \qquad (7)$$

$$h_i = 0.80839 \cdot T_i - 4.3416 \cdot 10^{-3} \cdot X_i T_i + 2.80315 \cdot 10^{-4} \cdot T_i^2 \qquad (8)$$

T_i, $i = 1, \cdots, 4$, are the solution temperatures in each effect, and T_{s0} is the vapor temperature that enters to the first effect. T_{si}, $i = 1, \cdots, 4$, are the vapor temperatures that leave each effect. The heat transfer coefficients are:

$$U_i = \frac{490 \cdot \left(D^{0.57} \cdot W_{si}^{3.6/L} \right)}{\mu_i^{0.25} \cdot \Delta T_i^{0.1}} \qquad (9)$$

where, the Arrhenius type equation for the viscosity is:

$$\mu_i = \mu_0 \cdot e^{\frac{A \cdot X_i}{100 - B \cdot X_i}} \qquad (10)$$

$$A = C_1 + \frac{C_2}{T_i} \qquad (11)$$

$$B = C_3 + C_4 \cdot T_i \qquad (12)$$

The global heat-transfer coefficients are directly influenced by the viscosity and indirectly by the temperature and concentration in each effect. The constants C_1, C_2, C_3, C_4 depend on the type of product to be concentrated (Kaya, 2002).

Although the model could be improved, the accuracy achieved is enough to incorporate a control structure.

4. Standard LTR procedure

4.1 The basic approach

Consider a linear time-invariant system with state characterization is given by:

$$\dot{x} = Ax(t) + Bu(t) + v(t) \tag{13}$$

$$y(t) = Cx(t) \tag{14}$$

where $x(t) \in R^n$, $u(t) \in R^m$, $v(t) \in R^m$, $y(t) \in R^l$, A, B and C have consistent dimensions. We further assume that is a wide sense stationary process with covariance matrix Q.

We then have that the system transfer matrix function is given by:

$$G(s) = C(sI - A)^{-1}B \tag{15}$$

If the state feedback law:

$$u(t) = -Fx(t) \tag{16}$$

is applied, we obtain an input sensitivity function is given by:

$$S_0(s) = |I + H(s)|^{-1} \tag{17}$$

where:

$$H(s) = F(sI - A)^{-1}B \tag{18}$$

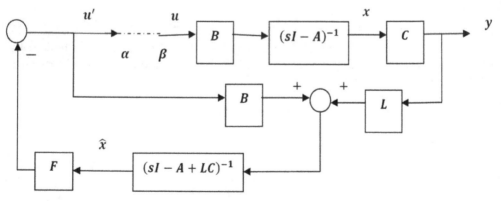

Fig. 2. Optimal LQG Scheme

The complete LQG control system appears in figure 2. The question of loop transfer recovery deals with the problem of keeping the sensitivity given in equation (17) when the control law is implemented with an observer of the state (Stein, 1987), i.e. the control $u(t)$ is generated trough:

$$u(t) = -F\hat{x}(t) \tag{19}$$

where $\hat{x}(t)$ is the output of a state observer is given by:

$$\dot{\hat{x}}(t) = A\hat{x}(t) + Bu(t) + L\{y(t) - C\hat{x}(t)\} \tag{20}$$

If the observer is designed using standard Kalman filter theory, then the filter gain L satisfies:

$$L = \Sigma C^T \tag{21}$$

where Σ is the symmetric nonnegative definite solution of the algebraic Riccati equation:

$$A\Sigma + \Sigma A^T - \Sigma C^T C \Sigma + Q = 0 \tag{22}$$

In this case the input sensitivity is given by:

$$S_{obs}(s) = \{I + [I + F(sI - A + LC)^{-1}B]^{-1}F(sI - A + LC)^{-1}LC(sI - A)^{-1}B\}^{-1} \tag{23}$$

After some elementary matrix manipulation, we obtain:

$$S_{obs}(s) = S_o(s)\{I + F(sI - A + LC)^{-1}B\} \tag{24}$$

Or

$$S_{obs}(s) = S_o(s)\{I + F\phi[B - L(sI - A + LC)^{-1}C\phi B]\} \tag{25}$$

where:

$$\phi = (sI - A)^{-1} \tag{26}$$

It becomes then sensible to measure the amount of recovery by the relative sensitivity error (Turan, 1990) given by:

$$E(s) = S_o^{-1}\{S_{obs} - S_o\} \tag{27}$$

Using the equation (25) we obtain:

$$E(s) = F(sI - A + LC)^{-1}B \tag{28}$$

It has been shown (Doyle, 1979) that if $G(s)$ is a minimum-phase transfer matrix then complete recovery, i.e. $E(s) = 0$, can be achieved provided that:
• We first augment equation (13) to read:

$$\dot{x} = Ax(t) + B\{u(t) + Uw(t)\} + v(t) \tag{29}$$

where $w(t) \in R^m$ is a wide sense stationary process with covariance matrix q^2I and U is a unitary matrix. We assume that $v(t)$ and $w(t)$ are uncorrelated.
• We then solve the Riccati equation (10) substituting Q by $Q + qBB^T$
• We finally let $q \rightarrow \infty$. In this case $L(q) \rightarrow qBU$.
The above procedure yields:

$$S_{obs}(s) \rightarrow S_o(s) \tag{30}$$

4.2 A factorized form of non-minimum phase plants

It is known that a transfer matrix function $G(s)$ with zeros in C^+ (right-half complex plane) can be described as:

$$G(s) = G_m(s)B_z(s) \tag{31}$$

where $B_z(s)$ is a stable all-pass factor with zeros located at the non-minimum-phase zeros of $G(s)$ and satisfies $B_z(s)B_z^T(s) = I$.

One possible way to build the factorization of equation (31) has been proposed by Enns (Enns, 1984; Zhang, 1990). The main result can be stated as follows.

Lemma 2.1 Given a transfer matrix function $G(s) = C(sI - A)^{-1}B$ with $l \in C^+$ zeros (including multiplicity), $z_1, \cdots, z_l$, there exists a matrix B_m such that:

$$G(s) = C(sI - A)^{-1}B_m B_z(s) \tag{32}$$

where $G(s) = C(sI - A)^{-1}B_m$ is minimum-phase and $B_z(s)$ is an all-pass stable matrix factor. We then have that:

$$B_z(s) = B_{z_1}(s)B_{z_2}(s) \cdots B_{z_l}(s) \tag{33}$$

and

$$B_m = B_m^l \tag{34}$$

where, for $i = 1, \cdots, l$:

$$B_{z_i}(s) = I - \frac{2\Re\{z_i\}}{s + z_i^*} \eta_i \eta_i^H \tag{35}$$

and

$$B_m^i = B_m^{i-1} - 2\Re\{z_i\}\xi_i \eta_i^H \tag{36}$$

with $B_m^0 = B$, $G_m^i(s) := C(sI - A)^{-1}B_m^i$.

The symbol $\Re\{.\}$ denotes the real part operator. The vectors η_i and ξ_i are solutions of:

$$\begin{bmatrix} z_i I - A & -B_m^{i-1} \\ -C & 0 \end{bmatrix} \begin{bmatrix} \xi_i \\ \eta_i \end{bmatrix} = 0 \tag{37}$$

□ □ □

We also have the following useful results:

Lemma 2.2 For SISO systems, the sequence $\{B_m^k\}$ can be alternatively computer as:

$$B_m^k = \underbrace{\prod_{i=1}^k \{I - 2\Re(z_i)(z_i I - A)^{-1}\}}_{\equiv M_k} B \tag{38}$$

Proof:

A1.- $B_m^0 = B$

A2.- From (36) $B_m^1 = B_m^0 - 2\Re\{z_1\}\xi_1 \eta_1^H$.

But for SISO systems $\eta_1 = \eta_2 = \cdots = 1$

and from (37) $\xi_1 = (z_1 I - A)^{-1}B_m^0$

therefore $B_m^1 = \underbrace{\{I - 2\Re(z_1)(z_1 I - A)^{-1}\}}_{\equiv M_1} B$

A3.- From (36) $B_m^k = B_m^{k-1} - 2\Re\{z_k\}\xi_k$. But for SISO systems $\eta_k = 1$, and from (37) we have that $B_m^k = \{I - 2\Re(z_k)(z_kI - A)^{-1}\}B_m^{k-1}$ then if (37) is satisfied for $k - 1$, the result follows.

□ □ □

Corollary:

$$\xi_k = (z_kI - A)^{-1}M_{k-1}B \tag{39}$$

$$M_0 = I \tag{40}$$

$$M_1 = I - 2\Re(z_1)(z_1I - A)^{-1} \tag{41}$$

□ □ □

Theorem 2.1 Consider a non-minimum-phase system (A, B, C), and its minimum-phase counterpart (A, B_m, C), with B_m computed according to **lemma 2.1**. Let L and L_m be the optimal observer gains for these two systems, then $L_m = L$.
Proof: See Zhang & Freudenberg (Zhang, 1990).

4.3 Loop transfer recovery and non-minimum phase plants

Assume now that $G(s)$ is a non-minimum phase plant and that it is factorized as in equation (33). If the standard LTR procedure is applied to recover the input sensitivity, then when $q \to \infty$ the sensitivity function satisfies:

$$S_{obs}(s) = S_o(s)\{I + E(s)\} \tag{42}$$

where

$$E(s) := F(sI - A)^{-1}\{B - qB_mW(I + qC\phi B_mW)^{-1}C\phi B_mB_z(s)\} \tag{43}$$

then

$$E(s) = F(sI - A)^{-1}\{B - B_mB_z(s)\} \tag{44}$$

It has been also shown that:

$$E(s) = E^i(s) = \sum_{k=1}^{l} \frac{2\Re\{z_k\}}{s+z_k^*} F\xi_k\eta_k^H B_z^{k-1}(s) \tag{45}$$

From equation (44) it is evident that for this type of plants the amount of recovery at a frequency w depends on the value of $\|E(jw)\|$, where $\|.\|$ is a suitable norm. As in equation (41), $E(s)$ corresponds to the error of the sensitivity in loop with the LTR observer.
The results of the previous two sections can be appreciated if we consider a SISO system with one zero in $s = z \in R^+$. If the standard LTR procedure is applied we have that:

$$\lim_{q \to ss} S_{obs}(s) = S_o(s)\left\{1 + \frac{2z}{s+z}H(z)\right\} \tag{46}$$

where

$$H(z) = F(zI - A)^{-1}B \tag{47}$$

One can then notice that if $|H(z)|$ is small, i.e. when the LQR design bandwidth is small in comparison with the magnitude of the C^+ zero, then the recovery is almost complete. This case will be also the situation for high frequencies since the factor $\frac{2z}{s+z}$ is low-pass filter. The sensitivity resulting from a LQR/LTR applied to a non-minimum phase plant is very significant at low frequencies and decreases as the frequency increases. The inability of the LQR/LTR scheme to recover sensitivity is consistent with some fundamental design tradeoffs for non-minimum phase systems (Freudenberg, 1988).

4.4 LTR procedure with partial state feedback (LTR/PSF)

If we assume that, apart from the system output, there is one or more independent measurements, we can implement a control system originally designed to work with state with state feedback via a mixture of observed and measured states (Aros, 1991). We propose to use the scheme shown in figure 3, where Γ is a diagonal matrix with nonzero diagonal entries for the corresponding measures states. It then becomes clear that $\Gamma = 0$ corresponds to the standard LTR scheme and $\Gamma = I$ corresponds to the optimal regulator with full state feedback.

A key result to describe the degree of recovery in the non-minimum phase case is given in the next lemma.

Lemma 3.1 Assume that the plant $G(s) = C(sI - A)^{-1}B$ in non-minimum phase with $l \in C^+$ zeros and factorized according to lemma 2.1. Then if we use a LTR/PSF scheme and we let $q \rightarrow \infty$ the sensitivity function is given by:

$$S_\Gamma(s) = S_o(s)\{I + \sum_{k=1}^{l} F(I - \Gamma)\xi_k\eta_k^H W_k(s)\} \qquad (53)$$

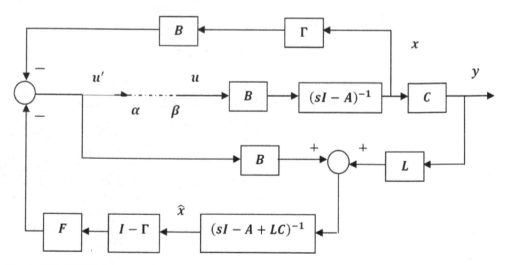

Fig. 3. LTR/PSF scheme.

where:

$$W_k(s) = \frac{2\Re e(z_k)}{s+z_k^*} B_z^{k-1}(s) \qquad (54)$$

$$B_z^{k-1}(s) = \prod_{i=1}^{k} B_{z_i}(s) \qquad (55)$$

$$B_{z_i}(s) = \frac{-s+z_i}{s+z_i^*} \tag{56}$$

Proof: Straightforward on using lemma 2.1 and equation (45).

□ □ □

Remark 3.1 For SISO systems $\eta_k = 1 \; \forall k$ and consequently (53) simplifies to:

$$S_{\Gamma}(s) = S_o(s)\{I + \sum_{k=1}^{l} F(I - \Gamma)\xi_k W_k(s)\} \tag{57}$$

Sufficient and necessary conditions for full recovery in SISO systems are given in the next theorem:

Theorem 3.1 Assume that a plant with transfer function $G(s)$ has $l \in C^+$ zeros denoted by $z_1, \cdots, z_l$. We apply the LTR/PSF procedure we obtain $E_{\Gamma}(s) = 0$, if $F(I - \Gamma)$ is orthogonal to ξ_k for $k = 1, 2, \cdots, l$ when $q \rightarrow \infty$.

Proof:

i. Sufficiency: straightforward on inspection of equation (53).

ii. Necessity: consider equation (57). We first notice that given the fact that functions $W_k(s)$ form a set of linearly independent functions, the only way to nullify the sum $\forall s$ is that the scalar $F(I - \Gamma)\xi_k$ be made equal to zero $\forall k$.

□ □ □

The user must then choose (if possible) the matrix Γ to satisfy the orthogonality condition in theorem 3.1. Equivalently, Γ must satisfy:

$$FT\zeta_k = F\xi_k \quad k = 1, 2, \cdots, l \tag{58}$$

The computation of Γ is given the next lemma.

Lemma 3.2 Consider a SISO plant as in theorem 3.1. If the LTR/PSF scheme is applied measuring, apart from the output, states $x_1, x_2 \cdots, x_\lambda$ then we obtain full recovery of the sensitivity if there exist $\gamma_1, \gamma_2 \cdots, \gamma_\lambda$, with $\Gamma = diag\{\gamma_1, \gamma_2, \cdots, \gamma_\lambda, 0, \cdots, 0\}$, satisfying:

$$\begin{bmatrix} \alpha_{1_1} & \cdots & \alpha_{\lambda_1} \\ \vdots & \ddots & \vdots \\ \alpha_{1_l} & \cdots & \alpha_{\lambda_l} \end{bmatrix} \begin{bmatrix} \gamma_1 \\ \vdots \\ \gamma_\lambda \end{bmatrix} = \begin{bmatrix} \sum_{i=1}^{n} \alpha_{i_1} \\ \vdots \\ \sum_{i=1}^{n} \alpha_{i_l} \end{bmatrix} \tag{59}$$

where

$$\alpha_{i_k} = f_i \xi_{k_i}; \quad i = 1, 2, \cdots, n \tag{60}$$

$$F = [f_1 \quad f_2 \quad \cdots \quad f_n] \tag{61}$$

$$\xi_\kappa = [\xi_{k_1} \quad \xi_{k_2} \quad \cdots \quad \xi_{k_n}]^T \tag{62}$$

Proof: By straight substitution.

□ □ □

Remark 3.2 From equation (53) it appears that full recovery is obtained $\forall \Gamma$ if η_k and ξ_k are orthogonal. This it shows that the LTR/PSF scheme maintains the standard LTR property claimed in Wall (Wall, 1980) and proved in Zhang (Zhang, 1990).

Remark 3.3 A complete analysis of the conditions the existence of none, one or an infinite number of solutions is out of the scope of this work, but some insight can be gained on analyzing the one RHP zero case and L_2 optimization. Both topics will be addressed below.

Theorem 3.2 Consider a scalar plant with transfer function $G(s)$ and one RHP zero located at $s = z$. If the LTR/PSF is applied measuring the input and one additional state variable (not proportional to the output) then $S_\Gamma(s) \longrightarrow S_o(s)$ when $q \longrightarrow \infty$.
Proof:
From (50) and (46), we can write:

$$\lim_{q \to ss} S_\Gamma(s) = S_o(s) \left\{ 1 + \frac{2z}{s+z^*} H(z) - \frac{2z}{s+z^*} H'(z) \right\} \tag{63}$$

where $H(s)$ is given in equation (47) and

$$H'(z) = F\Gamma(zI - A)^{-1}B \tag{64}$$

Without loss of generality we can assume that the state variable being fed back is $x_1(t)$. We can thus express Γ as:

$$\Gamma = \gamma\Gamma' \tag{65}$$

where

$$\Gamma' = diag\{1, 0, \cdots, 0\} \tag{66}$$

then full recovery is obtained if γ is chosen to satisfy:

$$\gamma == \frac{F(zI-A)^{-1}B}{F\Gamma'(zI-A)^{-1}B} \tag{67}$$

Remark 3.4 On examining equation (67) we note:
1.   If the output is proportional to x_1 there is not solution for γ since then $F\Gamma'(zI - A)^{-1}B = 0$. It certainly agrees with intuition, since nothing can be gained by measuring twice the same variable.
2.   There is not solution either when $F\Gamma' = 0$. This case also is intuitive since this situation corresponds to a control law where $x_1(t)$ was not required to be fed back.
These results also apply, mutatis mutandis, to MIMO systems, with the additional complexity which comes from the directionality properties of multivariable systems.

L_2 Optimization

When the designer don't have freedom to choose which state variable can be measured, due either to technical or economical reasons, then the feedback gains for the additional available measurements can be computed by solving an optimization problem. The simplest optimization problem can be posed in L_2. We examine that case for SISO systems.
Assume first that we measure and feed back the state variables $x_1(t), x_2(t), \cdots, x_\lambda(t)$ with gains $[\gamma_1, \gamma_2 \cdots, \gamma_\lambda]^T$. Then the L_2 optimization problem consists in finding a vector γ^o satisfying:

$$\gamma^o = \arg \min_{\gamma \in \Re^\lambda} J(\gamma) \tag{68}$$

where

$$J = \int_0^\infty |E_\Gamma(jw)|^2 \, dw \tag{69}$$

$$J = \int_0^\infty \left\| G_1(jw) + \gamma^T G_2(jw) \right\|^2 \, dw \tag{70}$$

with

$$G_1(jw) = F(jwI - A + LC)^{-1}B \qquad (71)$$

$$\gamma^T G_2(jw) = F\Gamma(jwI - A + LC)^{-1}B \qquad (72)$$

This problem has a unique solution if $G(jw)$ is not identical to zero. This unique solution is given by:

$$\gamma^o = -\left[\int_0^\infty G_2(jw)[G_2^*(jw)]^T dw\right]^{-1} \Re\left\{\int_0^\infty G_1(jw)G_2^*(jw)dw\right\} \qquad (73)$$

for $\lambda = 1$ equation (73) becomes:

$$\gamma^o = -\frac{\Re\left\{\int_0^\infty G_1(jw)G_2^*(jw)dw\right\}}{\int_0^\infty \|G_2(jw)\|^2 dw} \qquad (74)$$

5. Simulatinos results

5.1 Open loop
In figure 4, it shows the response of open loop system, when making a disturbance in one of the manipulated variables such as power flow; it represents the temperature of the first effect and concentration effect of the fourth output.

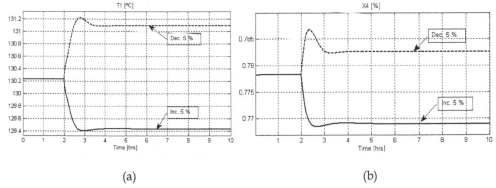

(a)   (b)

Fig. 4. Behavior of the concentration in the evaporator to a change of a step in the flow of food (up 5% - decrease of 5%)

In figure 5, it shows the response of open loop system, when making a disturbance in the steam temperature is the other manipulated variable; it represents the temperature of the first effect and concentration effect of the fourth output.
In figure 6, it shows the response of open loop system, when performing a step in one of the shocks as the concentration of power; it represents the temperature of the first effect and concentration effect of the fourth output.
In Figure 7, it shows the response of open loop system, when performing a step in the temperature of the food which is the other perturbations of the system; it represents the temperature of the first effect and concentration effect of the fourth output.

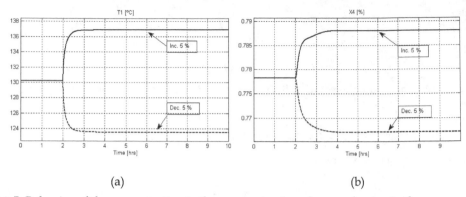

(a)   (b)

Fig. 5. Behavior of the concentration in the evaporator to a change of a step in the temperature of steam power (up 5% - decrease of 5%)

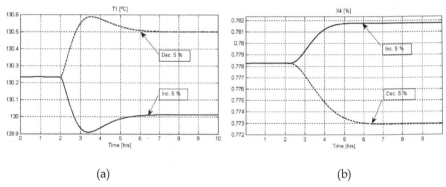

(a)   (b)

Fig. 6. Behavior of the concentration in the evaporator to a change of a step in the concentration of power (increase of 5% - decrease of 5%)

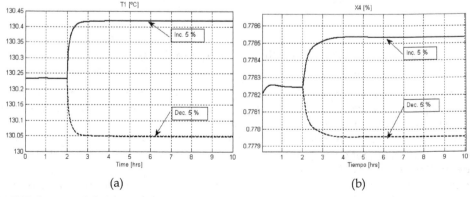

(a)   (b)

Fig. 7. Behavior of the concentration in the evaporator to a change of a step in the temperature of the input solution (5% increase - decrease of 5%)

5.2 Close loop

Controlled system response for optimal regulator, whereas white noise disturbances, as well as step-like variation to the inlet concentration to 50, and then a step 100 is added to the feed temperature at the entrance.

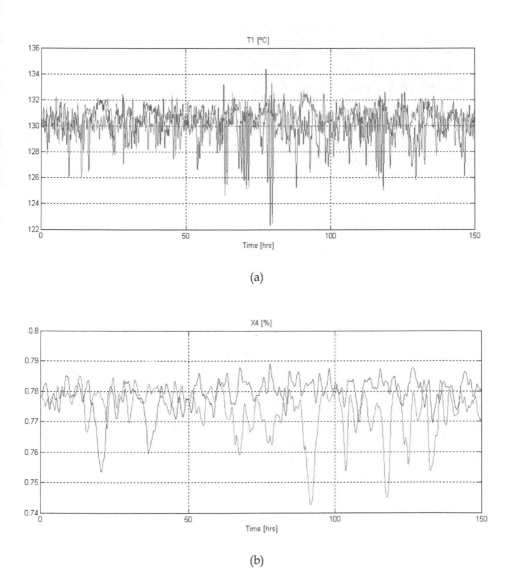

(a)

(b)

Fig. 8. Controlled system response to changes in the shocks in type of step and white noise (blue for changes of +5% - green changes -5%)

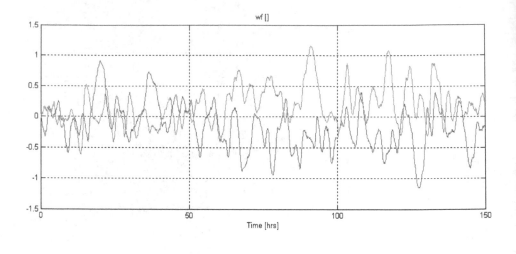

(a)

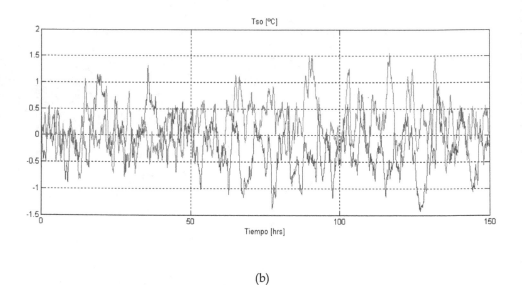

(b)

Fig. 9. Efforts to control the controlled system to changes in the shocks in type of step and white noise (blue for changes of +5% - green changes -5%)

5.3 LQG- design

Controlled system response for optimal regulator, whereas white noise disturbances, as well as like step variation of 5% for the inlet concentration to 50 and then to 100 adds a step is 5% of the feed temperature at the entrance.

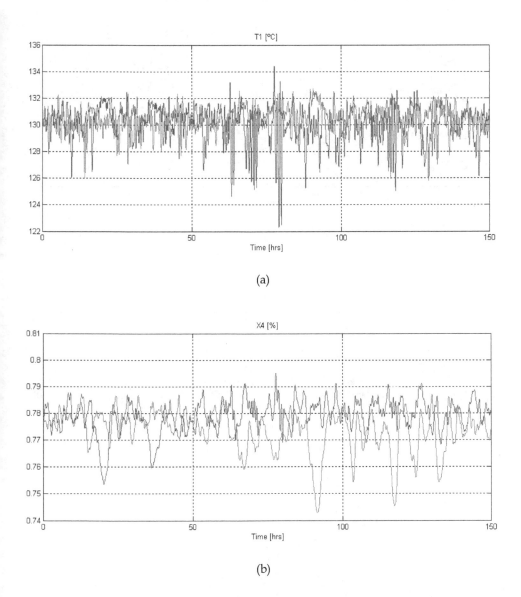

(a)

(b)

Fig. 10. LQG controlled system response to changes in the type shocks of step and white noise (blue for changes of +5% - green changes -5%)

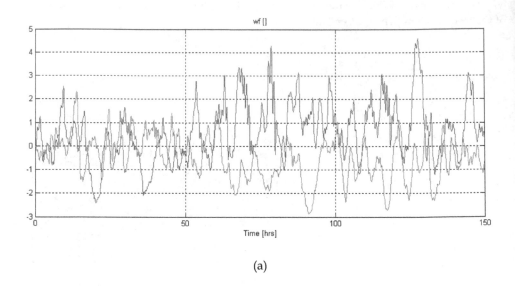

(a)

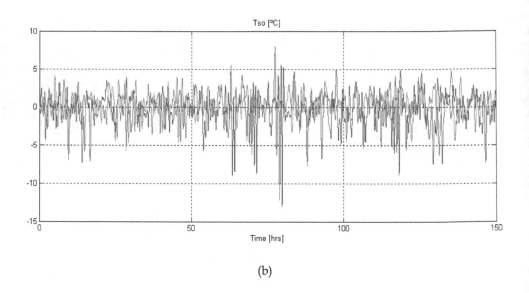

(b)

Fig. 11. Control efforts for the LQG-controlled system to changes in the type shocks of step and white noise (blue for changes of +5% - green changes -5%)

5.4 LQG/LTR

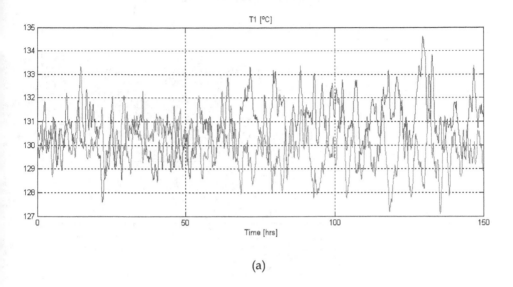

(a)

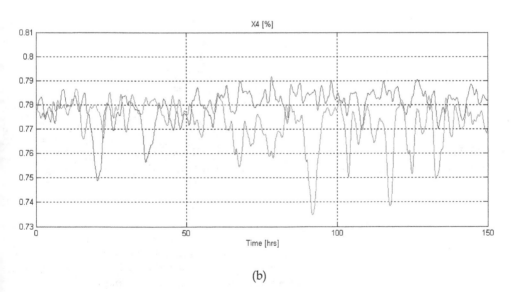

(b)

Fig. 12. Controlled system response LQG / LTR to changes in the type shocks of step and white noise (blue for changes of +5% - green changes -5%)

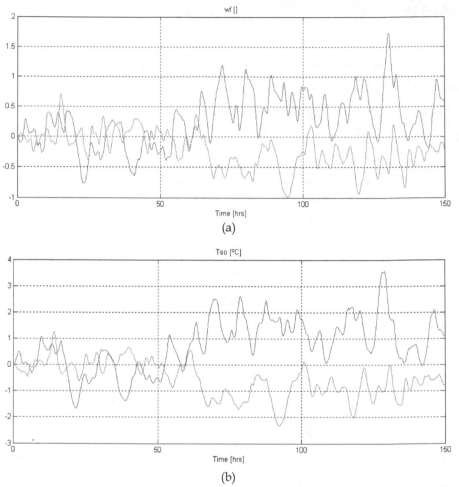

Fig. 13. Efforts to control the controlled system LQG / LTR to changes in the type shocks of step and white noise (blue for changes of +5% - green changes -5%)

6. Conclusions

Looking at the results presented in figures 4 to 7, show that it is appropriate to consider as manipulated variables steam temperature and feed rate of the solution to concentrate, and as measurable disturbance and characteristic of the system to the concentration the solution concentrated and the inlet temperature of food. You can check the analysis of these figures that the evaporation process presents a complex dynamic, high delay, coupling between the variables, high nonlinearities.

From the results shown in figures 8 to 13, on the behavior of the controlled system verifies that the design LQG/LTR has a better performance especially when control efforts are softer. Partly, it validates the robustness of the proposed control system, despite having analyzed only the rejection of disturbances, since these regulatory systems at the show a good response.

7. Acknowledgment

The authors gratefully acknowledge the financial support of the "Universidad de La Frontera"- Chile DIUFRO DI07-0102, "Universidad Nacional de San Juan"- Argentina, Project FI-I900. They are also grateful for the cooperation of "Mostera Rio San Juan".

8. References

(Anderson, 1971) Anderson B.D.O., Moore J.B., *Lineal Optimal Control Control*. Prentice Hall. Engleewood Cliffs, N.J.

(AOAC, 1995) *Official Methods of Analysis. Reference Tables Appendix C*

(Armaou, 2002) Armaou A., Christofides P.D., "Dynamic Optimization of Dissipative PDE Systems Using Nonlinear Order Reduction". Chemical Engineering Science 57 - 24, pp. 5083-5114.

(Aros, 1991) Aros N.H., *Recuperación de la Transferencia del Lazo por Realimentación Parcial del Estado*. M. Sc. Thesis. Universidad Técnica Federico Santa María, Chile.

(Barbieri, 1980) Barbieri, R., & Rossi, N. "Propietà Fisiche dei Mosti d'uva Concentrati". *Rivista de Viticol. e di Enologia*. Conegliano, No 1, 10–18.

(Bayindirli, 1992) Bayindirli, L. "Mathematical Analysis Of Variation Of Density And Viscosity Of Apple Juice With Temperature And Concentration". *Journal. Of Food Processing and Preservation* (16), 23-28.

(Bode, 1945) Bode H.W., *Network Analysis and Feedback Amplifier Design*. Van Nostrand, New York.

(Camacho, 1999) Camacho E., Bordons F.C., *Model Predictive Control*. Springer-Verlag.

(Crapiste, 1988) Crapiste, G.H. and Lozano, J.E. "Effect Of Concentration And Pressure On The Boiling Point Rise Of Apple Juice And Related Sugar Solutions". *Journal Food Science*. (53), 865-869

(Constela, 1989). Constenla D.T., Crapiste G.H. and Lozano J.E. "Thermophysical Properties Of Clarified Apple Juice As A Function Of Concentration And Temperature". *Journal. Food Science*.(54), 663-669.

(Di Leo, 1988) Di Leo, F. "Caratteristiche Fisico-chimiche dei Mosti Concentrati Rettificati. *Valutazione gleucometrica*". *Vignevini*, 15(1/2), 43–45.

(Doyle, 1979) Doyle J.C., Stein G., "Robustness with observers". *IEEE Trans. on Auto. Control, Vol. AC-24, April*.

(Enns, 1984) Enns D., *Model reduction for control systems design*. Ph. D. Thesis. Stanford University.

(El-Farra, 2003) El-Farra N.H., Armaou A., Christofides P.D., "Analysis and Control of Parabolic PDE Systems with Input Constraints". *Automatica 39 – 4, pp. 715-725*.

(Freudenberg, 1988) Freudenberg J., Looze D., *Frequency Domain Properties of Scalar and Multivariable Feedback Systems*. Springer Verlag, Berlín.

(Friedland, 1989) Friedland B., "On the properties of reduced-orden Kalman filters". *IEEE Trans. on Auto. Control, Vol. AC-34, March*.

(Ibarz, 1993) Ibarz, A., & Ortiz, J. "Reología de Zumos de Melocotón". Alimentación, Equipos y Tecnología. Octubre, 81–86, Instituto Nacional de Vitivinicultura. *Síntesis básica de estadística vitivinícola argentina, Mendoza*. Varios números.

(Kam, 1999) Kam K.M., Tade M.O., "Case studies on the modelling and control of evaporation systems". *XIX Interamerican Congress of Chemical Engineering COBEQ*.

(Kam, 2000) Kam K.M., Tade M.O., "Simulated Nonlinear Control Studies of Five Effect Evaporator Models". *Computers and Chemical Engineering, Vol. 23, pp. 1795 - 1810*.

(Kaya, 2002) Kaya A., Belibagh K.B., "Rheology of solid Gaziantep Pekmez". *Journal of Food Engineering, Vol. 54, pp. 221-226*.

(Middleton, 1990) Middleton R.H., Goodwin G.C., *Digital Control and Estimation. A Unified Approach.* Prentice Hall, Englewood Cliffs, N.J.

(Moressi, 1984). Moressi, M., & Spinosi, M. "Engineering factors in the production of concentrated fruit juices, II, fluid physical properties of grapes". *Journal of Food Technology*, 5(19), 519–533.

(Niemann, 1995) Niemann H.H., Stoustrup J., Shafai B., Beale S., "LTR design of proportional-integral observers". *Int. Journal Robust Nonlinear Control, pp. 671-693.*

(Pandolfi, 1991) Pandolfi, C., Romano, E. & Cerdán, A. Composición de los Mostos Concentrados Producidos en Mendoza y San Juan, Argentina. Ed. Agro Latino. *Viticultura/Enología profesional* 13, 65–74.

(Perry, 1997) Perry R., *Perry's Chemical Engineers Handbook.* 7TH Edition McGraw Hill.

(Pilati, 1998) Pilati, M. A., Rubio, L. A., Muñoz, E., Carullo, C. A., Chernikoff, R.E. & Longhi, M. F. "Evaporadores Tubulares de Circulación Forzada: Consumo de Potencia en Distintas Configuraciones. III Jornadas de Investigación. FCAI – UNCuyo. Libro de Resúmenes, 40.

(Rao, 1984) Rao, M. A., Cooley, H. J., & Vitali, A. A. "Flow Properties of Concentrated Juices at Low Temperatures. *Food Technology*, 3(38), 113–119.

(Rubio, 1998) Rubio, L. A., Muñoz, E., Carullo, C. A., Chernikoff, R. E., Pilati, M. A. & Longhi, M. F. "Evaporadores Tubulares de Circulación Forzada: Capacidad de Calor Intercambiada en Distintas Configuraciones". *III Jornadas de Investigación. FCAI – UNCuyo. Libro de Resúmenes,* 40.

(Sáenz 1986) Sáenz, C., & Costell, E. "Comportamiento Reológico de Productos de Limón, Influencia de la Temperatura y de la Concentración". *Revista de Agroquímica y Tecnología de Alimentos,* 4(26), 581–588.

(Saravacos, 1970) Saravacos, G. D. "Effect of Temperature on Viscosity of Fruit Juices and Purees". *Journal of Food Science,* (35), 122–125.

(Schwartz, 1986) Schwartz, M., & Costell, E. "Influencia de la Temperatura en el Comportamiento Reológico del Azúcar de Uva (cv, Thompson Seedless)". *Revista de Agroquímica y Tecnología de Alimentos,* 3(26), 365–372.

(Stefanov, 2003) Stefanov Z.I., Hoo K.A., "A Distributed-Parameter Model of Black Liquor Falling Film Evaporators". *Part I. Modeling of Single Plate. Industrial Engineering Chemical Research* 42, 1925-1937.

(Stein, 1987) Stein G., Athans, M., "The LQG/LTR procedure for multivariable feedback control design". IEEE Trans. on Auto. Control, Vol. AC-32, February.

(Suarez, 2010) Suarez G.I., Ortiz O.A., Aballay P.M., Aros N.H., "Adaptive neural model predictive control for the grape juice concentration process". *International Conference on Industrial Technology, IEEE-ICIT 2010, Chile.*

(Turan, 1990) Turan L., Mingori D.L., Goodwin G.C., "Loop transfer recovery design biased and unbiased controllers". Technical Report EE9021, February.

(Wall, 1980) Wall J.E., Doyle J.C, Harvey C.A., "Tradeoffs in the design of multivariable feedback systems". Proc.18th Allerton Conf., October.

(Zang, 1990) Zang Z., Freudenberg J.S., "Loop transfer recovery for nonminimum phase plants". *IEEE Trans. Automatic Control, Vol. 35, pp. 547-553.*

(Zheng, 2002) Zheng D., Hoo K. A., "Low-Order Model Identification for Implementable Control Solutions of Distributed Parameter Systems". *Computers and Chemical Engineering 26 7-8, pp. 1049-1076.*

(Zuritz, 2005) Zuritz C.A., Muñoz E., Mathey H.H., Pérez E.H., Gascón A., Rubio L.A., Carullo C.A., Chemikoff R.E., Cabeza M.S., "Density, viscosity and soluble solid concentration and temperatures". *Journal of Food Engineering, Vol. 71, pp. 143 - 149.*

Reactive Distillation: Control Structure and Process Design for Robustness

V. Pavan Kumar Malladi[1] and Nitin Kaistha[2]
[1]Department of Chemical Engineering,
National Institute of Technology Calicut, Kozhikode,
[2]Department of Chemical Engineering,
Indian Institute of Technology Kanpur, Kanpur,
India

1. Introduction

Reactive Distillation (RD) is the combination of reaction and distillation in a single vessel (Backhaus, 1921). Over the past two decades, it has emerged as a promising alternative to conventional "reaction followed by separation" processes (Towler & Frey, 2002). The technology is attractive when the reactant-product component relative volatilities allow recycle of reactants into the reactive zone via rectification/stripping and sufficiently high reaction rates can be achieved at tray bubble temperature. For equilibrium limited reactions, the continuous removal of products drives the reaction to near completion (Taylor & Krishna, 2000). The reaction can also significantly simplify the separation task by reacting away azeotropes (Huss et al., 2003). The Eastman methyl acetate RD process that replaced a reactor plus nine column conventional process with a single column is a classic commercial success story (Agreda et al., 1990). The capital and energy costs of the RD process are reported to be a fifth of the conventional process (Siirola, 1995).

Not withstanding the potentially significant economic advantages of RD technology, the process integration results in reduced number of valves for regulating both reaction and separation with high non-linearity due to the reaction-separation interaction (Engell & Fernholtz, 2003). Multiple steady states have been reported for several RD systems (Jacobs & Krishna, 1993; Ciric & Miao 1994; Mohl et al., 1999). The existence of multiple steady states in an RD column can significantly compromise column controllability and the design of a robust control system that effectively rejects large disturbances is a principal consideration in the successful implementation of the technology (Sneesby et al., 1997).

In this Chapter, through case studies on a generic double feed two-reactant two-product ideal RD system (Luyben, 2000) and the methyl acetate RD system (Al-Arfaj & Luyben, 2002), the implications of the non-linear effects, specifically input and output multiplicity, on open and closed loop column operation is studied. Specifically, steady state transitions under open and closed loop operation are demonstrated for the two example systems. Input multiplicity, in particular, is shown to significantly compromise control system robustness with the possibility of "wrong" control action or a steady state transition under closed loop operation for sufficiently large disturbances.

Temperature inferential control system design is considered here due to its practicality in an industrial setting. The design of an effective (robust) temperature inferential control system requires that the input-output pairings be carefully chosen to avoid multiplicity in the vicinity of the nominal steady state. A quantitative measure is developed to quantify the severity of the multiplicity in the steady-state input output relations. In cases where an appropriate tray temperature location with mild non-linearity cannot be found, it may be possible to "design" a measurement that combines different tray temperatures for a well-behaved input-output relation and consequently robust closed loop control performance. Sometimes temperature inferential control (including temperature combinations) may not be effective and one or more composition measurements may be necessary for acceptable closed loop control performance. In extreme cases, the RD column design itself may require alteration for a controllable column. RD column design modification, specifically the balance between fractionation and reaction capacity, for reduced non-linearity and better controllability is demonstrated for the ideal RD system. The Chapter comprehensively treats the role of non-linear effects in RD control and its mitigation via appropriate selection/design of the measurement and appropriate process design.

2. Steady state multiplicity and its control implications

Proper regulation of an RD column requires a control system that maintains the product purities and reaction conversion in the presence of large disturbances such as a throughput change or changes in the feed composition etc. This is usually accomplished by adjusting the column inputs (e.g. boil-up or reflux or a column feed) to maintain appropriate output variables (e.g. a tray temperature or composition) so that the purities and reaction conversion are maintained close to their nominal values regardless of disturbances. The steady state variation in an output variable to a change in the control input is referred to as its open loop steady state input-output (IO) relation. Due to high non-linearity in RD systems, the IO relation may not be well behaved exhibiting gain sign reversal with consequent steady state multiplicity.

From the control point of view, the multiplicity can be classified into two types, namely, input multiplicity and output multiplicity as shown in Figure 1. In case of output multiplicity, multiple output values are possible at a given input value (Figure 1(a)). Input multiplicity is implied when multiple input values result in the same output value (Figure 1(b)).

To understand the implications of input/output multiplicity on control, let us consider a SISO system. Let the open loop IO relation exhibit output multiplicity with the nominal operating point denoted by '*'(Figure 1(a)). Under open loop operation, a large step decrease in the control input from u_0 to u_1 would cause the output to decrease from y_0 to y_1. Upon increasing the input back to u_0, the output would reach a different value y_0' on the lower solution branch. For large changes in the control input (or alternatively large disturbances), the SISO system may exhibit a steady state transition under open loop operation. For RD systems, this transition may correspond to a transition from the high conversion steady state to a low conversion steady state. The transition can be easily prevented by installing a feedback controller with its setpoint as y_0. Since the output values at the three possible steady states corresponding to u_0 are distinct, it is theoretically possible to drive the system to the desired steady state with the appropriate setpoint (Kienle & Marquardt, 2003). Note that for the IO relation in Figure 1(a), the feedback controller would be reverse acting for y_0/y_0' and direct acting for y_0'' as the nominal steady state.

The implications of input multiplicity in an IO relation are much more severe. To understand the same, consider a SISO system with the IO relation in Figure 1(b) and the point marked '*' as the nominal steady state. Assume a feedback PI controller that manipulates u to maintain y at y_0. Around the nominal steady state, the controller is direct acting. Let us consider three initial steady states marked a, b and c on the IO relation, from where the controller must drive the output to its nominal steady state. At a, the initial error $(y^{SP}-y)$ is positive and the controller would decrease u to bring y to the desired steady state. At b, the error is again positive and the system gets driven to the desired steady state with the controller reducing u. At c, due to the y^{SP} crossover in the IO relation, the error signal is negative and the direct acting controller would increase u, which is the *wrong* control action. Since the IO relation turns back, the system would settle down at the steady state marked '**'. For large disturbances, a SISO system with input multiplicity can succumb to wrong control action with the control input saturating or a steady state transition if the IO relation exhibits another branch with the same slope sign as the nominal steady state. Input multiplicity or more specifically, multiple crossovers of y^{SP} in the IO relationship thus severely compromise control system robustness.

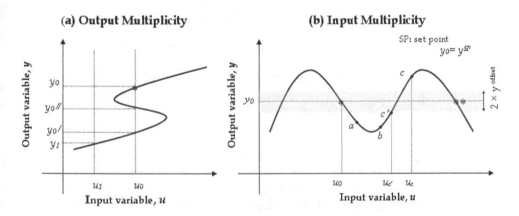

Fig. 1. Steady state multiplicity, (a) Output multiplicity, (b) Input multiplicity

The suitability of an input-output (IO) pairing for RD column regulation can be assessed by the steady state IO relation. Candidate output variables should exhibit good sensitivity (local slope in IO relation at nominal operating point) for adequate muscle to the control system where a small change in the input drives the deviating output back to its setpoint. Of these candidate sensitive (high open loop gain) outputs, those exhibiting output multiplicity may be acceptable for control while those exhibiting input multiplicity may compromise control system robustness due to the possibility of wrong control action. The design of a robust control system for an RD column then requires further evaluation of the IO relations of the sensitive (high gain) output variables to select the one(s) that are monotonic for large changes in the input around the nominal steady state and avoid multiple y^{SP} crossovers. If such a variable is not found, the variable with a y^{SP} crossover point (input multiplicity), that is the furthest from the nominal operating point should be selected. It may also be possible to combine different outputs to design one that avoids crossover (input multiplicity). The magnitude $|u_0-u_c|$, where u_c is the input value at the nearest y^{SP} crossover can be used as a criterion to screen out candidate outputs. For robustness, Kumar & Kaistha (2008) define the rangeability, r, of an IO relation as

$$r = |u_0 - u_c'|$$

where u_c' is obtained for $y = y^{SP} - y^{offset}$ as shown in Figure 1(b). The offset from the actual crossover point ensures robustness to disturbances such as a bias in the measurement. In extreme cases, where a suitable output variable is not found that can effectively reject large disturbances, the RD column design may require alteration for improving controllability. Each of these aspects is demonstrated in the following example case studies on a hypothetical two-reactant two-product ideal RD column and an industrial scale methyl acetate RD column.

3. RD control case studies

To demonstrate the impact of steady state multiplicity on RD control, two double feed two-reactant two-product RD columns with stoichiometric feeds (neat operation) are considered in this work. The first one is an ideal RD column with the equilibrium reaction $A + B \leftrightarrow C + D$. The component relative volatilities are in the order $\alpha_C > \alpha_A > \alpha_B > \alpha_D$ so that the reactants are intermediate boiling. The RD column consists of a reactive section with rectifying and stripping trays respectively above and below it. Light fresh A is fed immediately below and heavy fresh B is fed immediately above the reactive zone. Product C is recovered as the distillate while product D is recovered as the bottoms. The rectifying and stripping trays recycle the reactants escaping the reactive zone and prevent their exit in the product streams. This hypothetical ideal RD column was originally proposed by Luyben (2000) as a test-bed for studying various control structures (Al-Arfaj & Luyben, 2000).

In terms of its design configuration, the methyl acetate column is similar to the ideal RD column with light methanol being fed immediately below and heavy acetic acid being fed immediately above the reactive section. The esterification reaction $CH_3COOH + CH_3OH \leftrightarrow CH_3COOCH_3 + H_2O$ occurs in the reactive zone with nearly pure methyl acetate recovered as the distillate and nearly pure water recovered as the bottoms.

Figure 2 shows a schematic of the two RD columns. The ideal RD column is designed to process 12.6 mol s^{-1} of stoichiometric fresh feeds to produce 95% pure C as the distillate product and 95% pure D as the bottoms product. Alternative column designs with 7 rectifying, 6 reactive and 7 stripping trays or 5 rectifying, 10 reactive and 5 stripping trays are considered in this work. For brevity, these designs are referred to as 7/6/7 and 5/10/5 respectively. The methyl acetate RD column is designed to produce 95% pure methyl acetate distillate. The 7/18/10 design configuration reported by Singh et al. (2005) is studied here. Both the columns are operated neat with stoichiometric feeds. The reaction and vapor liquid equilibrium model parameters for the two systems are provided in Table 1.

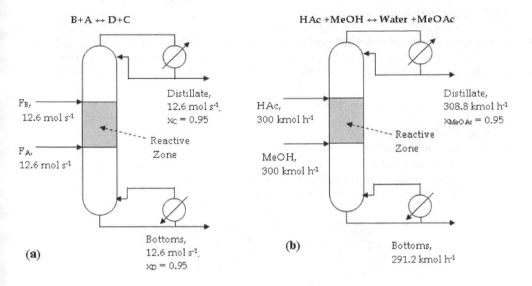

Fig. 2. Schematics of example RD columns. (a) Ideal, (b) Methyl acetate

	Ideal RD column	Methyl acetate RD column
Reaction	B+A ↔ D+C	Acetic acid + Methanol ↔ Water + Methyl Acetate
Relative volatility	$\alpha_C : \alpha_A : \alpha_B : \alpha_D$ $= 8 : 4 : 2 : 1$	Extended Antonie Equations are used for the estimation of saturation vapour pressure, temperature dependent
Liquid phase activity	Ideal	Wilson
Vapour phase	Ideal	Ideal with Marek Method (Marek, 1995) (Vapour dimerization of Acetic acid)
Reaction kinetics	$r_C(mol\,/\,mol\,s^{-1})$ $= k_f x_A x_B - k_b x_C x_D$	$r_{MeOAc} = \dfrac{M_C k_f \left[a_{HAc} a_{MeOH} - \dfrac{a_{MeOAc} a_{H_2O}}{K_{eq}} \right]}{\left[1 + K_{HAc} a_{HAc} + K_{MeOH} a_{MeOH} + K_{MeOAC} a_{MeOAC} + K_{H_2O} a_{H_2O} \right]^2}$
	$k_f = 2.4260 \times 10^{16} e^{15098.1/T}$ $k_b = 2.11768 \times 10^{-6} e^{5032.47/T}$	$K_{HAc} = 3.18; K_{MeOH} = 4.95; K_{H_2O} = 10.5$ $K_{MeOAc} = 0.82$ $k_f(kmol\,/\,kg_{cat}\,/\,h) = 69.42 \times 10^9 e^{-52275.93/(RT)}$ $K_{eq} = 2.32 e^{782.98/T}$
Heat of reaction	- 41840 kJ/kmol Temperature independent	- 33566.80 kJ/kmol at 330 K Temperature dependent

Table 1. VLE and reaction parameters of the example RD systems

3.1 Output multiplicity effects

To demonstrate the impact of output multiplicity on column operation, the 7/6/7 design with 1 kmol reaction holdup per reactive tray is considered for the ideal RD system. For 95% pure distillate and 95% pure bottoms, the reflux ratio and vapor boilup is found to be 2.6149 and 28.32 mol s^{-1}, respectively. For the methyl acetate RD column, the 7/18/10 design is considered. At the nominal design, the reflux ratio and reboiler duty is 1.875 and 4.6021 MW respectively for 95% methyl acetate distillate and 96.33% water bottoms.

3.1.1 Ideal RD column

The variation in the bottoms D purity with respect to the vapor boilup at constant reflux rate in the 7/6/7 ideal RD column design is shown in Figure 3(a). Both input and output multiplicity are present in the relation with respect to the nominal steady state. Output multiplicity is observed with three distinct purities for the product D other than the basecase

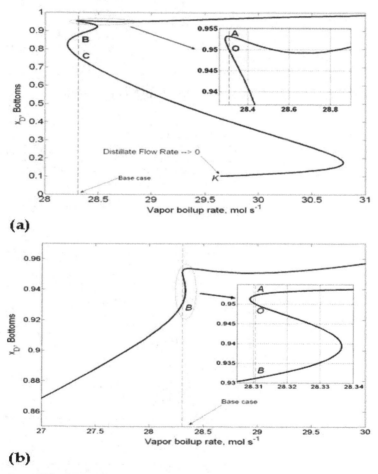

Fig. 3. Variation of ideal RD column bottom product purity with boilup at (a) fixed reflux rate, (b) fixed reflux ratio

design purity of 95%. At point K on the solution diagram, the distillate flow rate almost reaches 0 beyond which a steady solution is not found.

Figure 3(b) shows that IO relation of bottoms purity with vapor boilup at constant reflux to distillate ratio, a common operating policy implemented on distillation columns. Output multiplicity at the nominal steady state is evident in the Figure. Notice that a feasible steady state solution now exists for boilups below its nominal value, unlike for column operation at fixed reflux rate. From the column operation standpoint, maintaining reflux in ratio with the distillate is therefore a more pragmatic option as a feasible steady state exists for large changes in the vapor boilup in either direction.

To understand the implication of the observed steady state solution diagrams on column operation, the dynamic column response to a ±5% pulse change of one hour duration in the vapor boilup is obtained at a fixed reflux rate or at a fixed reflux ratio. The reflux drum and bottom sump levels are maintained using respectively the distillate and the bottoms flow (P controller with gain 2). The dynamic response is plotted in Figure 4. At constant reflux rate (Figure 4(a)), for the -5% boilup step change, the distillate rate quickly goes down to zero corresponding to no feasible solution in the solution diagram. For the +5% pulse change, the distillate rate settles at a slightly higher value of 12.623 mol s^{-1} (nominal value: 12.6 mol s^{-1}) implying an open loop steady state transition. This new steady state corresponds to Point B in the bifurcation diagram in Figure 3(a). For the -5% pulse, the distillate valve shuts down due to the absence of a feasible steady state solution for a large reduction in the boilup.

At fixed reflux ratio, a stable response is obtained for the ±5% pulse in boilup (Figure 4(b)). The column however ends up transitioning to different steady states for a +5% and a -5% pulse change, respectively. This is in line with the bifurcation diagram in Figure 3(b) with the column transitioning to a high conversion steady state (A) or a low conversion steady state (B) solution under open loop column operation.

Given the possibility of an open loop steady state transition due to output multiplicity, a PI controller is implemented that adjusts the reflux rate/reflux ratio to hold the distillate purity at 95%. The loop is tuned using the ATV method (Astrom & Hagglund, 1984) with Tyreus-Luyben settings (Tyreus & Luyben, 1992). At constant reflux rate, a boilup pulse change of -5% is handled with the column returning to its nominal steady state. In addition, a -5% step change is also handled with a stable response implying the existence of a steady state solution (feasibility) at low boilups with the distillate purity held constant. This is in contrast to the no feasible solution at reduced boilups for column operation at constant reflux rate. With the composition control loop on automatic, an unstable response is however observed for a large - 20% step change which is likely due to the absence of a feasible steady state for low boilups at constant distillate composition. With the composition control loop, a +5% pulse change in the vapor boilup does not result in a steady state transition unlike for column operation at constant reflux and the column returns to its nominal steady state.

The implementation of a feedback loop controlling distillate purity by adjusting the reflux ratio results in the column returning to its nominal steady state for a ±5% pulse change in the boilup. The open loop steady state transition observed for the same pulse disturbance at constant reflux ratio is thus prevented. In addition, a -20% step change in the boilup results in a stable response with the column settling at a new steady state implying feasibility. These dynamic results serve to highlight that the implementation of feedback control serves to mitigate the non-linear effects of output multiplicity so that an open loop steady transition is prevented (Dorn et al., 1998). Feedback control also ensures feasible operation over a larger disturbance range.

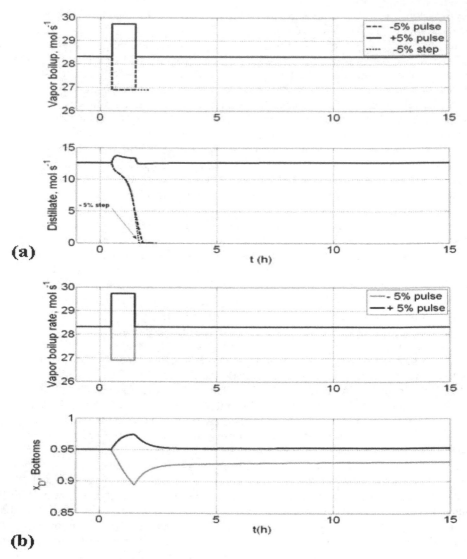

(a)

(b)

Fig. 4. Open loop dynamics of ideal RD column (7/6/7 design), (a) fixed reflux rate, (b) fixed reflux ratio

3.1.2 Methyl acetate RD column

The 7/18/10 methyl acetate RD column design is studied (Singh et al., 2005). The steady state variation of reaction conversion with respect to reboiler duty at a fixed reflux ratio and a fixed reflux rate is shown in Figure 5. At fixed reflux ratio, the nominal steady state is unique with a 97.77% conversion while two additional low conversion steady states (conversion: 72.95% and 59.66%) are observed at fixed reflux rate. The column dynamic response to a 5 hour duration -3% pulse in the reboiler duty at alternatively, a fixed reflux rate, a fixed reflux ratio or controlling a reactive tray temperature using reflux rate is shown in Figure 6. The liquid levels in the reflux and reboiler drums are controlled using the distillate and bottoms, respectively (P controller with gain 2). Whereas the column returns to its nominal steady state for a fixed reflux ratio or for reactive tray temperature control using reflux, a steady state transition to a low conversion steady state is observed at a fixed reflux rate. This transition is attributed to the output multiplicity at constant reflux rate in Figure 5. Maintaining the reflux in ratio with the distillate is thus a simple means of avoiding output multiplicity and the associated open loop column operation issues (Kumar & Kaistha, 2008).

3.2 Input multiplicity and its implications on controlled variable selection
As discussed, the existence of input multiplicity in an IO pairing can severely compromise control system robustness due to the possibility of wrong control action. In this section, we demonstrate wrong control action in the ideal and methyl acetate RD systems. We also demonstrate the systematic use of steady state IO relations to choose CVs (controlled variables) that are better behaved (more robust) in terms of their multiplicity behavior and the consequent improvement in control system robustness for the two example RD systems.

3.2.1 Ideal RD column
The 5/10/5 design with 1 kmol reaction holdup per reactive tray is considered here. For 95% distillate and bottoms purities, the reflux ratio and vapor boilup are respectively 2.6915 and 29.27 mol s^{-1} respectively. As with the 7/6/7 design, maintaining reflux in ratio with the distillate mitigates nonlinear effects and is therefore implemented. The simplest policy of operating the column at fixed reflux ratio is first considered.

At a fixed reflux ratio, there are three available inputs for control, namely the fresh A feed (F_A), the fresh B feed (F_B) and the vapor boilup (V_S). Of these, one of the inputs must be used

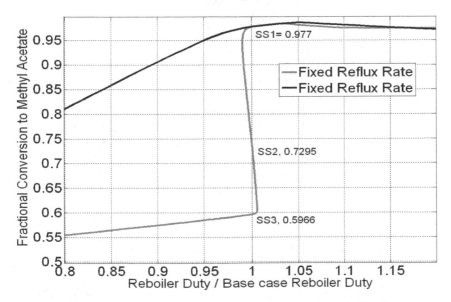

Fig. 5. Steady state conversion to methyl acetate with respect to reboiler duty

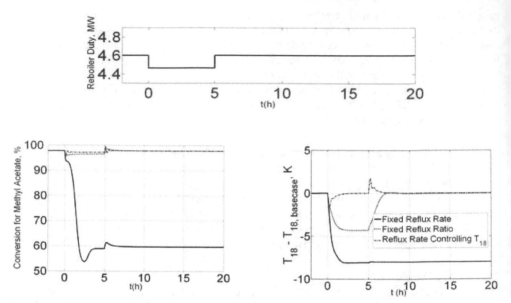

Fig. 6. Dynamic response of methyl acetate RD column for a pulse change in reboiler duty

to set the production rate (throughput) with the remaining two inputs available for column regulation. F_B is chosen as the throughput manipulator as the dynamic response of the tray temperatures (potential controlled outputs) to F_B is sluggish compared to V_S or F_A due to the associated large liquid hydraulic lags. V_S and F_A would thus be more effective manipulation handles for column regulation. From sensitivity analysis, a stripping tray temperature is the most sensitive to a change in F_A. Accordingly, F_A is paired with the sensitive stripping tray temperature (T_2, bottom-up tray numbering). V_S is then used as the manipulation handle for controlling a non-stripping (reactive or rectifying) tray temperature. Sensitivity analysis shows T_{18} to be the most sensitive rectifying tray temperature with T_{12} being the most sensitive reactive tray temperature, which is however lower than T_{18}. We therefore consider two alternative pairings namely T_{18}-V_S or T_{12}-V_S. A schematic of the two-temperature control structure is shown in Figure 7. The Niederlinski Index and Relative Gain Array of the two alternative control loop pairings are also given in the Figure and are found to be acceptable. These local metrics suggest T_{18} to be the better controlled variable.

The steady state input-output relations between the manipulated and controlled variables are now evaluated for multiplicity. The variation of three tray temperatures (T_2, T_{18} and T_{12}) with respect to all three inputs (F_B, F_A and V_S) is plotted in Figure 8. For easy comparison, the difference in the temperature from its nominal value is plotted with respect to percentage change in the inputs around the nominal steady state. Input-output relations are nearly monotonic with respect to V_S with an increase in V_S causing the tray temperature to increase. Although gain sign reversal is seen in T_{12} and T_2 for large negative change in V_S, the IO relations remain away from a crossover. On the other hand, crossover is seen with respect to F_B. In the T_{18}–F_B IO relation, crossover is observed at -22.5% and -30.8% and +22.7% change in F_B. With respect to F_A, directionality in response is observed with no change in T_{12} or T_{18} for an increase in F_A but a visible change for a decrease in F_A. The response of T_2 (controlled using F_A) is better behaved with gain sign reversal for a decrease in F_A. But the IO relation remains away from crossover for a ±35% input change.

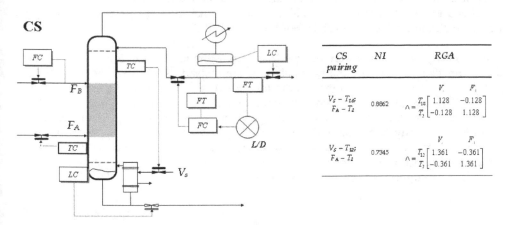

CS pairing	NI	RGA		
			V	F_1
$V_S - T_{16};$ $F_A - T_2$	0.8862	$\Lambda =$ $\begin{matrix} T_{18} \\ T_2 \end{matrix}$	$\begin{matrix} 1.128 \\ -0.128 \end{matrix}$	$\begin{matrix} -0.128 \\ 1.128 \end{matrix}$
			V	F_1
$V_S - T_{12};$ $F_A - T_2$	0.7345	$\Lambda =$ $\begin{matrix} T_{12} \\ T_2 \end{matrix}$	$\begin{matrix} 1.361 \\ -0.361 \end{matrix}$	$\begin{matrix} -0.361 \\ 1.361 \end{matrix}$

Fig. 7. Two temperature control structure with *Niederlinski Index (NI)* and *Relative Gain Array (RGA)* of control loop pairings

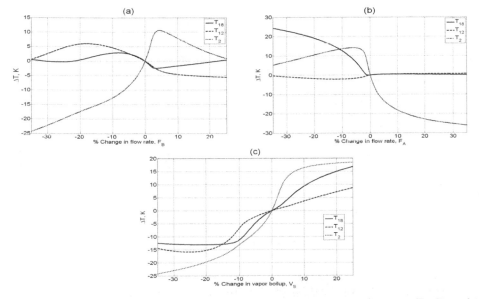

Fig. 8. Open loop variation of ideal RD column tray temperatures with inputs (F_B, F_A and V_S)

The open loop IO relation that a control loop 'sees' can be significantly different depending on whether the other loop is on manual (its input is fixed) or automatic (its output is fixed). To evaluate the same, open loop IO relations for the T_{18}-V_S pairing and T_2-F_A pairing are obtained with the output for the other loop (T_2 or T_{18}) maintained at its setpoint (nominal value). Similarly the T_{12}-V_S (T_2 fixed) and T_2-F_A (T_{12} fixed) IO relations are also obtained.

These are shown in Figure 9. The nominal steady state is marked O and the corresponding crossover points are marked A, B etc. A non-nominal steady state on a solution branch is stable if the local slope in the IO relation has the same sign as for the nominal steady state O, else it is unstable. Accordingly, the stable solution branch is shown as a continuous curve while the unstable solution branch is shown as a dashed curve.

For the T_{18}-V_S and T_2-F_A pairing, the input multiplicity steady states A and B are unstable with respect to controller action (reverse or direct) as the local slope sign of at least one of the IO relations is opposite the nominal slope sign. Steady state C on the other hand is stable. Disturbances that push the column towards A i.e., cause a large decrease in F_A/V_S, can result in wrong control action with saturation of a control input. On the other hand, disturbances that cause large increases in F_A/V_S can result in a closed loop steady state transition to steady state solution C. For the T_{12}-V_S and T_2-F_A pairing, both the input multiplicity steady states A' and B' are unstable with respect to controller action so that wrong control action with consequent valve saturation is expected for large changes in F_A/V_S in either direction (increase or decrease).

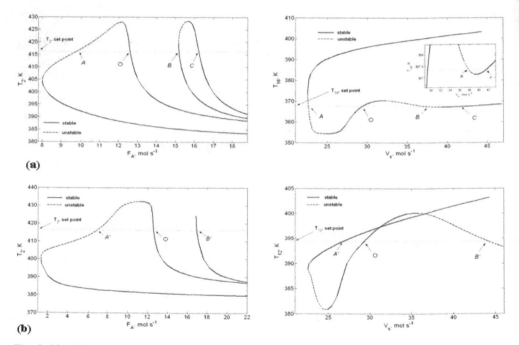

Fig. 9. Ideal RD column IO relations,
(a) T_2-F_A (fixed T_{18}) & T_{18}-V_S (fixed T_2) (b) T_2-F_A (fixed T_{12}) & T_{12}-V_S (fixed T_2)

Which pairing (T_{18}-V_S/T_2-F_A versus T_{12}-V_S/T_2-F_A) would handle larger disturbances without succumbing to wrong control action depends on the degree of tightness of control of the outputs. Usually tightest tray temperature control is usually possible with boilup as the manipulation handle. T_{18}/T_{12} is therefore likely to be controlled tightly without significant deviations from its nominal setpoint. Larger deviations in T_2 (controlled using F_A) can result in wrong control action due to input multiplicity corresponding to higher F_A feed into the column (Figure 8 and Figure 9). In the T_2-F_A IO relation (Figure 9), notice that a crossover in T_2 occurs earlier when T_{18} is held constant compared to when T_{12} is held constant. Accordingly, one would expect controlling T_{12} to handle larger disturbances without wrong control action.

Using T_{18}/T_{12} and T_2 as controlled variables to manipulate V_S and F_A respectively, two different series of step changes are given to the throughput manipulator F_B to demonstrate the impact of input multiplicity under closed loop operation. The temperature controllers are tuned individually using the relay feedback test. The T_{18}-V_S loop must be detuned by a factor of 5 from its Tyreus Luyben settings to avoid a highly oscillatory response while not detuning is necessary when the T_{12}-V_S loop is implemented. In the first (second) series of step changes, the F_B flow rate value is decreased (increased) to 15% (20%) and then 30% (40%) below its basecase value at time 0 and 15 hr respectively, and then restored back to its nominal value of 12.6 mol s^{-1} at 30 hour. The closed dynamic results for these step changes when T_{18} is controlled are shown in Figure 10(a).

For the first series of step changes, stable closed loop responses are obtained for the changes made at 0 and 15 hr (Figure 10(a)). Tight control of the product purities with less than 1% deviations is achieved suggesting that two-point temperature inferential control provides effective column regulation holding the reaction and separation close to the nominal steady state. Upon restoration of the F_B flow rate to its nominal value at 30 hrs with a large 30% step increase, the F_A and V_S valves are completely closed. A sudden large increment of F_B

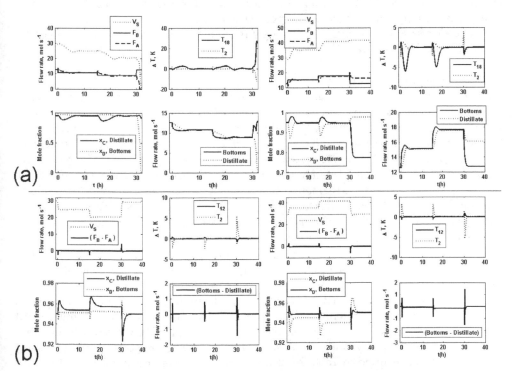

Fig. 10. The closed loop dynamics of ideal RD column for the two different series of step changes in F_B when (a) T_{18} (b) T_{12} is controlled variable

flow rate from 8.82 to 12.6 mol s^{-1} brings the column operation in the vicinity of point A in Figure 9 (relatively low F_A) with the consequent wrong control action causing a valve shutdown.

For the second series of step changes (+20%, +20% and -40%), a stable and well behaved response is observed for the two +20% step changes with acceptably small product purity deviations. However, for the -40% step change to bring F_B back to its nominal value, the column drifts to new steady state, i.e., settles at steady state C in Figure 9. The large F_B flow value decrease 17.64 to 12.6 mol s^{-1} at 30 hr, results in excess A input which causes a steady state transition to the stable steady state C in Figure 9. The same series of step changes in F_B (-15%, -15%, +30% and +20%, +20%, -40%) is effectively handled with no valve saturation or steady state transition due to wrong control action when T_{12} is used as the controlled variable manipulating V_S instead of T_{18}. The closed loop dynamic response is shown in Figure 10(b). The small steady state product purity deviations for the large throughput changes again highlight two-point temperature inferential control as an effective means of column regulation.

These results clearly demonstrate that proper choice of the controlled output variable can significantly improve the robustness of the control system in rejecting large disturbances. The results also highlight that the conventional wisdom of choosing controlled variables using local steady state metrics such as open loop gain or Niederlinski Index/relative gain may lead to the wrong conclusions. In the current example, the open loop sensitivity and relative gain for the T_{18}-V_S pairing are better than for the T_{12}-V_S pairing. A more comprehensive bifurcation analysis however reveals T_{12} to be the more robust CV. Such a comprehensive steady state analysis is strongly recommended for designing robust control systems for highly non-linear RD systems.

3.2.2 Methyl acetate RD column

In this RD column, column trays are numbered from top to bottom with the condenser as tray 0. As seen earlier, column operation at fixed reflux ratio avoids output multiplicity. Accordingly, the simple constant reflux ratio policy is implemented leaving the remaining three inputs, namely acetic acid feed (F_{HAc}), methanol feed (F_{MeOH}) and reboiler duty (Q_r) for column regulation. Sensitivity analysis shows that the temperature of tray 18 in the reactive section is very sensitive with respect to F_{HAc} and Q_r. In the stripping section, temperature of tray 34 is sensitive to all three inputs. Based on these sensitivities, two decentralized temperature inferential control structures, labelled CS1 and CS2, are synthesized, which are schematically depicted in Figure 11. In CS1, Q_r is the throughput manipulator, F_{HAc} controls a reactive tray and F_{MeOH} controls a stripping tray. This control structure was originally proposed by Roat et al. (1986). In CS2, F_{HAc} is the throughput manipulator with a reactive tray temperaure controlled using Q_r and a stripping tray temperature controlled using F_{MeOH}.

Further analysis is now conducted to check for multiplicity in the IO relations. As shown in Figure 12(a), all reactive tray temperatures (including the most sensitive T_{18}) exhibit input multiplicity with respect to changes in F_{HAc} and Q_r. To quantify the severity of input multiplicity, the rangeability (with a 3K offset) of the reactive tray temperatures with respect to Q_r and F_{HAc} are reported in Table 2. Even as reactive tray temperature, T_{18}, is the most sensitive to F_{HAc} and Q_r as evidenced from the slope at the nominal steady state in Figure 12(a), its rangeability is lower compared to reactive tray temperature T_{20}. To eliminate a

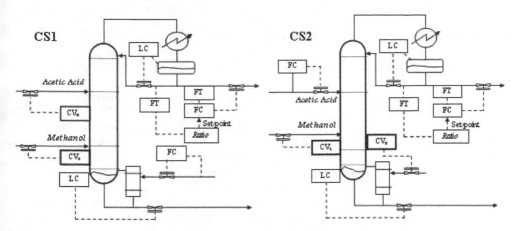

Fig. 11. Schematics of two temperature control structures used for the methyl acetate RD column

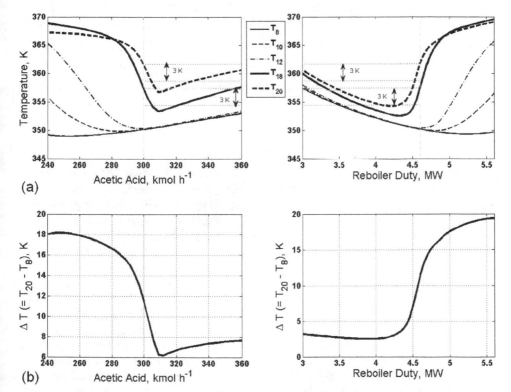

Fig. 12. Variation of (a) reactive tray temperatures and (b) $\Delta T = T_{20} - T_8$ with F_{HAc} and Q_r

crossover in the IO relations for high rangeability, we also consider a combination of tray temperatures. The difference between two reactive tray temperatures ($\Delta T = T_{20} - T_8$) was found to avoid input multiplicity with respect to F_{HAc} and Q_r with the corresponding IO relations in Figure 12(b).

In the T_{34}-F_{MeOH} IO relation, a crossover does not occur (data not shown) so that this pairing is fixed in both CS1 and CS2. For the reactive tray temperature control loop, there are three candidate controlled outputs in both CS1 and CS2, namely, T_{18}, T_{20} and ΔT (T_{20} − T_8). Superscripts 'a', 'b' and 'c' are appended to the control structure label (CS1 or CS2) corresponding to T_{18}, T_{20} and ΔT, respectively, as the controlled reactive zone measurement. Note that T_{18} exhibits the highest sensitivity but low rangeability, T_{20} exhibits reasonable sensitivity with higher rangeability while ΔT exhibits the best rangeability with reasonable sensitivity. The three variants of each control structure are tested using rigorous dynamic simulations for the maximum throughput change handled in the worst-case direction. From the IO relations in Figure 12(a), for CS1, a step decrease in Q_r is the worst-case direction due to input multiplicity at reduced Q_r while for CS2, a step increase in F_{HAc} is the worst-case direction due to input multiplicity at increased F_{HAc}.

Tray Number	HAc		Reboiler Duty		MeOH	
	Decrease	Increase	Decrease	Increase	Decrease	Increase
16	>20	0	0	>20	>20	0
17	>20	0	6.9	>20	>20	0
18	>20	8.8	17.32	>20	>20	0
19	>20	10.9	24.63	>20	>20	0
20	>20	11.1	25.19	>20	>20	0
21	19.2	7	31.14	>20	>20	0

Values are in % change about their basecase values
A 3K offset is used in calculating rangeability

Table 2. Rangeability of reactive tray temperatures

The PI temperature loops are systematically tuned (Kumar & Kaistha, 2008). The two level controllers are P only with a gain of 2. The column pressure is assumed fixed, which is reasonable as in practice tight pressure control is achieved by manipulating the condenser duty. Also instantaneous flow control is assumed which is again reasonable in that tray temperature dynamics are significantly slower than flow dynamics.

Table 3 reports the maximum throughput step change handled by the different variants of the two control structures. CS1[a] and CS1[b] fail for a 20% and 30% throughput decrease respectively while CS1[c] effectively handles 40% (larger changes not tested). The throughput increase for which CS2[a] and CS2[b] fail are respectively 25% and 40% while CS2[c] works even for a 50% throughput increase (larger increase not tested). The trend in both CS1 and CS2 is in direct agreement with the increasing rangeability of the controlled outputs T_{18} (CS1/2[a]), T_{20} (CS1/2[b]) and ΔT (CS1/2[c]). The result confirms the direct relationship between control system robustness and input multiplicity with rangeability being a useful metric for selecting 'robust' controlled variables. The result also shows that a well designed controlled variable such as ΔT with high rangeability and acceptable sensitivity results in a robust control system that effectively rejects large disturbances.

CS	CS1a		CS1b		CS1c		CS2a		CS2b		CS2c	
	-15%	40%	-25%	40%	-40%	40%	-40%	20%	-40%	35%	-40%	40%

Table 3. Maximum throughput change in either direction handled by the control structures

For the sake of brevity, the dynamic response to throughput change for CS1 and CS2 is not shown and may be found in Kumar & Kaistha (2008). These dynamic results show that controlling ΔT better prevents the breakthrough of heavy acetic acid from the reactive zone. In fact, the cause of input multiplicity in the IO relations is heavy acetic acid moving down and breaking through the reactive zone. This breakthrough would occur if the F_{HAc} is sufficiently increased above F_{MeOH} or if Q_r is sufficiently reduced, which results in the input multiplicity in the IO relations in Figure 12(a). For successful regulation of the RD column, such accumulation or breakthrough of acetic acid must be prevented and the same is effectively achieved by controlling ΔT.

In this example, an appropriate temperature based measurement could be designed that does not exhibit output multiplicity for robust column control. If such a temperature-based measurement is not evident for an RD system, controlling an appropriate tray composition may be considered. Even as online composition measurements are expensive, the additional expense would be justified in order to make the practical implementation of RD technology feasible.

4. RD design for controllability

The two case studies on control of RD columns clearly demonstrate that the existence of steady state multiplicity can result in hard-to-fathom nonlinear dynamic phenomena such as an open loop or a closed loop steady state transition, which can be particularly confusing for operators. In extreme cases where the non-linear effects cannot be sufficiently mitigated by appropriate choice/design of the controlled variable (including composition control), it may be necessary to alter the design of the column to mitigate the non-linearity for better controllability.

How to alter the column design to mitigate the non-linear effects? Several researchers have attempted to address this question for the ideal RD system with often contradictory claims (Huang et al., 2006; Kumar & Kaistha, 2008a, 2008b). To us, it appears that design modifications that help prevent escape of reactants from the reactive zone improve the controllability. To that end, for RD systems with exothermic reactions, the extension of the reactive zone into the stripping section with catalyst redistribution helps prevent the breakthrough of the heavy reactant from the reactive zone. Alternatively, the lower feed tray location may be moved up into the reactive zone. Reduced energy consumption has been demonstrated using a catalyst redistribution and lower feed tray location alteration. With respect to the original 5/10/5 ideal RD column design, controllability improves with catalyst redistribution only but deteriorates significantly when the lower feed tray location is moved up. A combination of the two provides acceptable controllability with significant energy savings. The extension of reactive zone into the rectifying section or upper feed tray alteration does not help improve controllability or energy consumption as the exothermic reaction causes the light reactant to escape up the top. For an endothermic reaction however, such a strategy may have merit (Huang et al., 2006).

For the methyl acetate column studied earlier, input multiplicity caused the control system to succumb to wrong control action for large throughput changes. Redistributing the catalyst onto the adjacent eight stripping trays results in significantly improved controllability and energy savings (Kumar & Kaistha, 2008b). Figure 13 plots the variation in the methyl acetate purity with reboiler duty at a fixed reflux rate for this alternative design. Notice that unlike the original 7/18/10 design with conventional feed tray locations, the revised design does not exhibit output multiplicity with respect to the nominal steady state (compare with Figure 5). The non-linearity is thus mitigated in this alternative design with expectedly improved control performance. Thus for example, where CS1 for the original design with the most sensitive reactive and stripping tray temperatures as the controlled outputs succumbs to wrong control action for a -20% step change in the reboiler duty, the corresponding change is easily handled in the revised design (Kumar & Kaistha, 2008b).

The IO relation of product purity (top or bottom) with respect to a column input can be a useful tool to screen out poor designs exhibiting output/input multiplicity with respect to the nominal steady state. To demonstrate this for the ideal RD system, we consider the 7/6/7 design which is the most difficult to control using temperature inferential control (Luyben, 2000). The catalyst hold up on each tray is kept fixed at 1 kmol. Keeping the distillate rate equal to the fresh feed rate, the reflux ratio can be adjusted for reaction conversions of 90%, 95% or 98.5% with corresponding product purities of 90%, 95% and 98.5%. As shown in Figure 14, for a column pressure of 9 bars, the distillate and bottoms purity IO relations exhibit input and output multiplicity with respect to the nominal steady state for high conversions (and purities) of 95% and 98.5%. The multiplicity disappears for 90% conversion suggesting that high conversion RD columns are likely to exhibit multiplicity and therefore susceptible to consequent non-linear dynamic phenomena.

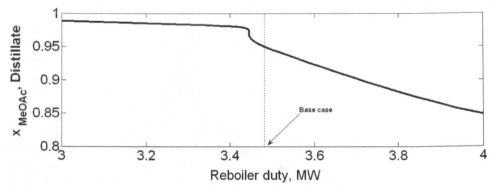

Fig. 13. Steady state variation of methyl acetate purity with respect to reboiler duty

We now consider column re-design for the highest considered conversion (and purity) of 98.5%. Holding the number of stripping trays equal to the number of rectifying trays, the number of reactive trays is increased and the IO relation of the distillate purity with respect to vapor boilup at constant reflux ratio is obtained. Similarly, holding the number of reactive trays constant, the number of stripping trays (equal to rectifying trays) is altered and the distillate purity-boilup IO relation is generated. Table 4 reports whether input or output multiplicity is observed in the different designs. From the Table, observe that simply reducing the number of rectifying (and stripping) trays from 7 to 4 causes the IO relation to be well behaved with no input/output multiplicity. The boilup is however too high and the design is uneconomical. No multiplicity is also observed for column designs with higher number of reactive trays and not too many fractionation trays, specifically, in the 4/9/4 and 7/12/7 designs. Of these, the latter consumes much less energy with a 30.17% lower boilup than the former. This design thus appears to be a good one both from the process economics and controllability perspectives.

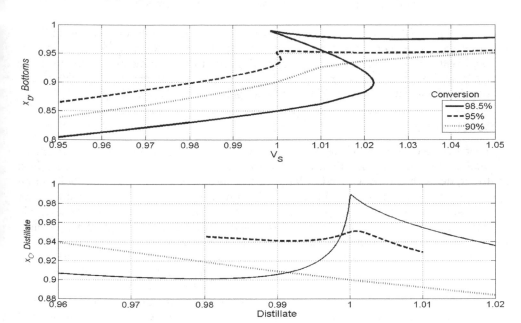

Fig. 14. Variation of $x_C{}^D$ & $x_D{}^B$ with vapour boilup and distillate for ideal RD 7/6/7 design

Design	Input multiplicity	Output multiplicity	Reflux ratio	Vapor boilup, mol s⁻¹
4/6/4	No	No	12.4400	151.4698
7/6/7	Yes	Yes	3.2841	36.1073
10/6/10	Yes	Yes	2.8155	30.2030
13/6/13	Yes	Yes	2.7311	29.1397
4/9/4	No	No	4.0037	45.1734
7/9/7	Yes	Yes	2.8312	30.4013
10/9/10	Yes	Yes	2.7868	29.8415
13/9/13	Yes	Yes	2.7774	29.7223
4/12/4	No	No	3.0407	33.0401
7/12/7	No	No	2.9055	31.3368
10/12/10	No	Yes	2.9007	31.2766
13/12/13	No	Yes	2.8996	31.2621
16/12/16	No	Yes	2.8989	31.2543

Table 4. Nature of the IO relation of bottom product purity versus vapour boilup (Ideal RD)

The multiplicity trends in the Table also suggest that excess fractionation capacity causes output multiplicity to 'appear' in the IO relations (compare e.g. 4/9/4 design with 7/9/7 design). The process design must therefore seek the appropriate balance between reaction capacity and fractionation capacity for well behaved IO relations (Bisowarno et al., 2004). For an economical design, sufficient reaction capacity must be provided.

We have dynamically tested both the 4/9/4 and 7/12/7 designs of 95% conversion (x_C, $Distillate = x_D$, $Bottoms = 0.95$) using two-point temperature inferential control structures similar to the ones studied earlier. Large throughput changes (up to 40%) in either direction are handled without wrong control action suggesting that these designs are inherently more controllable. This simple example demonstrates the power of steady state bifurcation analysis in arriving at economical RD column designs with good controllability.

5. Conclusions

To conclude, we hope that this Chapter has convinced the reader that a systematic evaluation of steady state multiplicity in RD systems is fundamental for designing robust control systems that effectively reject large disturbances. Specifically, the possibility of an open loop steady state transition due to output multiplicity and wrong control action under closed loop operation due to input multiplicity has been demonstrated for the example systems studied here. To improve the robustness of the control system, the controlled variables should be selected with care for a larger operating window around the nominal steady state without a crossover in the IO relation. In conjunction with local linear tools such as open loop gain, Niederlinski Index and relative gain, the proposed rangeability metric is a useful tool for selecting 'robust' controlled variables and rejecting poor choices that may potentially succumb to non-linear dynamic phenomena. The steady state IO relations (bifurcation analysis) can also help in arriving at an inherently more controllable and economical RD process design.

6. References

Agreda, V.H., Partin, L.R., Heise, W.H. (1990). High-purity methyl acetate via reactive distillation, *Chemical Engineering Progress, 86(2)*, pp.40 – 46.

Al-Arfaj, M.A., Luyben, W.L. (2000). Comparison of alternative control structures for an ideal two-product reactive distillation column, *Industrial and Engineering Chemitsry Research*, 39(9), pp.3298-3307.

Al-Arfaj, M.A., Luyben, W.L. (2002). Comparative control study of ideal and methy acetate reactive distillation, *Chemical Engineering Science, 57*, pp.5039-5050.

Astrom, K. J., Hagglund. (1984). Automatic tuning of simple regulators with specifications on phase and amplitude margins, *Automatica, 20*, pp.645-651.

Backhaus, A. A. (1921). Continuous Processes for the Manufacture of Esters, US patent 1400849.

Bisowarno, B., Tian, Y.-C., Tadé, M. O. (2004). Interaction of separation and reactive stages on ETBE reactive distillation columns, *AIChE Journal*, 50(3), pp.646-653.

Ciric, A.R., Miao, P. (1994). Steady state multiplicities in an ethylene glycol reactive distillation column, *Industrial and Engineering Chemistry Research, 33*, pp.2738-2748.

Dorn, C., Guttinger, T.E., Wells, G.J., Morari, M., Kienle, A., Klein, E., Gilles, E.-D. (1998). Stabilization of an unstable distillation column, *Industrial and Engineering Chemistry Research*, 37(2), pp.506-515.

Engell, S., Fernholz, G. (2003). Control of a reactive separation process, *Chemical Engineering and Processing, 42*, pp.201-210.

Huang, K., Nakaiwa, M., Tsutsumi, A. (2006). Towards further internal heat integration in design of reactive distillation columns. – Part 2: The process dynamics and operation, *Chemical Engineering Science*, 61(16), pp.5377-5392.

Huss, R. S., Chen, F., Malone, M. F., Doherty, M. F. (2003). Reactive distillation for methyl acetate production, *Computers and Chemical Engineering, 27*, pp.1855-1866.

Jacobs, R., Krishna, R. (1993). Multiple solutions in reactive distillation for methyl-tert-butyl ether synthesis, *Industrial and Engineering Chemistry Research, 32*, pp.1706-1709.

Kienle, A., Marquardt, W. (2003). Nonlinear dynamics and control of Reactive distillation processes. In K. Sundmacher and A. Kienle, Eds.; *Reactive distillation – status and future directions*. Wiley-VCH:Weinheim, 241-281. ISBN 978-3527305797

Kumar, M.V.P., Kaistha, N. (2008). Role of multiplicity in reactive distillation control system design, *Journal of Process Control*, 18 (7-8), pp.692-706.

Kumar, M.V.P., Kaistha, N. (2008a). Internal heat integration and controllability of double feed reactive distillation columns, 1. Effect of feed tray location, *Industrial and Engineering Chemistry Research*, 47(19), pp.7294-7303.

Kumar, M.V.P., Kaistha, N. (2008b). Internal heat integration and controllability of double feed reactive distillation columns, 1. Effect of catalyst redistribution, *Industrial and Engineering Chemistry Research*, 47(19), pp.7304-7311.

Luyben, W.L. (2000). Economic and dynamic impact of use of excess reactant in reactive distillation systems, *Industrial and Engineering Chemistry Research, 39*, pp.2935-2946.

Mohl, K., Kienle, A., Gilles, E., Rapmund, P., Sundmacher, K., Hoffmann, U. (1999) Steady-state multiplicities in reactive distillation columns for the production of fuel ethers MTBE and TAME: theoretical analysis and experimental verification, *Chemical Engineering Science, 54(8)*, pp.1029-1043.

Roat, S., Downs, J., Vogel, E., Doss, J., 1986. Integration of rigorous dynamic modeling and control system synthesis for distillation columns. In Morari, M., McAvoy, T.J., (Eds), Chemical Process Control; CPC III, Elsevier: Amesterdam, The Netherlands.

Siirola, J. J. (1995). An industrial perspective on process synthesis, *A.I.Ch.E. Symposium Series, 91 (304)*, pp.222-233.

Singh, B.P., Singh, R., Kumar, M.V.P., Kaistha, N. (2005). Steady state analysis of reactive distillation using homotopy continuation method, *Chemical Engineering Research and Design*, 83A, 959-968.

Sneesby, M.G., Tade, M.O., Datta, R., Smith, T.N. (1997). ETBE synthesis via reactive distillation. 2. Dynamic simulation and control aspects, *Industrial and Engineering Chemistry Research, 36*, pp.1870-1881.

Taylor, R., Krishna, R. (2000). Modeling of reactive distillation, *Chemical Engineering Science, 55*, 5183–5229.

Towler, G.P., Frey, S.J., (2001). Reactive Distillation, Kulpratipanja, S., Ed. In *Reactive Separation Processes*, Taylor & Francis. ISBN 978-1560328254

Tyreus, B.D., Luyben, W.L., 1992. Tuning PI controllers for integrator/deadtime processes, *Industrial and Engineering Chemistry Research*, 31, pp.2625-2628.

3

Robust Multivariable Control of Ill-Conditioned Plants – A Case Study for High-Purity Distillation

Kiyanoosh Razzaghi and Farhad Shahraki
Department of Chemical Engineering,
University of Sistan and Baluchestan, Zahedan
Iran

1. Introduction

Distillation is one of the most important unit operations in the chemical industry. Among various distillation operations, control of high-purity column poses difficult control due to a number of characteristics of these systems, including strong directionality, ill-conditioning and strongly nonlinear behavior. At the same time, the potential benefits that can be obtained through tight and economic control of the product compositions are very large. This is due to different reasons including the large energy consumption required by the columns and the market requirements which are becoming stricter and stricter. Because of these obvious features of high-purity distillation, this type of column has been studied extensively.

Control systems for chemical processes are typically designed using an approximate, linear, time-invariant model of the plant. The actual plant may differ from the nominal model due to many sources of uncertainty, such as nonlinearity, the selection of low-order models to represent a plant with inherently high-order dynamics, inaccurate identification of model parameters due to poor measurements or incomplete knowledge, and uncertainty in the manipulative variables. Considering the differences between the actual plant and nominal model, it is necessary to insure that the control system will be stable and meet some predetermined performance criteria when applied to the actual plant. The identification and control of distillation columns have been subjects of frequent study due to the ill-conditioned nature of the distillation process. An ill-conditioned plant is very close to singular, and unless care is taken, very small errors can make the model useless. In distillation, this means that a model may have features that are in conflict with physical knowledge (Luyben, 1987; Jacobsen & Skogestad, 1994; Böling & Häggblom, 1996). In addition, ill-conditioned dynamics of high-purity distillation columns leads to high sensitivity to uncertainties in the manipulated variables (Skogestad & Morari, 1988). This effect causes even small errors in the manipulated variables show significant deterioration of the product quality, a fact which explains why open-loop control of high-purity distillation columns is hardly ever satisfactory. The model of a high-purity distillation process has a steady-state gain matrix with a high condition number. The gain matrix is almost singular and its determinant may be affected by quite small model errors, and if determinant of the gain matrix of the model and that of the plant have different signs, no controller with integral action exists that can stabilize both the model and plant (Grosdidier et al., 1985).

Many control design techniques have been applied to the high-purity distillation columns (e.g. Georgiou et al., 1988; Skogestad and Lundström, 1990; Sriniwas et al., 1995; Christen et al., 1997; Shin et al., 2000; Razzaghi & Shahraki, 2005, 2007; Biswas et al., 2009). Some possible improvements for linear multivariable predictive control of high-purity distillation columns are proposed by Trentacapilli et al. (1997) and a simple way of inserting a local model that contains part of the process nonlinearity into the controller is described also. In addition, a reliable model of the column is generally considered as a prerequisite for the design of efficient two-product control by multivariable methods. Another important aspect of distillation control design is the choice of a good configuration. In fact, poor control performance can result from the improper choice of manipulated/controlled variable pairing (Hurowitz et al., 2003). Some authors have been considered control configuration selection (Shinskey, 1984; Skogestad and Morari, 1987a; Finco et al., 1989; Stichlmair, 1995; Heath et al., 2000; Hurowitz et al., 2003; Luyben, 2005; Hori & Skogestad, 2007; Razzaghi & Shahraki, 2009), but there is no general agreement among these authors in choosing the best control configuration, however, a complete review in this field is performed by Skogestad et al. (1990). The main works for selection of manipulated/controlled variable pairings have focused upon using controllability measures, such as relative gain array (Bristol, 1966) and structured singular value μ (Doyle, 1982). The relative gain array (RGA) provides a steady-state measure of coupling in multivariable systems and can be used to evaluate the steady-state coupling of configurations. RGA is still the most commonly used tool for control structure selection for single-loop controllers. Shinskey (1984) used the relative gain array to choose configuration which is applied widely in industry. Several authors such as Skogestad et al. (1990) and Kariwala et al. (2006) have demonstrated practical applications of the RGA that it depends on the plant model only, that it is scaling independent and that all possible configurations can be evaluated base on the a single matrix. The structured singular value (SSV) approach provides necessary and sufficient conditions for robust stability and performance for the situation in which uncertainty occurs simultaneously and independently in various parts of the overall control system (e.g. input and output uncertainty) but the perturbation matrix is still norm-bounded. One of the most difficult steps in analysing the robust stability and performance of any control system is the specification of an estimate of the uncertainty associated with the nominal process model. This is a critical step because an overestimation of the model inaccuracy will lead to extensively poor control performance and an underestimation may lead to instability (McDonald et al., 1988). Several papers discuss ways in which model inaccuracy can be described and methods that can be used for assessing robust stability. The most common multivariable approaches that use singular values (Doyle and Stein, 1981; Arkun et al., 1984) and structured singular values assume that the actual plant can be described by a norm-bounded perturbation matrix in the frequency domain. In chemical process control, nonlinearity is one of the most significant sources of model inaccuracy. We usually have some knowledge about the structure of model inaccuracy due to nonlinearity, however, and this knowledge should be exploited in our robustness studies. In formulating the SSV problem, use of physically-based uncertainty description is important. Simplified models that predict gain and time constant changes as the process is perturbed over the expected operating regime can be used to characterise the uncertainty (McDonald et al., 1988).

The objective in this chapter is to show that acceptable closed-loop performance can be achieved for an ill-conditioned high-purity distillation column by use of the structured singular value μ. The distillation column model used in this case study is a high-purity column, referred to as "column at operating point A" by Skogestad and Morari (1988). Table 1 summarizes the steady-state data of the model in detail. The following simplifying assumptions are also made for the column: (1) binary separation, (2) constant relative volatility, and (3) constant molar flows. To include the effect of neglected flow dynamics, we will add uncertainty when designing and analysing controller.

Column data	
Relative volatility	$\alpha = 1.5$
Number of theoretical trays	$N_T = 40$
Feed tray (1 = reboiler)	$N_F = 21$
Feed composition	$z_F = 0.50$
Operating data	
Distillate composition	$y_D = 0.99$
Bottom composition	$x_B = 0.01$
Distillate to feed ratio	$D/F = 0.500$
Reflux to feed ratio	$L/F = 2.706$

Table 1. Steady-state data for distillation column.

2. Process description

A simple two time-constant dynamic model presented by Skogestad and Morari (1988) is chosen as the basis for the controller design. The model is derived assuming the flow and composition dynamics to be decoupled, and then the two separate models for the composition and flow dynamics are simply combined. The nominal model of the column is given by

$$dy_D = \frac{87.8}{1+194s}dL + \left(\frac{1.4}{1+15s} - \frac{87.8}{1+194s}\right)dV,$$

$$dx_B = \frac{108.2}{1+194s}g_L(s)\,dL + \left(-\frac{1.4}{1+15s} - \frac{108.2}{1+194s}\right)dV. \tag{1}$$

$g_L(s)$ expresses the liquid flow dynamics:

$$g_L(s) = \frac{1}{[1+(2.46/n)s]^n} \tag{2}$$

where n is the number of trays in the column ($N_T - 1$). Fig. 1 shows a schematic of a binary distillation column that uses reflux and vapor boilup as manipulated inputs for the control of top and bottom compositions, respectively. This is denoted as the LV-configuration (structure). This structure is commonly used in industry for one-point composition control.

However, severe interactions often make two-point control difficult with this configuration. Although the closed-loop system may be extremely sensitive to input uncertainty when the LV-configuration is used, while it is shown that it is possible to obtain good control behavior (i.e. good performance) with the LV-configuration when model uncertainty and possible changes in the operating point are included (Skogestad and Lundström, 1990). The simultaneous control of overhead and bottoms composition in a binary distillation column using reflux and steam flow as the manipulated variables often proves to be particularly difficult because of the coupling inherent in the process. The result of this coupling, which cause the two control loops to interact, leads to a deterioration in the control performance of both composition control loops compared to their performance if the objective were control of only one composition. Since high-purity distillation columns can be very sensitive to uncertainties in the manipulated variables, it is important for successful implementation that a controller guarantees its performance in the presence of uncertainties. This particular design task is frequently solved by modeling a multiplicative uncertainty for a nominal plant model and subsequently calculating the controller using μ-synthesis (Doyle, 1982).

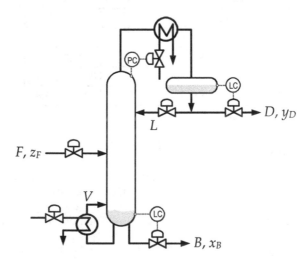

Fig. 1. Schematic of a binary distillation column using the LV-configuration. L and V: manipulated inputs; x_B and y_D: controlled outputs.

2.1 General control problem formulation

Fig. 2 shows general control problem formulation, where G is the generalized plant and C is the generalized controller. The controller design problem is divided into the analysis and synthesis phases. The controller C is synthesized such that some measure, in fact a norm, of the transfer function from w to z is minimized, e.g. the H_∞-norm. Then the controller design problem is to find a controller C (that generates a signal u considering the information from v to mitigate the effects of w on z) minimizing the closed-loop norm from w to z. For the analysis phase, the scheme in Fig. 2 is to be modified to group the generalized plant G and the resulting synthesized controller C in order to test the closed-loop performance achieved with C. To get meaningful controller synthesis problems, weights on the exogenous inputs w and outputs z are incorporated. The weighting matrices are usually frequency dependent and typically selected such that the weighted signals are of magnitude one, i.e. the norm from w to z should be less than one.

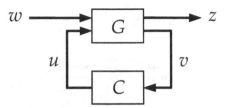

Fig. 2. General control problem formulation with no model uncertainty.

Once the stabilizing controller C is synthesized, it rests to analyze the closed-loop performance that it provides. In this phase, the controller for the configuration in Fig. 2 is incorporated into the generalized plant G to form the system N, as it is shown in Fig. 3. The expression for N is given by

$$N = G_{11} + G_{12}C(\mathbf{I} - G_{22})^{-1}G_{21} \equiv F_l(G,C) \tag{3}$$

where $F_l(G, C)$ denotes the lower Linear Fractional Transformation (LFT) of G and C. In order to obtain a good design for C, a precise knowledge of the plant is required. The dynamics of interest are modeled but this model may be inaccurate and may not reflect the changes suffered by the plant with time. To deal with this problem, the concept of model uncertainty comes out. The plant G is assumed to be unknown but belonging to a class of models, $\mathbf{P}$, built around a nominal model G_o. The set of models $\mathbf{P}$ is characterized by a matrix Δ, which can be either a full matrix or a block diagonal matrix that includes all possible perturbations representing uncertainty to the system. The general control configuration in Fig. 2 may be extended to include model uncertainty as it is shown in Fig. 4.

Fig. 3. General block diagram for analysis with no model uncertainty.

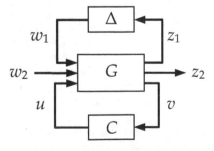

Fig. 4. General control problem formulation including model uncertainty.

The block diagram in Fig. 4 is used to synthesize the controller C. To transform it for analysis, the lower loop around G is closed by the controller C and it is incorporated into the generalized plant G to form the system N as it is shown in Fig. 5. The same lower LFT is obtained as in Eq. (3) where no uncertainty was considered.

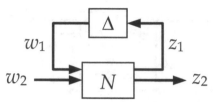

Fig. 5. General block diagram for analysis including model uncertainty.

To evaluate the relation between $w = [w_1\ w_2]^T$ and $z = [z_1\ z_2]^T$ for a given controller C in the uncertain system, the upper loop around N is closed with the perturbation matrix Δ. This results in the following upper LFT:

$$F_u(N,\Delta) \equiv N_{22} + N_{21}\Delta(I - N_{11})^{-1}N_{12} .\tag{4}$$

To represent any control problem with uncertainty by the general control configuration in Fig. 4, it is necessary to represent each source of uncertainty by a single perturbation block Δ_i, normalized such that $\bar{\sigma}(\Delta_i) \leq 1$. The individual uncertainties Δ_i are combined into one large block diagonal matrix Δ,

$$\Delta = \text{diag}\{\Delta_1, \Delta_2, ..., \Delta_m\} ,\tag{5}$$

satisfying

$$\bar{\sigma}(\Delta) \leq 1 .\tag{6}$$

Structured uncertainty representation considers the individual uncertainty present on each input channel and combines them into one large diagonal block. This representation avoids the norm-physical coupling at the input of the plant that appears with the full perturbation matrix Δ in an unstructured uncertainty description. Consequently, the resulting set of plants is not so large as with an unstructured uncertainty description and the resulting robustness analysis is not so conservative (Balas et al., 1993).

2.2 Robust performance and robust stability
For obtaining good set point tracking, it is obvious that some performance specifications must be satisfied in spite of unmeasured disturbances and model-plant mismatch, i.e. uncertainty. The performance specification should be satisfied for the worst-case combination of disturbances and model-plant mismatch (robust performance). In order to achieve robust performance, some specifications have to be satisfied. The following terminologies are used:
1. *Nominal Stability* — The closed-loop system has Nominal Stability (NS) if the controller C internally stabilizes the nominal model G_o, i.e. the four transfer matrices N_{11}, N_{12}, N_{21} and N_{22} in the closed-loop transfer matrix N are stable.
2. *Nominal Performance* — The closed-loop system has Nominal Performance (NP) if the performance objectives are satisfied for the nominal model G_o, i.e. $\|N_{22}\|_\infty < 1$.

3.   *Robust Stability*—The closed-loop system has Robust Stability (RS) if the controller C internally stabilizes every plant $G \in \mathbf{P}$, i.e. in Fig. 5, $F_u(N, \Delta)$ is stable and $\|\Delta\|_\infty \leq 1$.

4.   *Robust Performance*—The closed-loop feedback system has Robust Performance (RP) if the performance objectives are satisfied for $G \in \mathbf{P}$, i.e. in Fig. 5, $||F_u(N, \Delta)||_\infty < 1$ and $||\Delta||_\infty \leq 1$.

The structured singular value is used as a robust performance index. To use this index one must define performance using the H_∞ framework. The H_∞-norm of a transfer function $G(s)$ is the peak value of the maximum singular value over all frequencies

$$\|G(s)\|_\infty \equiv \sup_\omega \bar{\sigma}(G(j\omega)) . \tag{7}$$

Uncertainties are modeled by the perturbations and uncertainty weights included in G. These weights are chosen such that $||\Delta||_\infty \leq 1$ generates the family of all possible plants to be considered (Fig. 4). Δ may contain both real and complex perturbations, but in this case study only complex perturbations are used. The performance is specified by weights in G which normalized w_2 and z_2 such that a closed-loop H_∞-norm from w_2 to z_2 of less than one (for worst-case Δ) means that the control objectives are achieved. Fig. 6 is used for robustness analysis where N is a function of G and C, and Δ_P ($||\Delta_P||_\infty \leq 1$) is a fictitious "performance perturbation" connecting z_2 to w_2.

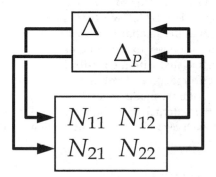

Fig. 6. General block diagram for robustness analysis.

Provided that the closed-loop system is nominally stable, the condition for robust performance (RP) is

$$RP \Leftrightarrow \mu_{RP} = \sup_\omega \mu_\Delta(N(j\omega)) < 1 , \tag{8}$$

where $\Delta = \text{diag}\{\Delta, \Delta_P\}$. μ is computed frequency-by-frequency through upper and lower bounds. Here we only consider the upper bound which is derived by the computation of non-negative scaling matrices D_l and D_r defined within a set $\mathbf{D}$ that commutes with the structure Δ:

$$\mu_\Delta(N) \leq \inf_{D \in \mathbf{D}} \bar{\sigma}(D_l N D_r^{-1}) , \tag{9}$$

where $\mathbf{D} = \{D | D\Delta = \Delta D\}$. A detailed discussion on the specification of such a set $\mathbf{D}$ of scaling matrices can be found in Packard and Doyle (1993).

2.3 Design procedure

The design procedure of a control system usually involves a mathematical model of the dynamic process, the plant model or nominal model. Consequently, many aspects of the real plant behavior cannot be captured in an accurate way with the plant model leading to uncertainties. Such plant-model mismatching should be characterized by means of disturbances signals and/or plant parameter variations, often characterized by probabilistic models, or unmodelled dynamics, commonly characterized in the frequency domain.

The modern approach to characterizing closed-loop performance objectives is to measure the size of certain closed-loop transfer function matrices using various matrix norms. Matrix norms provide a measure of how large output signals can get for certain classes of input signals. Optimizing these types of performance objectives, over the set of stabilizing controllers is the main thrust of recent optimal control theory, such as L_1, H_2, H_∞ and optimal control (Balas et al., 1993). Usually, high performance specifications are given in terms of the plant model. For this reason, model uncertainties characterization should be incorporated to the design procedure in order to provide a reliable control system capable to deal with the real process and to assure the fulfillment of the performance requirements. The term *robustness* is used to denote the ability of a control system to cope with the uncertain scheme. It is well known that there is an intrinsic conflict between performance and robustness in the standard feedback framework (Doyle and Stein, 1981; Chen, 1995). The system response to commands is an open-loop property while robustness properties are associated with the feedback. Therefore, one must make a trade-off between achievable performance and robustness. In this way, a high performance controller designed for a nominal model may have very little robustness against the model uncertainties and the external disturbances. For this reason, worst-case robust control design techniques such as μ-synthesis, have gained popularity in the last thirty years.

3. Modeling of the uncertain system

Analyzing the effect of uncertain models on achievable closed-loop performance and designing controller to provide optimal worst-case performance in the face of the plant uncertainty are the main features that must be considered in robust control of an uncertain system. Skogestad et al. (1988) recommended a general guideline for modeling of uncertain systems. According to this, three types of uncertainty can be identified:

1.   Uncertainty of the manipulated variables which is referred to input uncertainty.
2.   Uncertainty because of the process nonlinearity, and
3.   Unmodelled high-frequency dynamics and uncertainty of the measured variables which is referred to output uncertainty.

Fig. 7(a) shows a block diagram of a distillation column with related inputs (u, d) and outputs (y, y_m). In Fig. 7(b), we have added two additional blocks to Fig. 7(a). One is the controller C, which computes the appropriate input u based on the information about the process y_m. The other block, Δ, represents the model uncertainty. $\hat{G}$ and G are models only, and the actual plant is different depending on Δ. Based on the measurements y_m, the objective of the controller C is to generate inputs u that keep the outputs y as close as possible to their set points in spite of disturbances d and model uncertainty Δ. The controller C is often non-square, as there are usually more measurements than manipulated variables. For the design of the controller C, information about the expected model uncertainty should be taken into account. Usually, there are two main ways for adding uncertainty to a constructed model: additive and multiplicative uncertainty. Fig. 7(c) represents additive uncertainty. In this case, the perturbed plant gain G_p will be $G + \Delta$ where Δ is unstructured uncertainty. Fig. 7(d) represents multiplicative uncertainty where the perturbed plant is equal to $G\,(\mathbf{I} + \Delta)$.

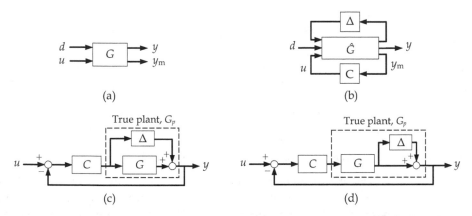

(a)   (b)

(c)   (d)

Fig. 7. (a) Schematic representation of distillation column; (b) general structure for studying any linear control problem; (c) additive unstructured uncertainty, $G_p = G + \Delta$; (d) multiplicative unstructured uncertainty, $G_p = G\,(\mathbf{I} + \Delta)$.

Here we will consider only input and output uncertainties:

Input uncertainty – Input uncertainty always occurs in practice and generally limits the achievable closed-loop performance (Skogestad et al., 1988). Ill-conditioned plants can be very sensitive to errors in the manipulated variables. The bounds for the relative errors of the column inputs u are modeled in the frequency domain by a multiplicative uncertainty with two frequency-dependent error bounds w_u. These two bounds are combined in the diagonal matrix $W_u = w_u \mathbf{I}$. In this case

$$\tilde{u}(j\omega) = \left[\mathbf{I} + \Delta_u(j\omega)W_u(j\omega)\right]u(j\omega) \quad \text{with} \quad \left\|\Delta_u(j\omega)\right\|_\infty \leq 1. \tag{10}$$

The value of the bound W_u is almost very small for low frequencies (we know the model very well there) and increases substantially as we go to high frequencies where parasitic parameters come into play and unmodelled structural flexibility is common. If all flow measurements are carefully calibrated, an error bound of 10% for the low frequency range is reasonable (Christen et al., 1997). This error bound is not common among the researchers (e.g. Skogestad and Lundström, 1990, used an error bound of 20% at steady state). Higher errors must be assumed in the higher frequency range. Because of uncertain or neglected high-frequency dynamics or time delays, the input error exceeds 100%. The following weight is used as input uncertainty weight

$$w_u(s) = 0.1 \frac{1+10s}{1+s}. \tag{11}$$

The weight is shown graphically as a function of frequency in Fig. 8.

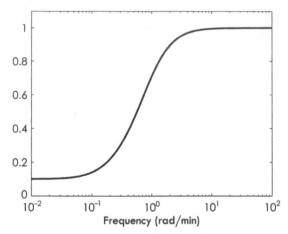

Fig. 8. Input uncertainty weight $|w_u(j\omega)|$ as a function of frequency.

Output uncertainty – Due to the nonlinear vapor/liquid equilibrium, the gains of the individual transfer functions between the two manipulated inputs and controlled outputs may change in opposite directions (gain directionality). This behavior can be described with independent multiplicative uncertainties for the two outputs of the model and a diagonal weighting matrix $W_y = w_y \mathbf{I}$. In mathematical form we can write

$$\tilde{y}(j\omega) = \left[\mathbf{I} + \Delta_y(j\omega) W_y(j\omega) \right] y(j\omega) \quad \text{with} \quad \left\| \Delta_y(j\omega) \right\|_\infty \leq 1. \tag{12}$$

For the low-frequency range, an uncertainty of 10% is assumed for the description of uncertainties in the measured outputs. The uncertainty weight is

$$w_y(s) = 0.1 \frac{1+180s}{1+2.5s}, \tag{13}$$

which has large gains in the high-frequency range that takes the effect of unmodelled dynamics into account.

Performance – The performance weight used in this study is the same in Skogestad and Morari (1988). The weight is defined as

$$w_P(s) = 0.5 \frac{1+10s}{10s}. \tag{14}$$

3.1 Controller

Skogestad and Lundström (1990) proposed two different approaches to tune controllers. The first approach is to fix the performance specification and minimize μ_{RP} by adjusting the controller tunings. The performance requirement is satisfied if μ_{RP} is less than one, and lower μ_{RP} values represent a better design. The second approach is to fix the uncertainty and find what performance can be achieved. In this approach, we adjust the time constant in the performance weight to make the optimal μ_{RP} values equal to one. The latter approach has two disadvantages: (1) it introduces an outer loop in the μ calculations, and (2) it may be impossible to achieve μ_{RP} equal to one by adjusting the time constant in the performance weight. Here the first approach is used for tuning the controller because of the mentioned disadvantages of the second approach.

A diagonal PID controller based on internal model control (IMC) (Rivera et al., 1986) is used to investigate the process. Optimal setting for single-loop PID controller is found by minimizing μ_{RP}. Furthermore, a μ-optimal controller is designed since it gives a good indication of the best possible performance of a linear controller.

3.2 Analysis of controller

Comparison of controller is based mainly on computing μ for robust performance. The main advantage of using the μ-analysis is that it provides a well-defined basis for comparison. μ-analysis is a worst-case analysis. It minimizes the H∞-norm with respect to the structured uncertainty matrix Δ. A worst-case analysis is particularly useful for ill-conditioned systems in the cross-over frequency range (Gjøsæter and Foss, 1997). This is due to the fact that such systems may provide large difference between nominal and robust performance.

The value of μ_{RP} is indicative of the worst-case response. If $\mu_{RP} > 1$, then the "worst-case" does not satisfy our performance objective, and if $\mu_{RP} < 1$ then the "worst-case" is better than required by our performance objective. Similarly, if $\mu_{NP} < 1$ then the performance objective is satisfied for the nominal case. However, this may not mean very much if the system is sensitive to uncertainty and μ_{RP} is significantly larger than one. It is shown that this is the case, for example, if an inverse-based controller is used for the distillation column (Skogestad and Morari, 1988). Controller was obtained by minimizing $\sup_\omega \mu_{RP}$ for the model using the input and output uncertainties and performance weight. The plots for RP for the μ-optimal controller are of particular interest since they indicate the best achievable performance for the plant. μ provides a much easier way of comparing and analyzing the effect of various combinations of controllers, uncertainty and disturbances than the traditional simulation approach. One of the main advantages with the μ-analysis as opposed to simulations is that one does not have to search for the worst-case, i.e. μ finds it automatically (Skogestad and Lundström, 1990).

3.3 Synthesis of controller

The structured singular value provides a systematic way to test for both robust stability and robust performance with a given controller C. In addition to this analysis tool, the structured singular value can be used to synthesize the controller C. The robust performance condition implies robust stability, since

$$\sup_\omega \mu_\Delta(N) \geq \sup_\omega \mu_\Delta(G). \tag{15}$$

Therefore, a controller designed to guarantee robust performance will also guarantee robust stability. Provided that the interconnection matrix N is a function of the controller C, the μ-optimal controller can be found by

$$\text{minimize}\left\{\sup_{\omega}\mu_{\Delta}(N)\right\} \tag{16}$$

At the present time, there is no direct method to find the controller C by minimizing (16), however, combination of μ-analysis and H_{∞}-synthesis which is called μ-synthesis or DK-iteration (Zhou et al., 1996) is a special method that attempts to minimize the upper bound of μ. Thus, the objective function (16) is transformed into

$$\min_{C}\left(\inf_{D_l,D_r\in\mathbf{D}}\sup_{\omega}\bar{\sigma}(D_lND_r^{-1})\right) \tag{17}$$

The DK-iteration approach involves to alternatively minimize

$$\sup_{\omega}\bar{\sigma}(D_lND_r^{-1}) \tag{18}$$

for either C or D_l and D_r while holding the other constant. For fixed D_l and D_r, the controller is solved via H_{∞} optimization; for fixed C, a convex optimization problem is solved at each frequency. The magnitude of each element of $D_l(j\omega)$ and $D_r(j\omega)$ is fitted with a stable and minimum phase transfer function and wrapped back into the nominal interconnection structure. The procedure is carried out until $\sup_{\omega}\bar{\sigma}(D_lND_r^{-1})<1$. Although convergence in each step is assured, joint convergence is not guaranteed. However, DK-iteration works well in most cases (Balas et al., 1993; Packard and Doyle, 1993). The optimal solutions in each step are of supreme importance to success with the DK-iteration. Moreover, when C is fixed, the fitting procedure plays an important role in the overall approach. Low order transfer function fits are preferable since the order of the H_{∞} problem in the following step is reduced yielding controllers of low order dimension. Nevertheless, the method is characterized by giving controllers of very high order that must be reduced applying model reduction techniques (Glover, 1984).

3.4 Simulation

Simulations are carried out with the nonlinear model of the column and using single-loop controller, which generally is insensitive to steady-state input errors (Skogestad and Morari, 1988). In addition, input and output uncertainties are included to get a realistic evaluation of the controller. Simulations are for both cases with and without uncertainty.

4. Model analysis

4.1 RGA-analysis of the model

Let $\times$ denote element-by-element multiplication. The RGA of the matrix G (Bristol, 1966) is defined as

$$\Lambda(G)=G\times(G^{-1})^{T}. \tag{19}$$

For 2×2 systems

$$\text{RGA}=\begin{pmatrix}\lambda_{11} & \lambda_{12}\\ \lambda_{21} & \lambda_{22}\end{pmatrix}=\begin{pmatrix}\lambda_{11} & 1-\lambda_{11}\\ 1-\lambda_{11} & \lambda_{11}\end{pmatrix}\text{ and }\lambda_{11}=\frac{1}{1-\left(g_{12}g_{21}/g_{11}g_{22}\right)}, \tag{20}$$

where g_{ij}s are open-loop gain from the jth input to the ith output of the process. The RGA has been considered as an important MIMO system information for feedback control. Controllers with large RGA elements should generally be avoided, because otherwise the closed-loop system is very sensitive to input uncertainty (Skogestad and Morari, 1987b). Fig. 9 shows the magnitude of the diagonal element of the RGA (λ_{11}). As seen in the figure, the plant is ill-conditioned at low frequencies, while at higher frequencies, the value of the RGA-element drops. This says that only based on the RGA plot, making a decision on the ill-conditionedness of the control problem may be misleading. On the other hand, the bandwidth area is located in a frequency range where the RGA elements are small or at lower frequencies where the RGA elements are large.

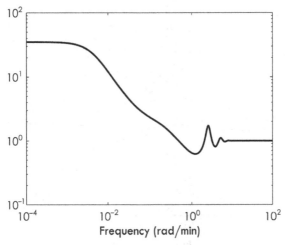

Fig. 9. Plot of $|\lambda_{11}|$ as a function of frequency.

4.2 Ill-conditionedness and process gain directionality

The common definition of an ill-conditioned plant is that it has a model with a large condition number (γ). The condition number is defined as the ratio between the largest and smallest singular values ($\bar{\sigma}/\underline{\sigma}$) of a process model. However, the condition number depends on the scaling of the process model. This problem arises from the scaling dependency of the Singular Value Decomposition (SVD). To eliminate the effect of scaling, the minimized condition number (γ_{min}) is defined as the smallest possible condition number that can be achieved by varying the scaling. Close relationship between γ_{min} and RGA is proposed by Grosdidier et al. (1985). For 2×2 systems

$$\gamma_{min}(G) = \|\Lambda(G)\|_1 + \sqrt{\|\Lambda(G)\|_1^2 - 1} , \tag{21}$$

where the 1-norm of the RGA is defined as

$$\|\Lambda\|_1 = \max_j \sum_{i=1}^m |\lambda_{ij}| . \tag{22}$$

According to the above relationship, a 2×2 system with small RGA elements always has a small γ_{min}. In particular, if $0 \le \lambda_{11} \le 1$ the minimized condition number is always equal to one. A process model with a large span in the possible gain of the model is said to show high directionality and a process model with the smallest singular value equal to the largest singular value is said to show no directionality. Waller et al. (1994) suggest redefined definition of process directionality. The definition divides the concept of process directionality into two parts. The minimized condition number is connected to stability aspects, whereas the condition number of a process model scaled according to the weight of the variables is connected to performance aspects. Fig. 10 shows the largest and smallest singular values and condition number of the process model as a function of frequency.

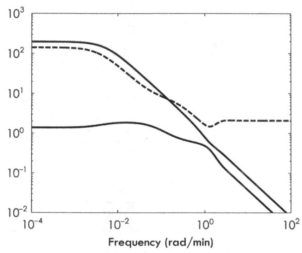

Fig. 10. Singular values (——) and condition number (- - - -) of the distillation column.

The condition number of the process is about 10 times lower at high frequencies than at low frequencies (steady state). Fig. 11(a) represents the values of γ and γ_{min} as a function of frequency. Values of γ and γ_{min} match each other from low to intermediate frequencies, but γ_{min} approaches one at high frequencies. For 2×2 systems (Grosdidier et al., 1985):

$$\left\| \Lambda \right\|_1 - \frac{1}{\gamma_{min}(G)} \le \gamma_{min}(G) \le \left\| \Lambda \right\|_1 . \tag{23}$$

Consequently, for 2×2 systems the difference between these quantities is at most one and $\left\| \Lambda \right\|_1$ approaches γ_{min} as $\gamma_{min} \to \infty$. Since $\left\| \Lambda \right\|_1$ is much easy to compute than γ_{min}, it is the preferred quantity to use. In Fig. 11(b), γ_{min} and $\left\| \Lambda \right\|_1$ are plotted as a function of frequency. The value of γ_{min} at low frequencies is approximately twice $\left\| \Lambda \right\|_1$. At high frequencies, both γ_{min} and $\left\| \Lambda \right\|_1$ approach one (after $\omega = 20$ rad/min). This is in agreement with the result obtained from λ_{11}-vs-frequency plot (Fig. 9). Since γ_{min} is independent of scaling, therefore it is better to use γ_{min} instead of γ, which is scale dependent.

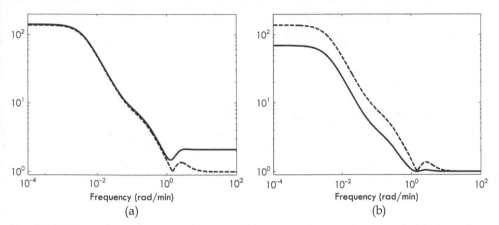

Fig. 11. (a) Plots of γ and γ_{min} as a function of frequency (— γ and ---- γ_{min}); (b) plots of $||\Lambda||_1$ and γ_{min} as a function of frequency (— $||\Lambda||_1$ and ---- γ_{min}).

4.3 Synthesis of the controller

The plots of the singular values of the sensitivity functions $S = (I + GC)^{-1}$ demonstrate good disturbance rejection properties, which indicate the closed-loop system is insensitive to uncertainties in inputs and outputs (Fig. 12(a)). The tracking properties of this controller are also adequate, which is illustrated by plots of the complementary sensitivity function, $T = I - S$ (Fig. 12(b)). Up to the mid-frequency range, the singular values are close to one and the maximum of the upper singular values is slightly greater than one.

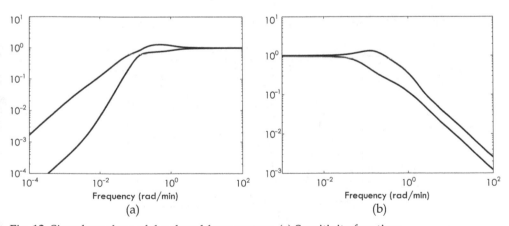

Fig. 12. Singular values of the closed-loop system. (a) Sensitivity function; (b) complementary sensitivity function.

4.4 PID-tuning of the controller

Table 2 summarizes the PID controller setting that is used for the column. Fig. 13 shows μ-plots of the controller. From a maximum peak-value point of view, it is seen that both robust and nominal performance plots are less than one which satisfy the criterion. The plots approach 0.5 as frequency approaches infinity.

Type of controller	k	τ_I (min)	τ_D (min)
PID Controller			
Top composition control loop	0.37	5.16	0.58
Bottom composition control loop	0.20	3.70	1.18
μ-Optimal Controller			
Top composition control loop	0.26	3.43	1.33
Bottom composition control loop	0.31	4.71	0.67

Table 2. Tuning parameters for PID and μ-optimal controllers.

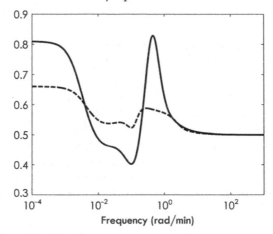

Fig. 13. μ plots for PID controller: — robust performance; ---- nominal performance.

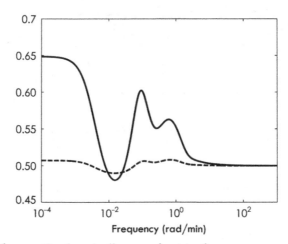

Fig. 14. μ-plots for the μ-optimal controller: — robust performance; ---- nominal performance.

4.5 Comparison with μ-optimal controller

Nominal and robust performance plots of the μ-optimal controller is shown in Fig. 14. Comparison of nominal performance of the controllers shows that for the μ-optimal controller, the plot is nearly flat over a large frequency range which indicates that an optimal controller is achieved. Comparing robust performance of the controllers indicates that obtaining robust performance with the LV-configuration is also possible. This is also in agreement with the results presented by Skogestad and Lundström (1990).

5. Simulations

Simulations of a set-point change in y_D using the PID- and μ-optimal controllers are shown in Figs. 15 and 16, respectively. As it is seen, the introduced uncertainties do not seriously affect the performance of the μ-optimal controller, while for the PID-controller, the effect of uncertainties is more rather the μ-optimal controller. It should be noted that the reference signal is filtered by a prefilter with a time constant of 5 min. Fig. 16 also shows that the PID controller has a slow return to steady state. This is due to the high μ_{NP} value at lower frequencies compared with the μ-optimal controller (Figs. 13 and 14). In Table 3, numerical values of μ for nominal and robust performance are presented.

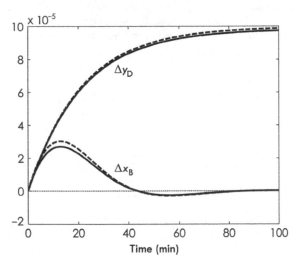

Fig. 15. Closed-loop response to small set-point change in y_D (μ-optimal controller): — no uncertainty; - - - - 10% uncertainty on input and output.

Controller	Nominal Performance	Robust Performance
PID	0.661	0.830
μ-optimal (both input and output uncertainties)	0.506	0.648
μ-optimal (only input uncertainty)	0.611	0.721

Table 3. μ values of the controllers.

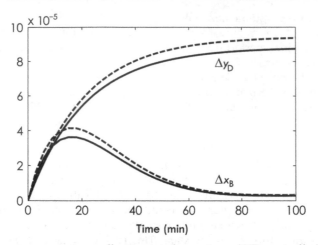

Fig. 16. Closed-loop response to small set-point change in y_D (PID controller): — no uncertainty; ---- 10% uncertainty on input and output.

Fig. 17 shows the closed-loop response of the μ-optimal controller to a 20% increase in feed flow rate. In Fig. 18, the closed-loop response for both controllers is shown simultaneously. As the figure shows, the PID controller needs considerably more times to reach steady state than the μ-optimal controller (see next page for the figures).

5.1 Effect of output uncertainty
Fig. 19 shows the effect of output uncertainty on closed-loop response of the μ-optimal controller. For the case that both input and output uncertainties are considered, the response is faster than for the case that only input uncertainty is considered, however, this difference is not so large. The reason for this again returns to the μ_{NP} values at low frequencies. The μ-values of nominal performance for the case including both input and output uncertainties is close to the case where only input uncertainty included (Table 3)

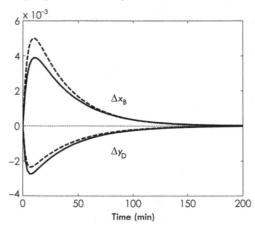

Fig. 17. Closed-loop response to a 20% increase in feed flow rate (μ-optimal controller): — no uncertainty; ---- 10% uncertainty on inputs and outputs.

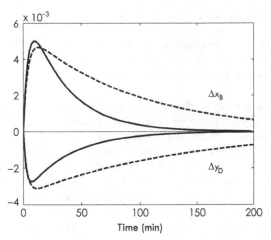

Fig. 18. Closed-loop response to a 20% increase in feed flow rate (including input and output uncertainties): — μ-optimal controller; - - - - PID controller.

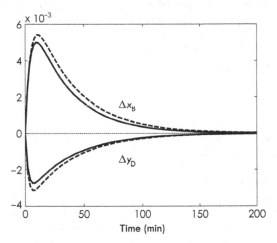

Fig. 19. Closed-loop response to a 20% increase in feed flow rate (μ-optimal controller): — both input and output uncertainty; - - - - input uncertainty only.

6. Discussion

The structured singular value (μ) is used to investigate the robust performance and robust stability of the PID controller. The control problem formulation used in this study is using weighted input and output uncertainties. Although other sources of uncertainty could be included, however, these two are the most severe uncertainties that may be considered. The inclusion of both input and output uncertainty prevents the control system from becoming sensitive to the uncertainties, as may happen with inverting controllers.

The solution of the problem leads to the inequality of Eq. (8). The numerical solution of this design task is difficult. At present, there is no direct method to synthesize a μ-optimal controller, however, combination of μ-analysis and H_∞-synthesis which called μ-synthesis or DK-iteration, often yields good results. This algorithm has two drawbacks. Firstly, the algorithm cannot guarantee convergence, and secondly, the algorithm requires a scaling of the plant in each iteration step, which increases the order of the plant.

The μ analysis advantageously avoids dealing explicitly with the bad condition of the plant. With the μ-approach, the upper bound for the bandwidth of the control system is provided by the uncertainty model, whereas the lower bound is a matter of optimization. μ-synthesis is ideally suited to deal with complex uncertainty models which takes into account such aspects as various operating points. A difficulty that one may encountered in synthesis of controller is high computation time, because the μ approach requires scaling in each iteration. If, however, loop-shaping ideas are used to form the augmented plant, H_∞-synthesis may be used to advantage. In this case, the results are as good as with the μ-synthesis, but are obtained with less numerical efforts (Christen et al., 1997).

In this case study, the LV-configuration is used. The use of this configuration for columns with high condition number may be doubtful, but under special considerations, this configuration may yield acceptable performance. It is shown (Skogestad and Lundström, 1990) that it is possible to achieve good control behavior using the LV-configuration for two-point composition control provided measurement delays are not too large (typically less than 1–2 min). In addition, severe interactions and poor control often reported with the LV-configuration may be almost eliminated if the loops are tuned sufficiently tight. However, this does not imply that the LV-configuration is the best structure to use. Shinskey (1984) showed that the use of the $(L/D)(V/B)$-configuration is probably better in most cases, and in particular for columns with large reflux.

7. Concluding remarks

Based on a structured uncertainty model, which describes the column dynamics within the entire operating range, a decentralized PID controller is calculated using the μ-synthesis technique. The controller was found to be robust with respect to model-plant mismatch, provided the RGA values of the column transfer function are not too large in the cross-over frequency range. The response of the system is improved by using a μ-optimal controller.

In spite of high condition number of the process, nominal and robust performance is achieved by insertion of input and output uncertainties in the control system and using the structured singular value to synthesis the controller. Good set-point tracking and disturbance rejection of the controller is observed by simulations that carried out for the closed-loop system. It was also shown that good control performance can be obtained by using the LV-configuration which is difficult to implement for two-point control. The obtained results also verify the findings of Skogestad and Lundström (1990).

Symbols

B	Bottom product
C	Controller
D	Distillate, scaling matrix
D	Set of scaling matrices
F	Feed flow rate, Linear Fractional Transformation (LFT)
g_L	Liquid flow dynamics
G	Plant transfer function

$\mathbf{I}$	Identity matrix
L	Reflux
n	Number of trays in the column
N	Lower LFT
N_T	Number of theoretical trays in the column
$\mathbf{P}$	Set of all possible plants
S	Sensitivity function
T	Complementary sensitivity function
u	Uncertain input
$\tilde{u}$	Weighted input
V	Vapor boilup
w	Scalar weight, input signal
W	Diagonal matrix weight
x_B	Bottom composition
y	Output
$\tilde{y}$	Weighted output
y_D	Distillate composition
z	Output signal
z_F	Feed composition
$\lVert \cdot \rVert_1$	1-norm
$\lVert \cdot \rVert_\infty$	∞-norm

Greek letters

α	Relative volatility
γ	Condition number
Δ	Perturbation matrix
Λ	Relative gain array
λ_{ij}	i, j element of the RGA
μ	Structured singular value (SSV)
σ	Singular value
τ	Time constant
ω	Frequency (rad/min)

Subscripts

D	Derivative
I	Integral
l	Lower, left
min	Minimized
NP	Nominal performance
o	Nominal
P	Performance
r	Right
RP	Robust performance
u	Input, upper
y	Output

8. References

Arkun, Y., Manousiouthakis, B. & Palazoglu, A. (1984). Robustness Analysis of Process Control Systems: A Case Study of Decoupling Control in Distillation. *Industrial and Engineering Chemistry Process Design and Development* 23(1), 93–101.

Biswas, P.P., Ray, S. & Samanta, A.N. (2009). Nonlinear Control of High Purity Distillation Column under Input Saturation and Parametric Uncertainty. *Journal of Process Control* 19(1), 75–84.

Böling, J.M. & Häggblom, K.E. (1996). Control-Relevant Identification of an Ill-Conditioned Distillation Column. *Proceedings of IEEE Conference on Control Applications*, Dearborn, MI, 570–575.

Bristol, E.H. (1966). On A New Measure of Interactions for Multivariable Process Control. *IEEE Transactions on Automatic Control* 11(1), 133–134.

Chen, J. (1995). Sensitivity Integral Relations and Design Trade-Offs in Linear Multivariable Feedback Systems. *IEEE Transactions on Automatic Control* 40(10), 1700–1716.

Christen, U., Musch, H.E. & Steiner, M. (1997). Robust Control of Distillation Columns: μ- vs. H_∞-Synthesis. *Journal of Process Control* 7(1), 19–30.

Doyle, J.C. (1982). Analysis of Feedback Systems with Structured Uncertainties. *IEE Proceedings* 129(6), 242–250.

Doyle, J.C. & Stein, G. (1981). Multivariable Feedback Design: Concepts for A Classical/Modern Synthesis. *IEEE Transactions on Automatic Control* 26(1), 4–16.

Finco, M.V., Luyben, W.L. & Polleck, R.E. (1989). Control of Distillation Columns with Low Relative Volatilities. *Industrial and Engineering Chemistry Research* 28(1), 75–83.

Georgiou, A., Georgakis, C. & Luyben, W.L. (1988). Nonlinear Dynamic Matrix Control for High-Purity Distillation Columns. *AIChE Journal* 34(8), 1287–1298.

Glover, K. (1984). All Optimal Hankel-Norm Approximations of Linear Multivariable Systems and Their L^∞-Error Bounds. *International Journal of Control* 39(6), 1115–1193.

Grosdidier, P., Morari, M. & Holt, B.R. (1985). Closed-Loop Properties from Steady-State Gain Information. *Industrial and Engineering Chemistry Fundamentals* 24(2), 221–235.

Heath, J.A., Kookos, I.K. & Perkins, J.D. (2000). Process Control Structure Selection Based on Economics. *AIChE Journal* 46(10), 1998–2016.

Hori, E.S. & Skogestad, S. (2007). Selection of Control Structure and Temperature Location for Two-Product Distillation Columns. *Chemical Engineering Research and Design* 85(3), 293–306.

Hurowitz, S., Anderson, J., Duvall, M. & Riggs, J.B. (2003). Distillation Control Configuration Selection. *Journal of Process Control* 13(4), 357–362.

Jacobsen, E.W. & Skogestad, S. (1994). Inconsistencies in Dynamic Models for Ill-Conditioned Plants: Application to Low-Order Models of Distillation Columns. *Industrial and Engineering Chemistry Research* 33(3), 631–640.

Kariwala, V., Skogestad, S. & Forbes, J.F. (2006). Relative Gain Array for Norm-Bounded Uncertain Systems. *Industrial and Engineering Chemistry Research* 45(5), 1751–1757.

Luyben, W.L. (1987). Sensitivity of Distillation Relative Gain Arrays to Steady-State Gains. *Industrial and Engineering Chemistry Research* 26(10), 2076–2078.

Luyben, W.L. (2005). Effect of Feed Composition on the Selection of Control Structures for High-Purity Binary Distillation. *Industrial and Engineering Chemistry Research* 44(20), 7800–7813.

McDonald, K.A., Palazoglu, A. & Bequette, B.W. (1988). Impact of Model Uncertainty Descriptions for High-Purity Distillation Control. *AIChE Journal* 34(12), 1996–2004.

Packard, A. & Doyle, J.C. (1993). The Complex Structured Singular Value. *Automatica* 29(1), 71–109.

Razzaghi, K. & Shahraki, F. (2005). Robust Multivariable PID-Controller Design for a High-Purity Distillation Column Using μ-Synthesis. *Proceedings of the 55th Canadian Chemical Engineering Conference*, Toronto, Ontario, Canada, October 16–19.

Razzaghi, K. & Shahraki, F. (2007). Robust Control of an Ill-Conditioned Plant Using μ-Synthesis: A Case Study for High-Purity Distillation. *Chemical Engineering Science* 62(5), 1543–1547.

Razzaghi, K. & Shahraki, F. (2009). A Survey for the Selection of Control Structure for Distillation Columns Based on Steady State Controllability Indexes. *Iranian Journal of Chemical Engineering* 6(2), 29–36.

Rivera, D.E., Morari, M. & Skogestad, S. (1986). Internal Model Control: 4. PID Controller Design. *Industrial and Engineering Process Design and Development* 25(1), 252–265.

Shin, J., Seo, H., Han, M. & Park, S. (2000). A Nonlinear Profile Observer Using Tray Temperatures for High-Purity Binary Distillation Column Control. *Chemical Engineering Science* 55(4), 807–816.

Shinskey, F.G. (1984). *Distillation Control*. 2nd ed., McGraw-Hill, New York.

Skogestad, S. & Lundström, P. (1990). Mu-Optimal LV-Control of Distillation Columns. *Computers and Chemical Engineering* 14(4–5), 401–413.

Skogestad, S., Lundström, P. & Jacobsen, E.W. (1990). Selecting the Best Distillation Control Configuration. *AIChE Journal* 36(5), 753–764.

Skogestad, S. & Morari, M. (1987a). Control Configuration Selection for Distillation Columns. *AIChE Journal* 33(10), 1620–1635.

Skogestad, S. & Morari, M. (1987b). Implications of Large RGA Elements on Control Performance. *Industrial and Engineering Chemistry Research* 26(11), 2323–2330.

Skogestad, S. & Morari, M. (1988). LV-Control of a High-Purity Distillation Column. *Chemical Engineering Science* 43(1), 33–48.

Skogestad, S., Morari, M. & Doyle, J.C. (1988). Robust Control of Ill-Conditioned Plants: High-Purity Distillation. *IEEE Transactions on Automatic Control* 33(12), 1092–1105.

Sriniwas, G.R., Arkun, Y., Chien, I.-L. & Ogunnaike, B.A. (1995). Nonlinear Identification and Control of a High-Purity Distillation Column: A Case Study. *Journal of Process Control* 5(3), 149–162.

Stichlmair, J. (1995). Conceptual Design of the Control Configurations of Distillation Columns. *Chemical Engineering and Processing* 34(2), 61–69.

Trentacapilli, M., Semino, D. & Brambilla, A. (1997). High-Purity Distillation Control: Some Issues Regarding the Application of Multivariable Control. *Distillation and Absorption '97*, Vol. 1, IChemE, 313–322.

Waller, J.B., Sågfors, M. & Waller, K.E. (1994). Ill-Conditionedness and Process Directionality — The Use of Condition Numbers in Process Control. *Proceedings of IFAC Symposium*, Kyoto, Japan, 465–470.

Zhou, K., Doyle, J.C. & Glover, K. (1996). *Robust and Optimal Control*. Prentice-Hall, Inc., Upper Saddle River, New Jersey.

Part 2

Power Plant and Power System Control

Wide-Area Robust H_2/H_∞ Control with Pole Placement for Damping Inter-Area Oscillation of Power System

Chen He[1] and Bai Hong[2]
[1]State Power Economic Research Institute, State Grid Corporation of China
[2]China Electric Power Research Institute
China

1. Introduction

The damping of inter-area oscillations is an important problem in electric power systems (Klein et al., 1991; Kundur, 1994; Rogers, 2000). Especially in China, the practices of nationwide interconnection and ultra high voltage (UHV) transmission are carrying on and under broad researches (Zhou et al., 2010), bulk power will be transferred through very long distance in near future from the viewpoints of economical transmission and requirement of allocation of insufficient resources. The potential threat of inter-area oscillations will increase with these developments. If inter-area oscillations happened, restrictions would have to be placed on the transferred power. So procedures and equipments of providing adequate damping to inter-area oscillations become mandatory.

Conventional method coping with oscillations is by using power system stabilizer (PSS) that provides supplementary control through the excitation system (Kundur, 1994; Rogers, 2000; Larsen et al., 1981), or utilizing supplementary control of flexible AC transmission systems (FACTS) devices (Farsangi et al., 2003; Pal et al., 2001; Chaudhuri et al., 2003, 2004). Decentralized construction is often adopted by these controllers. But for inter-area oscillations, conventional decentralized control may not work so well since they have not observability of system level. Maximum observability for particular modes can be obtained from the remote signals or from the combination of remote and local signals (Chaudhuri et al., 2004; Snyder, et al., 1998; Kamwa et al., 2001). Phasor measurement units (PMUs)-based wide-area measurement system (WAMS) (Phadke, 1993) can provide system level observability and controllability and make so-called wide-area damping control practical.

On the other hand, power system exists in a dynamic balance, its operating condition always changes with the variations of generations or load patterns, as well as changes of system topology, etc. From control theory point of view, these changes can be called uncertainty. Conventional control methods can not systemically consider these uncertainties, and often need tuning or coordination. Therefore, so-called robust models are derived to take these uncertainties into account at the controller design stage (Doyle et al., 1989; Zhou et al., 1998). Then the robust control is applied on these models to realize both disturbance attenuation and stability enhancement.

In robust control theory, H_2 performance and H_∞ performance are two important specifications. H_∞ performance is convenient to enforce robustness to model uncertainty, H_2 performance is useful to handle stochastic aspects such as measurement noise and capture the control cost. In time-domain aspects, satisfactory time response and closed-loop damping can often be achieved by enforcing the closed-loop poles into a pre-determined subregion of the left-half plane (Chilali et al., 1996). Combining there requirements to form so-called mixed H_2/H_∞ design with pole placement constrains allows for more flexible and accurate specification of closed-loop behavior. In recent years, linear matrix inequalities (LMIs) technique is often considered for this kind of multi-objective synthesis (Chilali et al., 1996; Boyd et al., 1994; Scherer et al., 1997, 2005). LMIs reflect constraints rather than optimality, compared with Riccati equations-based method (Doyle et al., 1989 ; Zhou et al., 1998), LMIs provide more flexibility for combining various design objectives in a numerically tractable manner, and can even cope with those problems to which analytical solution is out of question. Besides, LMIs can be solved by sophisticated interior-point algorithms (Nesterov et al., 1994).

In this chapter, the wide-area measurement technique and robust control theory are combined together to design a wide-area robust damping controller (WRC for short) to cope with inter-area oscillation of power system. Both local and PMU-provided remote signals, which are selected by analysis results based on participation phasor and residue, are utilized as feedback inputs of the controller. Mixed H_2/H_∞ output-feedback control design with pole placement is carried out. The feedback gain matrix is obtained through solving a family of LMIs. The design objective is to improve system damping of inter-area oscillations despite of the model changes which are caused mainly by load changes. Computer simulations on a 4-generator benchmark system model are carried out to illustrate the effectiveness and robustness of the designed controller, and the results are compared with the conventional PSS.

The rest of this chapter is organized as follows: In Section 2 a mixed H_2/H_∞ output-feedback control with pole placement design based on the mixed-sensitivity formulation is presented. The transformation into numerically tractable LMIs is provided in Section 3. Section 4 gives the benchmark power system model and carries out modal analyses. The synthesis procedures of wide-area robust damping controller as well as the computer simulations are presented in Section 5. The concluding remarks are provided in Section 6.

2. H_2/H_∞ Control with pole placement constrain

2.1 H_∞ mixed-sensitivity control

Oscillations in power systems are caused by variation of loads, action of voltage regulator due to fault, etc. For a damping controller these changes can be considered as disturbances on output $\mathbf{y}$ (Chaudhuri et al., 2003, 2004), the primary function of the controller is to minimize the impact of these disturbances on power system. The output disturbance rejection problem can be depicted in the standard mixed-sensitivity ($\mathbf{S}/\mathbf{KS}$) framework, as shown in Fig. 1, where sensitivity function $\mathbf{S}(s)=(\mathbf{I}-\mathbf{G}(s)\mathbf{K}(s))^{-1}$.

An implied transformation existing in this framework is from the perturbation of model uncertainties (e.g. system load changes) to the exogenous disturbance. Consider additive model uncertainty as shown in Fig. 2, The transfer function from perturbation $\mathbf{d}$ to controller output $\mathbf{u}$, $\mathbf{T}_{ud}$, equals $\mathbf{K}(s)\mathbf{S}(s)$. By virtue of small gain theory, $|\mathbf{T}_{ud}\Delta(s)|_\infty<1$ if and only if $|\mathbf{W}_2(s)\mathbf{T}_{ud}|_\infty<1$ with a frequency-depended weighting function $|\mathbf{W}_2(s)|>|\Delta(s)|$. So a system with additive model uncertain perturbation (Fig. 2) can be transformed into a disturbance rejection problem (Fig. 1) if the weighted H_∞ norm of transfer function form **d** to **u** is small than 1, and the weighting function $\mathbf{W}_2(s)$ is the profile of model uncertainty.

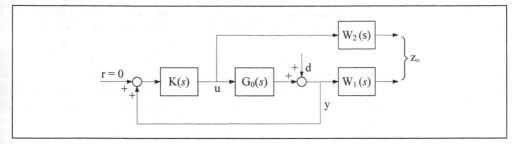

Fig. 1. Mixed sensitivity output disturbance rejection

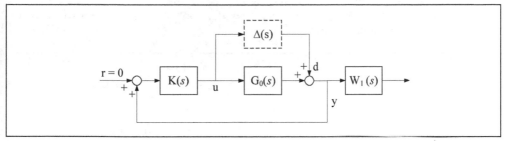

Fig. 2. System with additive model uncertainty

The design objective of standard mixed-sensitivity design problem, shown in Fig. 1, is to find a controller $\mathbf{K}(s)$ from the set of internally stabilizing controller $\mathbb{S}$ such that

$$\min_{K \in \mathbb{S}} \left\| \begin{bmatrix} \mathbf{W}_1(s)\mathbf{S}(s) \\ \mathbf{W}_2(s)\mathbf{K}(s)\mathbf{S}(s) \end{bmatrix} \right\|_\infty < 1 \qquad (1)$$

In (1), the upper inequality is the constraint on nominal performance, ensuring disturbance rejection, the lower inequality is to handle the robustness issues as well as limit the control effort. Knowing that the transfer function from **d** to **y**, $\mathbf{T}_{yd}$, equals $\mathbf{S}(s)$. So condition (1) is equivalent to

$$\min_{K \in \mathbb{S}} \left\| \begin{bmatrix} \mathbf{W}_1(s)\mathbf{T}_{yd} \\ \mathbf{W}_2(s)\mathbf{T}_{ud} \end{bmatrix} \right\|_\infty < 1 \qquad (2)$$

or

$$\min_{K \in \mathbb{S}} \left\| \mathbf{T}_{z_\infty d} \right\|_\infty < 1 \qquad (3)$$

The system performance and robustness of controlled system is determined by the proper selection of weighting function $\mathbf{W}_1(s)$ and $\mathbf{W}_2(s)$ in (1) or (2). In the standard H_∞ control design, the weighting function $\mathbf{W}_1(s)$ should be a low-pass filter for output disturbance rejection and $\mathbf{W}_2(s)$ should be a high-pass filter in order to reduce the control effort and to ensure robustness against model uncertainties. But in some cases, there would be a low-pass requirement on $\mathbf{W}_2(s)$ when the open-loop gain is very high by applying standard lower-pass design, which will result in a conflict in the nature of $\mathbf{W}_2(s)$ to ensure robustness and minimize control effort (Pal et al., 2001). So the determination of $\mathbf{W}_2(s)$ should be careful.

2.2 H_2 performance for control cost requirement

It is known that the control cost can be more realistically captured through H_2 norm, see (Pal et al., 2001) and its reference, this enlightens directly adding H_2 performance on controller output $\mathbf{u}$ at the design stage, i.e. consider constraint

$$\left\| \mathbf{W}_3(s)\mathbf{T}_{ud} \right\|_2 < \gamma_2 \tag{4}$$

to constrain the control effort and mitigate the burden of selection of $\mathbf{W}_2(s)$. The weighting function $\mathbf{W}_3(s)$ is used to compromise between the control effort and the disturbance rejection performance, as shown in Fig. 3.

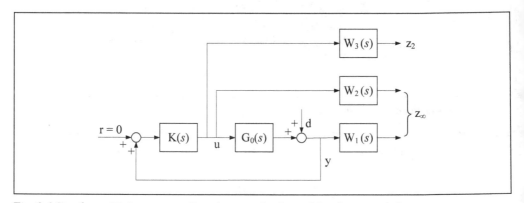

Fig. 3. Mixed sensitivity output disturbance rejection with other constraint

2.3 Pole placement constraint

H_2/H_∞ design deals mostly with frequency-domain aspects and provides little control over the transient behavior and closed loop pole location. Satisfactory time response and closed-loop damping can often be achieved by forcing the closed-loop poles into a suitable subregion of the left-half plane, and fast controller dynamics can also be prevented by prohibiting large closed-loop poles. Therefore, besides H_∞ and H_2 norm constraint, pole placement constraint that confine the poles to a LMI region is also considered.

A LMI region $S(a, r, \theta)$ is a set of complex number $x+jy$ such that $x < -a < 0$, $|x+jy| < r$, and $\tan(\theta)x < -|y|$, as shown in Fig. 4. Confining the closed-loop poles to this region can ensure a minimum decay rate a, and minimum damping ratio $\zeta = \cos(\theta)$, and a maximum undamped natural frequency $\omega_d = r\sin(\theta)$. The standard mathematical description of LMI region can be found in (Chilali et al., 1996).

The multiple-objective design including H_∞/H_2 norm and pole placement constrains can be formulated in the LMIs framework and the controller is obtained by solving a family of LMIs.

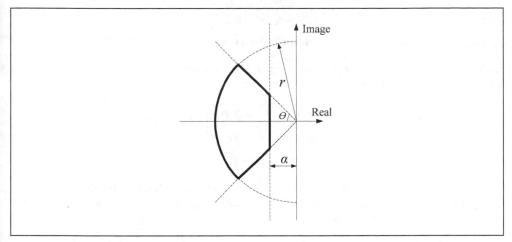

Fig. 4. LMI region $S(a, r, \theta)$

3. Multiple-objective synthesis using LMI method

General mixed H_2/H_∞ control with pole placement scheme has multi-channel form as shown in Fig. 5. **G**(s) is a linear time invariant generalized plant, **d** is vector representing the disturbances or other exogenous input signals, z_∞ is the controlled output associated with H_∞ performance and z_2 is the controlled output associated with H_2 performance, **u** is the control input while **y** is the measured output.

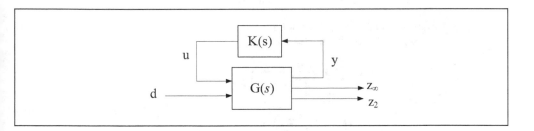

Fig. 5. Multiple-objective synthesis

The state-space description of above system can be written as

$$\left.\begin{aligned}
\dot{x} &= Ax + B_w d + B_u u \\
z_\infty &= C_\infty x + D_{\infty 1} d + D_{\infty 2} u \\
z_2 &= C_2 x + D_{21} d + D_{22} u \\
y &= C_y x + D_y d
\end{aligned}\right\} \tag{5}$$

The goal is to compute a output-feedback controller **K**(s) in the form of

$$
\left.
\begin{aligned}
\dot{\zeta} &= \mathbf{A}_K \zeta + \mathbf{B}_K \mathbf{y} \\
\mathbf{u} &= \mathbf{C}_K \zeta + \mathbf{D}_K \mathbf{y}
\end{aligned}
\right\}
\tag{6}
$$

such that the closed-loop system meets mixed H_2/H_∞ specifications and pole placement constraint. The closed-loop system can be written as

$$
\left.
\begin{aligned}
\dot{\mathbf{x}}_c &= \mathbf{A}_c \mathbf{x}_c + \mathbf{B}_c \mathbf{d} \\
\mathbf{z}_\infty &= \mathbf{C}_{c1} \mathbf{x}_c + \mathbf{D}_{c1} \mathbf{d} \\
\mathbf{z}_2 &= \mathbf{C}_{c2} \mathbf{x}_c + \mathbf{D}_{c2} \mathbf{d}
\end{aligned}
\right\}
\tag{7}
$$

By virtue of bounded real lemma (Boyd et al., 1994) and Schur's formula for the determinant of a partitioned matrix, matrix inequality condition (3) is equivalent to the existence of a symmetric matrix $\mathbf{X}_\infty > 0$ such that

$$
\begin{pmatrix}
\mathbf{A}_c \mathbf{X}_\infty + \mathbf{X}_\infty \mathbf{A}_c^{\mathrm{T}} & \mathbf{B}_c & \mathbf{X}_\infty \mathbf{C}_{c1}^{\mathrm{T}} \\
\mathbf{B}_c^{\mathrm{T}} & -\mathbf{I} & \mathbf{D}_{c1}^{\mathrm{T}} \\
\mathbf{C}_{c1} \mathbf{X}_\infty & \mathbf{D}_{c1} & -\mathbf{I}
\end{pmatrix} < 0
\tag{8}
$$

The closed-loop poles lie in the LMI region (see Fig. 4) $S(0, 0, \theta)$ if and only if there exists a symmetric matrix $\mathbf{X}_D$ such that (Chilali et al., 1996):

$$
\begin{pmatrix}
\sin(\theta)(\mathbf{A}\mathbf{X}_D + \mathbf{X}_D \mathbf{A}^{\mathrm{T}}) & \cos(\theta)(\mathbf{A}\mathbf{X}_D - \mathbf{X}_D \mathbf{A}^{\mathrm{T}}) \\
\cos(\theta)(\mathbf{X}_D \mathbf{A}^{\mathrm{T}} - \mathbf{A}\mathbf{X}_D) & \sin(\theta)(\mathbf{A}\mathbf{X}_D + \mathbf{X}_D \mathbf{A}^{\mathrm{T}})
\end{pmatrix} < 0
\tag{9}
$$

For H_2 performance, $\|W_3(s)T_{ud}(s)\|_2$ does not exceed γ_2 if and only if $\mathbf{D}_{c2}=0$ and there exist two symmetric matrices $\mathbf{X}_2 > 0$ and $\mathbf{Q} > 0$ such that

$$
\left.
\begin{aligned}
&\begin{pmatrix}
\mathbf{A}_c \mathbf{X}_2 + \mathbf{X}_2 \mathbf{A}_c^{\mathrm{T}} & \mathbf{B}_c \\
\mathbf{B}_c^{T} & -\mathbf{I}
\end{pmatrix} < 0 \\
&\begin{pmatrix}
\mathbf{Q} & \mathbf{C}_{c2} \mathbf{X}_2 \\
\mathbf{X}_2 \mathbf{C}_{c2}^{\mathrm{T}} & \mathbf{X}_2
\end{pmatrix} > 0, \ \mathrm{Trace}(\mathbf{Q}) < \gamma_2{}^2
\end{aligned}
\right\}
\tag{10}
$$

This condition can be deduced from the definition of H_2 norm (Chilali et al., 1996 ; Scherer et al., 1997). The multiple-objective synthesis of controller is through solving matrix inequality (8) to (10). But this problem is not jointly convex in the variable and nonlinear, for example nonlinear entry $\mathbf{A}_c \mathbf{X}_\infty$ in (8), so they are not numerically tractable. Choosing a single Lyapunov matrix $\mathbf{X}=\mathbf{X}_\infty=\mathbf{X}_2=\mathbf{X}_D$ and linearizing change of variables can cope with this problem. Choosing a single Lyapunov matrix makes the resulting controller not globally optimal, but is not overly conservative from the practical point of view. The linearizing change of variables is important for multiple-objective output feedback robust synthesis based LMIs. The details can be found in (Chilali et al., 1996 ; Scherer et al., 1997) and the references in them. Finally the result can be obtained as

$$\begin{cases} \min \ \mathbf{c}^T\mathbf{x} \\ \text{s.t. linearized LMIs constraints from (8) to (10)} \end{cases} \tag{11}$$

This standard LMI problem (Boyd et al., 1994) is readily solved with LMI optimization software. An efficient algorithm for this problem is available in *hinfmix*() function of the LMI control toolbox for Matlab (Gahinet et al., 1995).

4. A Benchmark system with undamped inter-area oscillation

4.1 Low frequency oscillation in power system
One of the major problems in power system operation is low frequency (between 0.1 and 2 Hz) oscillatory instability. Normally no apparent warning can be identified for the occurrence of such kinds of growing oscillations caused by the changes in the system's operating condition or by improper-tuned sustained excitation.

The change in electrical torque of a synchronous machine following a perturbation can be resolved as $\Delta T_e = T_S\Delta\delta + T_D\Delta\omega$, where $T_S\Delta\delta$ is the component of torque change in phase with the rotor angle perturbation $\Delta\delta$ and is referred as the synchronizing torque component, T_S is the synchronizing torque coefficient. Lack of sufficient synchronizing torque will result in aperiodic drift in rotor angle. $T_D\Delta\omega$ is the component of torque in phase with the speed deviation $\Delta\omega$ and is referred to as the damping torque component, T_D is the damping torque coefficient. Lack of sufficient damping torque will result in oscillatory instability.

In next section, an example will be used to illustrate the low frequency oscillation of a weak-tied system and the design of a wide-robust damping controller (WRC) to effectively increase the damping ratio of inter-area mode.

4.2 System model and modal analysis
A 4-generator benchmark system shown in Fig. 6 is considered. The system parameters is from (Klein et al., 1991) or (Kundur, 1994). However some modifications have been made to facilitate the simulations. The generator G2 is chosen as angular reference to eliminate the undesired zero eigenvalues. Saturation and speed governor are not modeled. Excitation system is chosen by thyristor exciter with a high transient gain. All loads are represented by constant impedance model and complete system parameters are listed in Appendix.

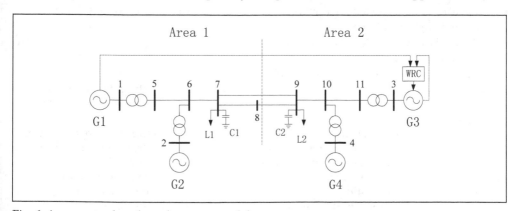

Fig. 6. 4-generator benchmark system model

After linearization around given operating condition and elimination of algebraic variables, the following state-space representation is obtained.

$$\left.\begin{array}{l} \dot{x}=Ax+B_u u \\ y=C_y x \end{array}\right\} \tag{12}$$

where x is state vector; u is input vector, y is output vector; A is the state matrix depending on the system operating conditions, B_u and C_y are input and output matrices, respectively. The number of the original state variables is 28, since generator 2 has been chosen as angular reference, 2 sates are eliminated, so the number of state variables is 26.

Following the small-signal theory (Kundur, 1994), the eigenvalues of the test system and corresponding frequencies, damping ratios and electromechanical correlation ratios are calculated. The results are classified in Table 1. It can be found that mode 3 is undamped, which means that the disturbed system can not hold transient stability.

The electromechanical correlation ratio in Table 1 is determined by a ratio between summations of eigenvectors relating to rotor angle and rotor speed and summations of other eigenvectors. If the absolute value of one entry (correlation ratio) is much higher than 1, the corresponding mode is considered as electromechanical oscillation.

No.	Mode	Frequency (Hz)	Damping Ratio (%)	Electromechanical Correlation Ratio
1	-0.7412 ± 6.7481	1.0740	0.1092	5.7087
2	-0.7154 ± 6.9988	1.1139	0.1017	5.6918
3	0.0196 ± 3.9141	0.6229	-0.0050	13.2007

Table 1. Results of Modal Analysis

A conception named participation phasor is used to facilitate the positioning of controller and the selection of remote feedback signal. Participation phasor is defined in this easy way: its amplitude is participation factor (Klein et al., 1991; Kundur, 1994) and its phase angle is angle of eigenvector. The analysis results are shown in Fig. 7, in which all vectors are originated from origin (0, 0) and vector arrows are omitted for simplicity.

It can be seen that

- Mode 1 is a local mode between G1 and G2. The Participation phasor of G3 and G4 are too small to be identified;
- Mode 2 is a local mode between G3 and G4. The Participation phasor of G1 and G2 are too small to be identified;
- Mode 3 is an inter-area mode between G1, G2 and G3, G4.

Wide-area controller is located in G3, which has highest participation factor than others. Even if using local signal only, the controller locating in G3 will have more effects than locating in other generators.

Often the residue indicates the sensitivity of eigenvalues to feedback transfer function (Rogers, 2000), that is to say if residue is 0 then feedback control have no effects on controlled system, so residue is used to select suitable remote feedback signal provided by PMU. The residue corresponding to the transfer function between rotor speed output of G1 and excitation system input of G3 is 1.58 (normalized value), while the residue corresponding to the transfer function between rotor speed output of G2 and excitation system input of G3 is 1 (normalized value). So the remote signal is chosen from G1.

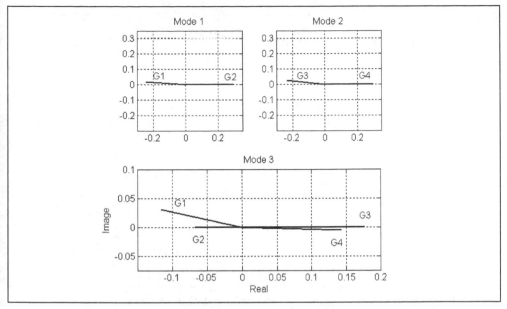

Fig. 7. Participation phasors of considered power system

The positioning of controller and the selection of signals are shown in Fig. 6. Both local and remote feedback signals are rotor speed deviation $\Delta\omega$, in this way the component of torque (see in section 4.1) can be increased directly, and controller output u of WRC is an input to the automatic voltage regulators (AVRs) of G3. The configuration of WRC, excitation system and voltage transducer is shown in Fig. 8.

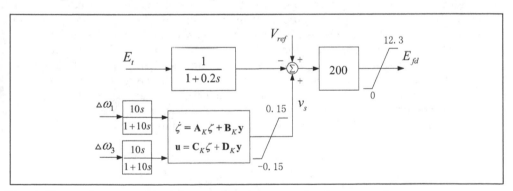

Fig. 8. The configuration of WRC, excitation system and voltage transducer

5. Wide-area robust damping controller design

5.1 Designprocedure

The basic steps of controller design are summarized as below.

(1) Reduce the original system model through Schur balanced truncation technique (Zhou et al., 1998), a reduced 9-order system model can be obtained. The frequency responses of

original and reduced model are compared in Fig. 9, it shows that reduced system has proper approximation to original system within considered frequency range.

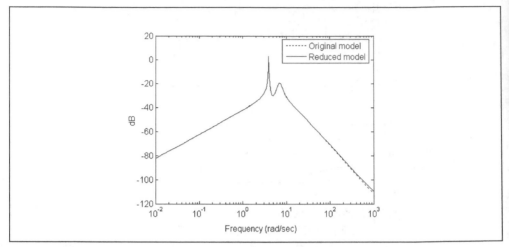

Fig. 9. Frequency response of original system model and reduced system model

(2) Formulate the generalized plant in Fig. 5 using the reduced model and the weighting function. The weighting functions are chosen as follows:

$$\mathbf{W}_1(s) = \frac{80}{s+41}, \quad \mathbf{W}_2(s) = \frac{8.6s+4}{s+4}, \quad \mathbf{W}_3(s) = 1 \qquad (13)$$

The weighting functions are in accordance with the basic requirements of mixed-sensitivity design. $\mathbf{W}_1(s)$ is a low-pass filter for output disturbance rejection, $\mathbf{W}_2(s)$ is a high-pass filter for covering the additive model uncertainty, and $\mathbf{W}_3(s)$ is a weight on H_2 performance.

(3) Controller design by using the Robust Control Toolbox in Matlab. The solution is numerically sought using suitably defined objectives in the arguments of the *hinfmix*() function of the Robust Control Toolbox. The LMI region is chosen as a conic sector with inner angle equals 2*acos(0.17) (corresponding damping ratio 17%) and apex at the origin.

(4) Controller reduction through Schur balanced truncation technique. A 4-order 2-input 1-output controller is obtained. The state-space representation of the designed controller is

$$\mathbf{A}_K = \begin{pmatrix} -5.4 & 11.6 & -4.0 & -0.1 \\ -1.9 & -14.2 & 16.1 & -0.5 \\ -9.3 & 25.2 & -14.5 & 0.0 \\ -3.3 & 125.6 & -10.4 & -2.7 \end{pmatrix}, \ \mathbf{B}_K = \begin{pmatrix} -0.36 & 6.66 \\ -0.36 & -8.82 \\ 0.72 & 14.94 \\ 8.1 & 25.52 \end{pmatrix}$$

$$\mathbf{C}_K = \begin{pmatrix} -19.5 & -25.7 & 60 & 2.1 \end{pmatrix}, \ \mathbf{D}_K = \begin{pmatrix} 0 \\ 0 \end{pmatrix}.$$

A washout filter 10s/(10s+1) is added in each feedback channel as shown in Fig. 8. This is a standard practice to prevent the damping controllers from responding to very slow variations in the system conditions (Kundur, 1994). A limit of [—0.15, 0.15] (pu) is imposed on the output of the designed controller.

5.2 Computer simulations and robustness validation

Computer simulations are carried out to test the effectiveness and performance of the designed controller and validate the robustness in different operating conditions. The simulation is carried out by Matlab-Simulink.

A 5%-magnitude pulse, applied for 12 cycles at the voltage reference of G1, is used to simulate the modes of oscillation. For comparison, one conventional PSS is also considered. The PSS has one gain, one washout and two phase compensations, the block diagram representation of the conventional PSS is shown in Fig. 10. The parameters are adopted directly from (Kundur, 1994).

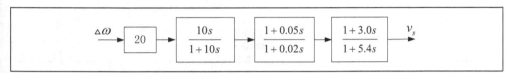

Fig. 10. Block diagram of conventional PSS

Figure 11 shows the tie line (transmission lines between bus 7 and bus 9 in Fig. 6) active power response to the pulse disturbance without any damping controller (with only AVRs in each generator). It shows that the open-loop system oscillates and is unstable.

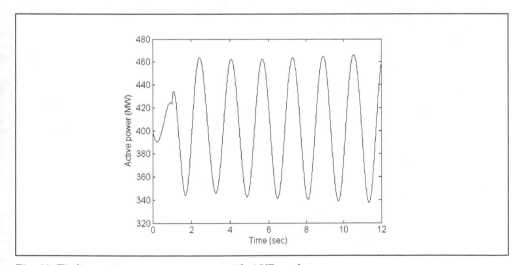

Fig. 11. Tie line active power response with AVRs only

The pulse response with the designed WRC is shown in Fig. 12, which is compared with the response with one conventional PSS located in G3. The state variable is the tie line active power. Both of the damping controllers can ensure the system asymptotic stable but better damping performance is achieved by the WRC.

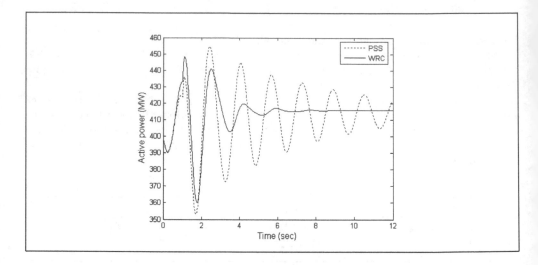

Fig. 12. Tie line active power response with one PSS and the WRC

Figure 13 shows the pulse responses of the system in the cases of open-loop, controlled by one PSS and by the WRC. The state variables in this figure are the rotor speeds of all the generators. The inter-area mode oscillation between G1, G2 and G3, G4 can be clearly identified from the open-loop responses. The rotor speed response of the designed controller shows better damping performance than that of conventional PSS.

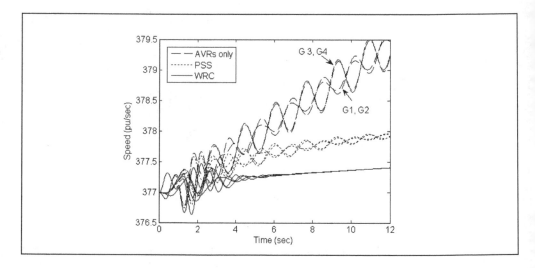

Fig. 13. Rotor speed responses of all the generators with AVRs only, one PSS and the WRC

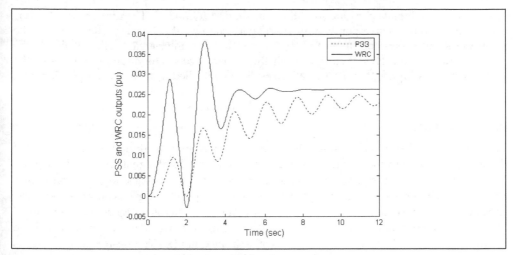

Fig. 14. Outputs of PSS and WRC

Figure 14 shows the outputs of the PSS and the WRC, the WRC show better transient performance and its output is not higher than 0.04 pu.

To test the robustness of the designed controller to changes of operating conditions (or model uncertainties), load changes are considered. Eight different operation conditions are considered, corresponding load L_1 and L_2 in normal conditions and change between ±5%and ±10%, respectively. The load change, making the tie line power change, is the primary factor affecting the eigenvalues of the matrix $\mathbf{A}$ (also the damping ratios) in system model (12), and also used to select the weighting function $\mathbf{W}_2(s)$. Fig. 15 shows the frequencies and damping ratios corresponding to these changes. The horizontal axis is the load changes

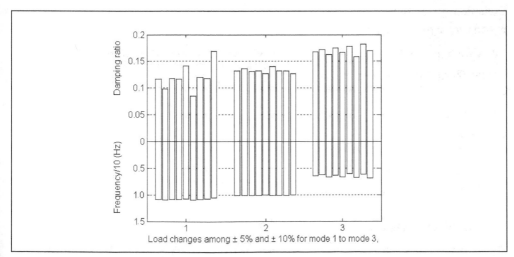

Fig. 15. Damping ratios and frequency corresponding to load change for mode 1 to mode 3

(including the nominal operating condition) for mode 1 to mode 3. The upper vertical axis is the damping ratios corresponding to each load change, the lower vertical axis is the frequencies corresponding to each damping ratio. For inter-area mode, mode 3, the damping ratios are higher than 0.15 in all these load levels. The damping rations of the whole system is higher than 0.08 in all cases. The controlled system has proper damping performance and keeps robustness against the variations of system loads.

6. Conclusion

This chapter applies robust control theory to power system, to design wide-area robust damping controller to cope with inter-area oscillation. Both local signal and suitable chosen PMU-provided remote signal are utilized to construct the feedback loop. A conception named participation vector is used for facilitating the positioning of controller, and the residue is utilized to select suitable remote signal. The controller is designed based on mixed H_2/H_∞ output-feedback control with pole placement, and the controller parameters are obtained through solving a family of linear matrix inequalities. The designed controller is applied on a 4-generator power system model. The computer simulations are performed for pulse disturbance as well as system operating changes. The designed controller shows better damping than conventional PSS and keeps robustness with load variations.

7. Appendix: Benchmark system model parameters

Synchronous machine data (pu)

X_d=1.8, X_d'=0.3, X_d''=0.25, X_q=1.7, X_q'=0.55, X_q''=0.25, X_l=0.2, R_a=0.0025, T_{d0}'=8, T_{d0}''=0.03, T_{q0}'=0.4, T_{q0}''=0.05, H_1=6.5, H_2=6.175.

Transmission system data in per unit

r=0.0001, x_L=0.001, b_C=0.0018, x_T=0.15.

Excitation system data (pu)

K_A=200, T_R=0.01, E_{FMAX}=12.3, E_{FMIN} =0.

Generation (power flow results calculated by Matlab-Simulink) (MW, MVar)

G1: P=700, Q=146.5; G2: P=678.9, Q=137.3;
G3: P=719, Q=138.1; G4: P=700, Q=109.1.

Load model (MW, MVar)

L1: P_L= 967, Q_L=100, Q_C=187;
L2: P_L= 967, Q_L=100, Q_C=187.

Shunt capacitor: (MVar)

C1: Q_C=100; C2: Q_C=250.

8. Acknowledgment

The authors thank Prof. Guangxiong Wang and Prof. Huijun Gao, Harbin Institute of Technology, for their kindly discussions on robust control theory.

9. References

Klein, M.; Rogers, G. J. & Kundur, P. (1991). A Fundamental Study of Inter-Area Oscillations in Power Systems. *IEEE Trans. Power Syst.*, Vol. 6, No. 3, pp. 914-921, ISSN: 0885-8950

Kundur, P. (1994). *Power System Stability and Control.* McGraw-Hill Professional, ISBN 007035958X, New York, USA

Rogers, M. G. (2000). *Power System Oscillations.* Springer, ISBN 978-0-7923-7712-2, Boston, USA

Zhou, X. X.; Yi, J.; Song, R. H.; Yang, X. Y.; Lia, Y. & Tang, H. Y. (2010) et al, An Overview of Power Transmission Systems in China, Energy, Vol. 35, Issue 11, pp. 4302-4312, ISSN: 1540-7977

Larsen, E. V. & Swann, D. A. (1981). Applying Power System Stabilizers, Part I-III. *IEEE Trans. Power Apparat. Syst.*, Vol. PAS-100, Issue.6, (February 1981), pp. 3017 - 3024, ISSN: 0018-9510

Farsangi, M. M.; Song, Y. H. & Tan, M.(2003). Multi-Objective Design of Damping Controllers of Facts Devices via Mixed H_2/H_∞ With Regional Pole Placement. *Electrical Power and Energy Systems*, Vol. 25, pp. 339-346, ISSN: 0142-0615

Pal, B. C.; Coonick, A. H. & Cory, B. J. (2001). Linear Matrix Inequality Versus Root-Locus Approach for Damping Inter-Area Oscillations in Power Systems, *Electrical Power and Energy Systems*, Vol. 23, No. 6, pp. 481-489, ISSN: 0142-0615

Chaudhuri, B.; Pal, B. C.; Zolotas, A. C.; Jaimoukha, I. M. & Green, T. C. (2003). Mixed-Sensitivity Approach to H_∞ Control of Power System Oscillations Employing Multiple Facts Devices, *IEEE Trans. Power Syst.*, Vol. 18, No. 3, pp. 1149-1156, ISSN: 0885-8950

Chaudhuri, B. & Pal, B. C. (2004). Robust Damping of Multiple Swing Modes Employing Global Stabilizing Signals With a TCSC, *IEEE Trans. Power Syst.*, Vol. 19, No. 1, pp. 499-506, ISSN: 0885-8950

Snyder, A. F.; Hadjsaid, N.; Georges, D.; Mili, L.; Phadke, A. G.; Faucon, O. & Vitet, S. (1998). Inter-Area Oscillation Damping With Power System Stabilizers and Synchronized Phasor Measurements, *Proceedings* of *International Conference on Power System Technology*, pp.790-794, ISBN: 0-7803-4754-4, Beijing , China, August 1998.

Kamwa, I.; Grondin, R.; & Hebert, Y. (2001). Wide-Area Measurement Based Stabilizing Control of Large Power Systems — A Decentralized/Hierarchical Approach, *IEEE Trans. Power Syst.*, Vol. 16, pp. 136-153, ISSN: 0885-8950

Phadke, A. G. (1993). Synchronized Phasor Measurement in Power Systems, *IEEE Computer Applications in Power*, Vol. 6, No. 2, pp. 10-15, ISSN: 0895-0156

Doyle, J. C.; Glover, K.; Khargonekar, P. P. & Francis B. A. (1989). State-space solutions to standard H_2 and H_∞ control problems, *IEEE Trans. Automat. Contr.*, Vol. 34, No. 8, pp. 831–847, ISSN: 0018-9286

Zhou, K.; Doyle, J. C. (1998). *Essentials of Robust Control.* Prentice Hall, ISBN 0-13-525833-2, New Jersey, USA

Chilali, M.; Gahinet, P. (1996). H_∞ Design With Pole Placement Constraints: An LMI Approach, *IEEE Trans. Automat. Contr.*, Vol. 41, No. 3, pp. 358-367, ISSN: 0018-9286

Boyd, S.; Ghaoui, L. El; Feron, E. & Balakrishnan, V. (1994). *Linear Matrix Inequalities in System and Control Theory*, Volume 15 of Studies in Applied Mathematics. SIAM, ISBN 0-89871-334-X, Philadelphia, PA, June 1994.

Scherer C. W. & Weiland S (2005). Lecture notes DISC course on linear matrix inequalities in control-2004/2005. Delft University of Technology, Netherlands. Compilation: pp. 70-71. [Online]. Available: http://www.cs.ele.tue.nl/sweiland/lmi.html

Scherer, C. W.; Gahinet, P.; Chilail, M. (1997). Multiobjective Output- Feedback Control via LMI Optimization, *IEEE Trans. Automat. Contr.*, Vol. 42, No. 7, pp. 896-911, ISSN: 0018-9286

Nesterov, Y. & Nemirovski, A. (1994). *Interior Point Polynomial Algorithms in Convex Programming*. SIAM publications, ISBN: 0898715156, Philadelphia, USA

Gahinet, P.; Nemirovskii, A.; Laub, A. J. & Chilali, M. (1995). *LMI Control Toolbox*. The MathWorks Inc, 1995.

5

A Robust and Flexible Control System to Reduce Environmental Effects of Thermal Power Plants

Toru Eguchi, Takaaki Sekiai, Naohiro Kusumi, Akihiro Yamada,
Satoru Shimizu and Masayuki Fukai
Hitachi Ltd.
Japan

1. Introduction

Regulations on environmental effects due to such issues as nitrogen oxide (NOx) and carbon monoxide (CO) emissions from thermal power plants have become stricter[1]; hence the need for compliance with these regulations has been increasing. To meet this need, several technologies with respect to fuel combustion, exhaust gas treatment and operational control have been developed[2-4]. The technologies for the fuel combustion and the exhaust gas treatment include a low NOx burner and an air quality control system, and they are capable of reducing impact on the environment as physical and chemical implementation methods. The operational control technology for the thermal power plants is constantly required to receive changes in operational conditions. It is difficult to realize operational control which responds to combustion properties.

To overcome this issue, the operational control must be able to reduce NOx and CO emissions flexibly in accordance with such changes. Robustness is also required in such control because the measured NOx and CO data often include noise. Therefore, a robust and flexible plant control system is strongly desired to reduce environmental effects from thermal power plants efficiently.

Several studies have proposed plant control technologies to reduce the environmental effects[4-10]. These technologies are classified into two types of methods: model based and non-model based methods. The former methods include an optimization algorithm and a numerical model to estimate plant properties using neural networks (NNs)[11,12] and multivariable model predictive control[13]. The optimization algorithm searches for optimal control signals to reduce NOx and CO emissions using the numerical model. The latter methods have no models and they generates the optimal control signals by fuzzy logic[14]. A fuzzy logic controller outputs the optimal control signals for multivariable inputs using fuzzy rule bases. The fuzzy rule bases are based on *a priori* knowledge of plant control, and they can be tuned by parameters.

These technologies require the measured plant data for initial tuning of the model properties and the parameters of rules when the technologies are installed in plants. It usually takes some time to collect enough plant data. In addition, the search for control signals can only be made in the past operating range, thus it is difficult to find the optimal control signals of they are located outside the range.

The authors have proposed a new plant control system for reducing environmental effects utilizing numerical calculation technology[15] to shorten the time for initial tuning and search the global optima. The system has one or more calculation databases (DBs) with respect to NOx and CO properties obtained by numerical calculation. Since the model can be tuned using the calculation DBs in advance, it is not necessary to take times for initial tuning when the control system is installed. Moreover, the proposed system obtains better control signals than the conventional technologies because it can model the NOx and CO properties including both inside and outside the operating range by the numerical calculation, which facilitates to search the optimal control signals.

After installation, the proposed control system is capable of tuning its model using the data measured in real time to reduce the model errors. In plant control, the shortest interval for changing operations is every 20 minutes because it often takes about 20 minutes to become static after an operation. The proposed system must be able to calculate the control signals during this interval, hence model tuning and searching for control signals should terminate within 20 minutes.

The proposed system employs radial basis function (RBF) network[16,17] and reinforcement learning (RL)[18]. The RBF network represents the NOx and CO properties to estimate their concentrations according to the control signals. The RL leads to the optimal control signals to achieve the control goals which is to reduce the estimated NOx and CO concentrations. The RBF network is one of the NNs having Gaussian basis functions. The RBF network usually learns the NOx and CO properties faster than ordinary NNs because the learning algorithm of the RBF network can be converted into matrix calculations without iterations. The RL is one of the machine learning methods[19] optimizing action rules of an agent by trial and error. It is preferable to apply the RL to the control system which requires real-time computing because the RL is a single point searching method and its computational cost is relatively small. It is also preferable to use the RL because the control history which can be utilized to improve the control logic can be traced in the RL control system. The proposed control system with the above features is expected to realize robustness, flexibility in control and real-time computing.

However, there are two practical problems to enhance these advantages more efficiently in the proposed control system. The first one is ensuring that the model can achieve enough estimation accuracy within practical computational times. Conventional methods to improve estimation accuracy of the model[11] are to adjust radii parameters of the Gaussian basis functions in RBF networks by calculating the estimation error for regression. However, with the conventional radius adjustment methods it might be difficult to adjust radii parameters within the time restriction because the adjustment of radii by regression requires many iterations. On the other hand, a radius adjustment method without calculation of estimation error has also been proposed[20]. This method determines the radii parameters using an equation considering learning data properties such as size and dimension. Its computational time is fast, but the estimation accuracy is worse than the method with regression. Therefore, it is desired to propose a new radius adjustment method for the plant control to achieve both higher estimation accuracy and faster computation.

The authors propose a novel radius adjustment method to overcome this first problem[21]. The proposed method focuses on the importance of covering input space properly where the model simulates the NOx and CO properties by the Gaussian basis functions to improve estimation accuracy. This method adjusts radii parameters considering distances among the learning data. Consequently, the Gaussian basis functions can cover the input space properly and both high estimation accuracy and practical computational speed are achieved.

The second problem is to improve flexibility of the learning algorithm. Performance of the RL depends on the definition of a reward function equivalent to an evaluation function. The reward function has to be defined so that the RL algorithm can obtain the desired goal for the problem. As for application of the RL to thermal power plant control, the properties of the model changes in accordance with operational changes, thus the reward function has to be changed flexibly for the operational changes. However, it is quite difficult to prepare the reward functions for all patterns of operational conditions in advance.

To overcome this second problem, the authors introduce a reward function which has variable parameters and they proposed an automatic reward adjustment method[22]. The proposed method adjusts the variable parameters of the reward function automatically based on the NOx and CO emissions obtained in the learning process. As a result, the proposed method can obtain proper reward functions for all kinds of operational conditions.

The following sections outline the proposed control system and its newly proposed methods. Simulations clarify the advantages of the proposed system with respect to the following points: estimation accuracy and computational time of the RBF network, flexibility of the control logic and robustness in control for the noise of data.

2. Proposed plant control system for reducing environmental effects

2.1 Basic structure

Figure 1 shows the basic structure of the proposed control system. This system consists of a plant property estimation part and an operation optimizing part. The plant property estimation part includes a statistical model and measurement and numerical calculation DBs. The statistical model estimates the NOx and CO emission properties in thermal power plants. It is difficult to express these properties as mathematical equations because they have strong nonlinearities. The proposed system employs the RBF network as the statistical model which can estimate NOx and CO emissions for control variables using data stored in the DBs. The measurement DBs store the measured NOx and CO data for some control variables, and the numerical calculation DB stores data consisting of NOx and CO values for control variables calculated by the combustion analysis[15]. The control variables correspond to input of the statistical model, and the estimated NOx and CO emissions correspond to output of it. The statistical model can be modified by measured data obtained during the plant operations.

Conventional studies have been made about the model based control technology to reduce environmental effects from thermal power plants[4,6-8], but none of them considered employing not only the measured DB, but also the numerical calculation DBs. As the model can be tuned using the calculation DBs in advance, it is not necessary to take times for initial tuning at the time of installation. In addition, it is possible to tune the model after the installation by the data in the measured DB.

The operation optimizing part includes a RL agent, a reward calculation module, a reward adjustment module and a learning result DB. The learning procedure is as follows. First, the statistical model calculates and outputs the model outputs for the model inputs changed by the RL agent. Secondly, the reward calculation module calculates a reward using the model inputs and gives it to the RL agent. Thirdly, the RL agent learns its control logic. Learning results are stored in the learning result DB, and they are converted into modification signals. The control signals of the plant are generated by adding the modification signals to original control signals of the basic controller. The reward adjustment module adjusts reward parameters using the model outputs and the calculated reward. Normalized Gaussian network (NGnet)[23] has been employed as the structure of the RL agent. The learning algorithm of the NGnet is an actor-critic learning method[18], and it is appropriate for learning in a continuous environment.

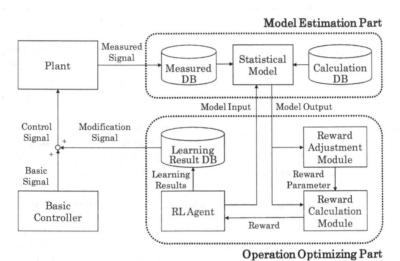

Fig. 1. Basic Structure of the Proposed Plant Control System

2.2 RBF network

The basic structure of the RBF network is shown in Fig. 2. The RBF network has three layers: an input layer, a hidden layer with Gaussian function, and an output layer. First, the J-dimensional vector is input in the input layer. Secondly, Gaussian function values are calculated using the input in the hidden layer. Finally, the P-dimensional vector is calculated by the Gaussian function values and weight parameters in the output layer. The RBF network is preferred for constructing a response surface due to the following properties.

- The RBF network avoids overfitting by the parameter of weight decay[16] to reduce the influences of noise included in the learning data.
- The RBF network does not need iterative calculations for learning of weight parameters like back propagation does[12].

Here, the input and output of the RBF network are denoted as $\mathbf{x}^T = \{x_1, ... x_j, ... x_J\}$ $(j \in J)$, $\mathbf{y}^T = \{y_1, ... y_p, ... y_P\}$ $(p \in P)$, then the p-th output y_p is calculated by Eqs. (1) and (2).

$$h_l(\mathbf{x}) = \exp\left(-\frac{(\mathbf{x} - \mathbf{c}_l)^T (\mathbf{x} - \mathbf{c}_l)}{r_l^2}\right) \tag{1}$$

$$y_p(\mathbf{x}) = \sum_{l=1}^{N_M} u_{lp} h_l(\mathbf{x}) \tag{2}$$

Here, $h_l(\mathbf{x})$ is the Gaussian function value of the l-th basis function, N_M is the number of basis functions, u_{lp} is the weight parameter between the hidden layer and output layer and $\mathbf{c}_l$, r_l are center coordinates and radius of the l-th basis function, respectively. The parameters $\mathbf{c}_l$ and r_l should be determined appropriately because they have much influence on estimation accuracy. In this chapter, the center coordinates are set to the learning data, and the radii are adjusted by the proposed radius adjusting method described later.

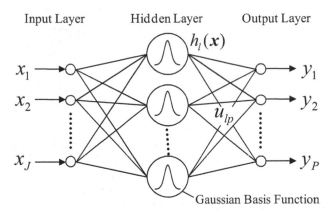

Fig. 2. Basic Structure of RBF Network

Learning of the RBF network corresponds to the determination of the weight parameter u_{lp} to minimize the energy function E_p given by Eq. (3) when the teaching data paired with learning data $\mathbf{x}_q$ are denoted as y_{pq}.

$$E_p = \sum_{q=1}^{N_D} (y_{pq} - y_p(\mathbf{x}))^2 + \lambda \sum_{l=1}^{N_M} u_{lp}^2 \tag{3}$$

Here, N_D is the number of learning data and λ is a weight decay reducing influences of noise included in learning data. The proposed control system can realize a robust control by tuning this parameter in accordance with the learning data. Then, the following matrices are defined.

$$\mathbf{U} = \begin{bmatrix} u_{11} & u_{12} & \cdots & u_{1P} \\ u_{21} & u_{22} & \cdots & u_{2P} \\ \vdots & \vdots & \ddots & \vdots \\ u_{N_M 1} & u_{N_M 1} & \cdots & u_{N_M P} \end{bmatrix} \tag{4}$$

$$
\mathbf{H} = \begin{bmatrix} h_1(\mathbf{x}_1) & h_2(\mathbf{x}_1) & \cdots & h_{N_M}(\mathbf{x}_1) \\ h_1(\mathbf{x}_2) & h_2(\mathbf{x}_2) & \cdots & h_{N_M}(\mathbf{x}_2) \\ \vdots & \vdots & \ddots & \vdots \\ h_1(\mathbf{x}_{N_D}) & h_2(\mathbf{x}_{N_D}) & \cdots & h_{N_M}(\mathbf{x}_{N_D}) \end{bmatrix} \tag{5}
$$

$$
\mathbf{Y} = \begin{bmatrix} y_{11} & y_{12} & \cdots & y_{1P} \\ y_{21} & y_{22} & \cdots & y_{2P} \\ \vdots & \vdots & \ddots & \vdots \\ y_{N_M 1} & y_{N_M 1} & \cdots & y_{N_M P} \end{bmatrix} \tag{6}
$$

$$
\Lambda = \lambda \mathbf{I} \tag{7}
$$

In Eq. (3), both sides are partially differentiated by u_{lp} and Eqs. (4)-(7) are substituted, then Eq. (8) is obtained[16]. The learning of the RBF network can be described as the calculation of the weight matrix $\mathbf{U}$ given by Eq. (8).

$$
\mathbf{U} = \left(\mathbf{H}^T \mathbf{H} + \Lambda \right)^{-1} \mathbf{H}^T \mathbf{Y} \tag{8}
$$

2.3 Reinforcement learning
2.3.1 Basic algorithm
The NGnet for learning of the RL agent learns its action, *i.e.*, control logic, and state value by putting Gaussian basis functions on its state space. Here, the state space is a mapping space to identify its status in the learning environment. The state value is a degree to evaluate how desirable the agent is in its current state. NGnet is known to be able to learn faster than other RL algorithms such as tile coding[18] because of the following features.
- NGnet can learn locally by the Gaussian basis functions.
- NGnet can reduce necessary basis function size by normalization.
- NGnet can add/delete the basis functions and parameter tuning.

Figure 3 shows the basic structure of NGnet. First, NGnet calculates activations of its Gaussian basis functions a_i and normalized activations b_i for the input $\mathbf{x}$ by Eqs. (9)-(11). Next, outputs of actor $\mathbf{m}(\mathbf{x}) = \{m_1, ... m_k, ... m_K\}$ ($k \in K$) *i.e.*, action and critic $V(\mathbf{x})$ *i.e.*, state value are calculated by Eqs. (12)-(14).

$$
a_i = \exp\left(-\frac{1}{2} (\mathbf{x} - \mathbf{\mu}_i)^T \sum_i^{-1} (\mathbf{x} - \mathbf{\mu}_i) \right) \tag{9}
$$

$$
\sum_i = diag(\sigma_i^2) \tag{10}
$$

$$
b_i = \frac{a_i}{\sum_{t=1}^{N_L} a_t} \tag{11}
$$

$$
m_k(\mathbf{x}) = m_k^{\max} f_{sig}\left(\sum_{i=1}^{N_L} w_{ki} b_i + \beta n_k \right) \tag{12}
$$

$$f_{sig}(z) = \frac{2}{1-\exp(-z)} - 1 \tag{13}$$

$$V(\mathbf{x}) = \sum_{i=1}^{N_L} v_i b_i \tag{14}$$

Here, i, j, k denote the subscripts of the basis functions of the agent, inputs and actor outputs, respectively. J, K also denote the dimensions of the inputs and actor outputs. In this chapter, the input of the statistical model is defined as becoming equal to that of the RL agent. In other words, the RL agent outputs the control bias to the input condition $\mathbf{x}$. The reward is calculated based on the results of control, *i.e.*, the outputs of the statistical model obtained after the control.

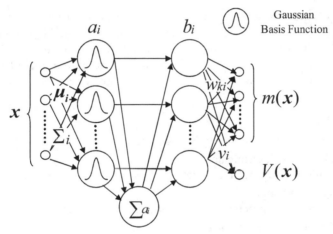

Fig. 3. Basic Structure of NGnet

Here, $\sum_i$ is the covariance matrix of the Gaussian basis function. $\mathbf{\mu}_i = \{\mu_{i1}, \dots \mu_{ij}, \dots \mu_{iJ}\}$, $\mathbf{\sigma}_i^2 = \{\sigma_{i1}^2, \dots \sigma_{ij}^2, \dots \sigma_{iJ}^2\}$ are the center and radii vectors, respectively. N_L is the basis function size. w_{ki}, v_i are the weight parameters of actor and critic, respectively.

The procedures to calculate the actor outputs m_k are as follows. First, the sum of the normalized activations b_i is added to a noise component to search for optimal actions. Next, they are converted to the region of $[-1.1]$ by a sigmoid function. Finally, the actor outputs m_k are calculated by multiplying the maximum values of the actor outputs m_k^{max} and the converted value. Here, n_k is normalized noise whose average is 0 and variance is 1. β is a noise ratio.

2.3.2 Learning algorithm
Learning of NGnet is executed by the following procedures: updating the weight parameters w_{ki}, v_i, adding/deleting of the Gaussian basis functions, and tuning $\mathbf{\mu}_i, \sigma_i^2$. TD

learning[17] is employed to update w_{ki}, v_i. The agent updates its input ($\mathbf{x} \rightarrow \mathbf{x'}$) by its actor outputs m_k, then the model outputs are calculated by the actor outputs. Eq. (15) calculates TD error δ by *reward* calculated by the model outputs and the state value $V(\mathbf{x'})$ calculated by the input $\mathbf{x'}$.

$$\delta = reward + \gamma V(\mathbf{x'}) - V(\mathbf{x}) \tag{15}$$

Here, γ is a discount ratio for the future reward. The actor of NGnet learns its actions to improve $V(\mathbf{x})$, and the critic of NGnet also learns to estimate $V(\mathbf{x})$ appropriately. w_{ki}, v_i are updated by Eqs. (16) and (17) using δ.

$$w_{ki} = w_{ki} + \alpha_A b_i \delta n_k \tag{16}$$

$$v_i = v_i + \alpha_C b_i \delta \tag{17}$$

Here, α_A and α_C denote the learning rates of w_{ki} and v_i, respectively.
The other learning procedures execute adding/deleting the Gaussian basis functions and tuning of μ_i, σ_i^2 so that the NGnet can obtain enough resolutions to learn its state space. The proposed control system employs the following algorithm: the sizes of basis functions of the NGnet are initialized to 0, and new basis functions are added adaptively in its learning.

Basis Addition Algorithm

Step 1. If the current basis function size N_L satisfies $N_L < N_L^{max}$, then the algorithm goes to **Step 2**. Otherwise, it terminates.

Step 2. The activations of the agent's current basis functions a_i are calculated for the input $\mathbf{x}$ during its learning.

Step 3. If there is no basis function i which meets $a_i \geq a_{min}$, then the algorithm goes to **Step 4**. Otherwise, it terminates.

Step 4. If $\delta > \delta_{min}$ is satisfied, the algorithm goes to **Step 5**. Otherwise, it terminates.

Step 5. A basis function whose center and radius is set to $\mathbf{x}$ and σ_i is added to NGnet, then the algorithm terminates.

Here, N_L^{max}, a_{min} and δ_{min} denote maximum basis function size, threshold value of activation and threshold value of TD error, respectively. This algorithm adds new basis functions in the regions of the state space which are not sufficiently covered with learned basis functions. In addition, the maximum basis function size N_L^{max} is set because it might be possible to add unnecessary basis functions by increasing variation of the TD error due to the proposed automatic reward adjustment method described later. Therefore, the agent can put only the necessary basis functions in its state space.

2.4 Learning flow of the proposed control system
The learning algorithm flow of the proposed control system consists of the following steps.

Learning Algorithm of the Proposed Control System

Step 1. Initialize learning parameters of the RBF network and RL.

Step 2. Adjust radii of the RBF network.

Step 3. Calculate weight parameters of the RBF network.

Step 4. Determine initial control variables.

Step 5. Change control variables by the RL agent.

Step 6. Calculate model outputs by the RBF network.

Step 7. Calculate reward.

Step 8. Calculate TD error.

Step 9. Update weight parameters of the RL agent.

Step 10. Add new basis functions of the RL agent.

Step 11. If the terminal condition of the episode is reached, go to **Step 12**. Otherwise, return to **Step 5**.

Step 12. Adjust the reward parameters.

Step 13. If the terminal condition of learning is reached, terminate the algorithm. Otherwise, return to **Step 4**.

In the above algorithm, an episode terminates after executing the processes between **Step 5** and **Step 10** for S times, and a trial of learning terminates after executing the processes between **Step 4** and **Step 12** for T times.

3. Adaptive radius adjustment method

3.1 Basic concepts

In the proposed control system, the outputs of the RBF network are calculated by the Gaussian basis functions according to the input space. To obtain high estimation accuracy, the radii should be adjusted so that the basis functions can cover the space sufficiently.

The proposed method focuses on the covering rate of the basis functions on the input space. It adjusts the radii based on the distances between a randomly generated input and the center of the basis functions selected to surround the input, where the learning data are located. As a result, the radii of basis functions whose distances to other data are short become small, and *vice versa*.

3.2 Algorithm of the proposed method

The algorithm of the proposed method consists of the following steps.

Algorithm of the Radius Adjustment Method

Step 1. Initialize the radii and adjusting parameters.

Step 2. Generate an input randomly.

Step 3. Select pairs of learning data by the k-SN (k-surrounded neighbor) method[24].

Step 4. Exclude the selected data from the data candidates for selection.

Step 5. If there are no data candidates, go to **Step 4**. Otherwise, return to **Step 3**.

Step 6. If there are no selected data, go to **Step 8**. Otherwise, go to **Step 7**.

Step 7. Update radii of the selected data

Step 8. If n reaches N, terminate the algorithm. Otherwise, increment n and return to **Step 2**.

In **Step 1**, the radii are initialized as a small value. In **Step 2**, an input condition x_n (n: suffix showing the number of iterations) is generated randomly. **In Step 3**, the pairs of learning data (x_m^1, x_m^2) (m: suffix showing the number of pairs) for which the radii are to be adjusted are selected for the generated $\mathbf{x}_n$ using the k-SN method. The k-SN method is a data extraction method to satisfy the condition of interpolation. It selects the pair of data ($\mathbf{x}_m^1, \mathbf{x}_m^2$) so that $\mathbf{x}_n$ is surrounded by them.

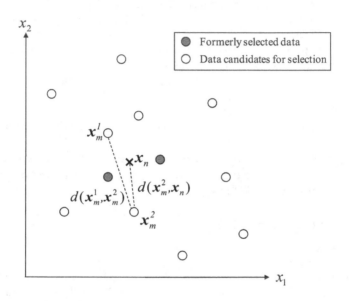

Fig. 4. Mechanism of k-SN method

Figure 4 shows the mechanism of the k-SN method in a 2-dimensional input space. The nearest datum $\mathbf{x}_m^1$ to $\mathbf{x}_n$ is selected from the data candidates available for selection, *i.e.,* learning data excluding the formerly selected data. Then the datum $\mathbf{x}_m^2$ paired with $\mathbf{x}_m^1$ is selected according to Eq. (18).

$$\mathbf{x}_m^2 = \arg\min_{z \in Z} d(\mathbf{x}_z, \mathbf{x}_n)$$

$$subject\ to\ d(\mathbf{x}_z, \mathbf{x}_n) < d(\mathbf{x}_m^1, \mathbf{x}_z) \tag{18}$$

Here, z denotes the suffix of the data candidates available for selection and $d(\mathbf{x}_z, \mathbf{x}_n)$ denotes the distance between $\mathbf{x}_z$ and $\mathbf{x}_n$. In **Step 4**, the selected data ($\mathbf{x}_m^1, \mathbf{x}_m^2$) are excluded from the data candidates. If there is no $\mathbf{x}_z$ satisfying Eq. (18), only $\mathbf{x}_m^1$ is excluded. In this way, the radii of basis functions in an interpolative relation with inputs are adjusted, then the basis functions can cover the input space sufficiently. This selection continues until all the data candidates have been selected.

In **Step 7**, the radii (r_m^1, r_m^2) set at the selected data are adjusted by Eqs. (19) and (20).

$$r_m^1 = r_m^1 + \alpha_{rad} \tau^n \left(d(\mathbf{x}_m^1, \mathbf{x}_n) - r_m^1 \right) \tag{19}$$

$$r_m^2 = r_m^2 + \alpha_{rad}\tau^n\left(d(\mathbf{x}_m^2, \mathbf{x}_n) - r_m^2\right) \tag{20}$$

Here, α_{rad} is an initial step size parameter of radius, and τ is a decay rate of the step size parameter ($0 < \tau < 1$). The second term in the right sides of both Eqs. (19) and (20) decays as iteration n increases, then the radii finally converge to certain values. These steps are iterated until n reaches N, then the radii are adjusted to certain values according to the distribution of learning data.

3.3 Simulations
In this section, some simulations are executed in order to evaluate the performances of the proposed radius adjustment method. The proposed method is compared with two conventional radius adjustment methods with respect to estimation accuracy and computational time using the test function data.

3.3.1 Simulation conditions
Simulations are executed in the following steps: a) determination of radii, b) calculation of weight parameters, and c) evaluation of estimation error. In step a), the proposed method, the Cross Validation (CV) method[11] and the radius equation method[20] are used to determine radii. The CV method adjusts radii with regression, and the radius equation method adjusts radii without regression. (See appendix). In step b), the weight parameters of the RBF network are calculated by Eq. (8). In step c), the estimation errors between the outputs of the RBF network and the test data are evaluated.

In the case of plant control, the shape of the response surface changes according to the plant properties, input dimensions and numbers of learning data. In order to simulate various response surfaces, the learning data are created for different test functions, input dimensions and numbers of data. The test functions $F_1(\mathbf{x})$ and $F_2(\mathbf{x})$ ($\mathbf{x} \in [-5,5]$) described as Eqs. (21) and (22) are used in the simulations. These functions are often used as benchmark problems of RBF networks[20].

$$F_1(\mathbf{x}) = \sum_{j=1}^{J}\left(x_j^4 - 16x_j^2 + 5x_j + 100\right) \tag{21}$$

$$F_2(\mathbf{x}) = \sum_{j=1}^{J}\left(\sum_{k=1}^{j} x_k\right)^2 \tag{22}$$

Table 1 shows settings of learning data and test data of the RBF network in the simulations. Here, the numbers of learning data and test data are denoted as N_D and N_{Test}, respectively. In simulations, the output dimension P is fixed to 1, while the input dimension J is varied from 2 to 10. The parameters of α_{rad}, τ and N are set to 0.01, 0.999 and 3000, respectively. They are set appropriately based on prior experimental results. The parameters of r^{min}, r^{max} and Δr used in the CV method are shown in Table 2. The common parameter, λ is set to 0.01. Each simulation is executed for 25 random sequences using a Linux machine (CPU clock: 2.8[GHz]).

Case	Function	Input Dimension J	Data Size N_D	N_{Test}
1			25	
2		2	50	25
3			100	
4			100	
5	$F_1(x)$	5	300	50
6			500	
7			100	
8		10	500	100
9			1000	
10			25	
11		2	50	25
12			100	
13			100	
14	$F_2(x)$	5	300	50
15			500	
16			100	
17		10	500	100
18			1000	

Table 1. Specifications of learning data and test data in the simulation cases

Case	r^{min}	r^{max}	Δr
1,2,3,10,11,12	0.1	10	0.1
4,13	5	15	0.1
5,14	5	15	0.5
6,15	5	15	1
7,16	5	20	0.1
8,9,17,18	5	20	1

Table 2. Parameter conditions in CV method

3.3.2 Results and discussions

In order to evaluate estimation accuracy of the proposed method, root mean square error $RMSE_{cn}$ calculated by Eq. (23) is used.

$$RMSE_{cn} = \sqrt{\sum_{t=1}^{N_{Test}} \frac{\left(y_{cn}(\mathbf{x}_t) - F_{cn}(\mathbf{x}_t)\right)^2}{N_{Test}}} \tag{23}$$

Here, $y_{cn}(\mathbf{x}_t)$ and $F_{cn}(\mathbf{x}_t)$ are an output value of the RBF network and the test data for the input $\mathbf{x}_t$ (t: suffix of the test data) in case cn ($cn = \{1,2,...18\}$), respectively.

First, convergence performance of the proposed method is studied using the RMSE and adjusted radii parameters. Figs. 5 and 6 show the RMSE and several radii parameters for iteration N in case 5 of Table 1. Case 5 is the most suitable condition for real plants with respect to input dimensions and numbers of learning data. The other cases also show the results similar to those of case 5. From Fig. 5, it is confirmed that the RMSE decreases and converges into a certain value with iteration.

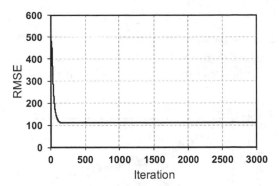

Fig. 5. RMSE curve obtained by the proposed method

Figure 6 shows the adjustment history of 10 typical radii selected from those of 300 Gaussian basis functions corresponding to the numbers of learning data in case 5. In this figure, the radii soon increase with iteration but converge into different values. The reason why the adjusted radii converge into different values is that the proposed method adjusts the radii based on the distribution of learning data. For the data whose distances to other data are short, the distances between the learning data and x_n become short. Consequently, the radii of the data in the region become shorter than those in the region whose distances are long. It is also confirmed by comparing Figs. 5 and 6 that the convergence of radii due to the decay of τ^n contributes to the convergence of RMSE.

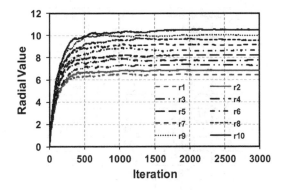

Fig. 6. Adjusting history of typical radial values by the proposed method

Next, Fig. 7 shows the radial values plotted for the crowding index ci of their basis functions calculated by Eqs. (24) and (25). The crowded index ci represents how the center coordinate c_i of the basis function i is covered with all the basis functions having uniform radii, thus this index of the data whose distances to other data are short usually becomes large.

$$h_t(c_i) = \exp\left(-\frac{(c_i - c_t)^T(c_i - c_t)}{r_{ci}^2}\right) \tag{24}$$

$$ci(\mathbf{c}_i) = \frac{1}{N_D} \sum_{t=1}^{N_D} h_t(\mathbf{c}_i) \tag{25}$$

Here, $h_t(\mathbf{c}_i)$ is the Gaussian function value of the basis function whose center is $\mathbf{c}_t$ and r_{ci} is the radius to which a certain constant value is set. In this simulation, r_{ci} is set to 3.89 considering the range of input values.

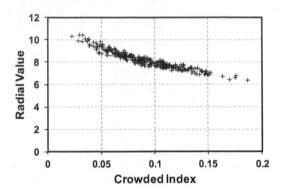

Fig. 7. Relation between the crowded index and radial values

In Fig. 7, the radial values with low crowded index are larger than those with high crowded index because the basis functions in the region where distances to data are long need to cover a wider input space. This result indicates that the proposed radius adjustment algorithm works properly.

Case	Proposed Method	CV Method	Radius Equation
1	76.0	83.5	96.5
2	71.4	70.9	99.7
3	29.5	36.1	63.3
4	138.3	130.3	186.5
5	116.6	115.4	170.1
6	107.2	113.3	153.1
7	201.0	234.1	272.7
8	174.4	166.8	230.7
9	164.0	158.4	239.3
10	7.9	6.1	14.2
11	2.7	2.7	10.5
12	1.5	2.3	9.3
13	39.8	35.3	79.1
14	16.4	12.9	58.5
15	8.9	10.9	48.4
16	268.1	292.2	294.7
17	82.0	58.8	173.5
18	63.9	38.2	175.6
Ave.	87.3	87.1	132.0

Table 3. Comparisons of the RMSEs obtained by the proposed and conventional methods

Table 3 compares the RMSEs of the proposed method and conventional methods. The case values in the table are the averages of 25 simulation results. The RMSEs of the proposed method are smaller than those for the radius equation in each case. The radius equation is usually applied to learning data having a uniform crowded index[20]. Therefore, it is difficult to apply it to plant control where the learning data usually have deviations of crowded index like Fig. 7. The proposed method can adjust the radii considering the distribution of the learning data, thus the RMSEs are an average of 33.9[%] better compared to those from the radius equation. The proposed method also has the same performances as the CV method.

Table 4 compares computational times of the proposed and conventional methods. These case results are also the averages of 25 simulation results. The computational times of the radius equation are enormously short because it spends time only in the calculation of Eq. (34) to adjust the radii. Regarding the CV method, the computational times increase exponentially with the number of data because error evaluations are needed for all learning data. There are some cases where the computational times are well beyond the limitation of practical use (20 minutes). Therefore, it is difficult to apply the CV method to plant control. On the other hand, the computational times of the proposed method in every case are within 20 minutes. These computational times are practical for plant control and it is confirmed that the proposed method is the most suitable for plant control.

These simulation results show that the proposed plant control system can construct a flexible statistical model having high estimation accuracy for various operational conditions of thermal power plants within a practical computational time. It is expected to improve effectiveness in reducing NOx and CO by learning with such a statistical model.

Case	Proposed Method	CV Method	Radius Equation
1	2.8E-02	6.5E-01	7.6E-06
2	9.9E-02	9.2E+00	2.8E-05
3	3.7E-01	1.5E+02	1.1E-04
4	4.6E-01	1.4E+02	1.4E-04
5	3.9E+00	2.6E+03	1.3E-03
6	1.1E+01	1.7E+04	3.6E-03
7	6.6E-01	2.2E+02	2.8E-04
8	1.6E+01	2.3E+04	6.9E-03
9	6.4E+02	6.5E+05	3.1E-02
10	2.7E-02	6.5E-01	7.6E-06
11	9.8E-02	9.2E+00	2.7E-05
12	3.7E-01	1.5E+02	1.1E-04
13	4.6E-01	1.4E+02	1.4E-04
14	3.9E+00	2.6E+03	1.3E-03
15	1.1E+01	1.6E+04	3.6E-03
16	6.6E-01	2.2E+02	2.8E-04
17	1.6E+01	2.3E+04	6.9E-03
18	6.4E+02	6.5E+05	3.1E-02

Table 4. Comparisons of the computational times [s] for the proposed and conventional methods

4. Automatic reward adjustment method

4.1 Basic concepts

When the RL is applied to the thermal power plant control, it is necessary to design the reward so that it can be given to the agent instantly in order to adapt to the plant properties which change from hour to hour. So far, studies with respect to designing reward of the RL have reported[25,26] that high flexibility could be realized by switching or adjusting the reward in accordance with change of the agent's objectives and situations. However, it would be difficult to apply this to thermal power plant control which needs instant reward designing for changes of plant properties because the reward design and its switching or adjusting depend on *a priori* knowledge.

The proposed control system defines a reward function which does not depend on the learning object and proposes an automatic reward adjustment method which adjusts the parameters of the reward function adaptively based on the plant property information obtained in the learning. It is possible to use the same reward function for different operating conditions and control objectives in this method, and the reward function is adjusted in accordance with learning progress. Therefore, it is expected possible to construct a flexible plant control system without manual reward design.

4.2 Definition of reward

The statistical model in the proposed control system has a unique characteristic due to specifications of applied plants, kinds of environmental effects and operating conditions. In case such a model is used for learning, the reward function should be generalized because it is difficult to design unique reward functions for various plant properties in real time. Thus the authors have defined the reward function as Eq. (26).

$$reward = \begin{cases} reward_{\max} \exp\left(\dfrac{\rho - f}{\phi}\right) & (f \geq \rho) \\ reward_{\max} & (f < \rho) \end{cases} \tag{26}$$

Here, $reward_{\max}$ and f are maximum reward value and sum of weighted model outputs calculated by Eq. (27), respectively. ϕ and ρ are the parameters to determine shapes of the reward function.

$$f = \sum_{p=1}^{P} C_p y_p \tag{27}$$

Here, C_p are the weight of the model output y_p, and p is a suffix for model output. In Eq. (26), the conditions $\phi > 0$, $\rho \geq 0$ are satisfied. If ϕ and ρ become larger, a larger reward is gotten for f. In addition, it is possible for f to weight y_p by C_p in accordance with control goals. Fig. 8 shows the shape of the reward function where $reward_{\max} = 1$, $\phi = 10$, $\rho = 20$ are set in Eq. (26).

The reward function defined as Eq. (26) can be applied for various kinds of statistical models where the operating conditions and the control goals are different because it is possible to define the reward only by ϕ, ρ and C_p. C_p is set in accordance with the control goals, and ϕ, ρ are adjusted automatically by the proposed automatic reward adjustment method.

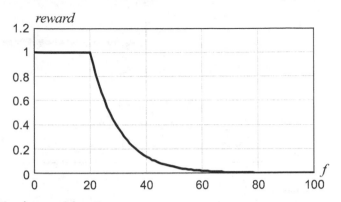

Fig. 8. Schematic of reward function

4.3 Algorithm of the proposed reward adjustment method

The proposed reward adjustment method adjusts the reward parameters ϕ, ρ using the model outputs which are obtained during the learning so that the agent can get the proper reward for (1) characteristics of the learning object and (2) progress of learning. Here, (1) means that this method can adjust the reward properly for the statistical models whose optimal control conditions and NOx/CO properties are different by adjusting ϕ, ρ. (2) means that this method makes it easier for the agent to get the reward and accelerate learning at the early stage, while also making the conditions to get the reward stricter and improving the agent's learning accuracy.

The reward parameters are updated based on the sum of weighted model outputs f obtained in each episode and the best f value obtained during the past episodes. Hereafter, the sum of weighted model outputs and the reward parameters at episode t are denoted as f_t, ϕ_t and ρ_t, respectively.

The algorithm of the proposed method is as follows. First, f_t is calculated by Eq. (28), then its moving average $\overline{f_t}$ is calculated.

$$\overline{f_t} = \varepsilon f_t + (1-\varepsilon)\overline{f_{t-1}} \tag{28}$$

Here, ε is a smoothing parameter of the moving average. The parameter ϕ_t is updated by Eqs. (29) and (30) where $\overline{f_t} > \rho_t$ is satisfied.

$$\phi_{t+1} = \phi_t + \alpha_\phi(\phi'_t - \phi_t) \tag{29}$$

$$\phi'_t = \frac{\rho_t - \overline{f_t}}{\ln(\theta_t / reward_{max})} \tag{30}$$

Here, ϕ'_t is an updating index of ϕ_t, θ_t is a threshold parameter to determine the updating direction (positive/negative), and α_ϕ is a step size parameter of ϕ_t. As shown in Fig. 9, ϕ'_t corresponds to the ϕ when the reward value for $\overline{f_t}$ becomes θ_t. The updating direction of ϕ_t becomes positive where θ'_t calculated by Eq. (31) is smaller than θ_t, and vice versa.

$$\theta_t' = reward_{max} \exp\left(\frac{\rho_t - \overline{f}_t}{\phi_t}\right) \tag{31}$$

θ_t is updated by Eq. (32) so that it becomes closer to θ_t'.

$$\theta_{t+1} = \theta_t + \alpha_\theta(\theta_t' - \theta_t) \tag{32}$$

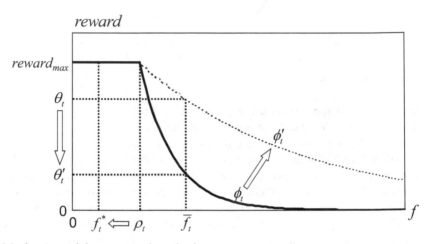

Fig. 9. Mechanism of the proposed method

Here, α_θ is a step size parameter of θ_t. θ_t is initialized to small value. As a result of updating θ_t by Eq. (32), finally ϕ_t' becomes equal to ϕ_t. This means that the reward is given to the agent appropriately for current $\overline{f}_t$. The value of θ_t depends on the learning object and progress, hence it is preferable to acquire empirically in the learning process. That is because θ_t', the reward value for $\overline{f}_t$ is defined according to the updating index of θ_t.

The parameter ρ_t is updated to approach the f_t^* by Eq. (33) which is the best value of f during past learning.

$$\rho_{t+1} = \rho_t + \alpha_\rho(f_t^* - \rho_t) \tag{33}$$

Here, α_ρ is a step size parameter of ρ_t.

The above algorithm is summarized as the following steps.

Reward Automatic Adjustment Algorithm

Step 1. Calculate $\overline{f}_t$ by Eq. (28).

Step 2. If $\overline{f}_t > \rho_t$ is satisfied, go to **Step 3**. Otherwise, go to **Step 5**.

Step 3. Update ϕ_t by Eqs. (29) and (30).

Step 4. Update θ_t by Eqs. (31) and (32).

Step 5. Update ρ_t by Eq. (33) and terminate the algorithm.

4.4 Simulations

In this section, simulations are described to evaluate the performances of the proposed control system with the automatic reward adjustment method when it is applied to virtual plant models configured on the basis of experimental data. The simulations incorporate changes of the plant operations several times and the data for the RBF network. The evaluations focus on the flexibility in control of the proposed reward adjustment method for the change of the operational conditions. In addition, the robustness in control for the statistical model including noise by tuning the weight decay parameter of RBF network is also studied.

4.4.1 Simulation conditions

Figure 10 shows the basic structure of the simulation. The objective of the simulation is to reduce NOx and CO emissions from a virtual coal-fired boiler model (statistical model) constructed with three numerical calculation DBs. The RL agent learns how to control three operational parameters with respect to air mass flow supplied to the boiler. Therefore, input and output dimensions (J,P) of the control system are 3 and 2, respectively. The input values are normalized into the range of $[0,1]$. The three numerical calculation DBs have different operational conditions, and each DB has 63 data whose input-output conditions are different. These data include some noise similar to the actual plant data.

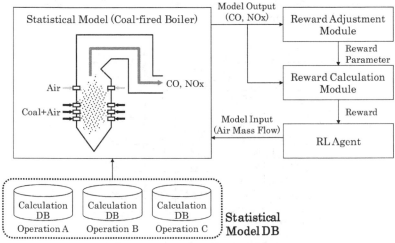

Fig. 10. Basic structure of thermal power plant control simulation

In this simulation, the robustness and flexibility of the proposed control system are verified by implementing the RL agent so that it learns and controls the statistical model which changes in time series. Two kinds of boiler operational simulations are executed according to Table 5. Each simulation case is done for six hours (0:00-6:00) of operation, and it is considered that the statistical model is changed at 0:00, 2:00 and 4:00. One of the simulations considers three kinds of operational conditions (A,B,C) where coal types and power outputs are different, and the other considers three kinds of control goals defined as Eq. (27), where the weight coefficients C_1,C_2 of CO and NOx, respectively in that equation are different.

The simulations are executed by two reward settings: the variable reward for the proposed reward adjustment method (proposed method) and the fixed reward (conventional method). Both reward settings are done under two conditions where the weight decay λ for the RBF network is set to 0, 0.01 to evaluate the robustness of control by λ settings. The RL agent learns at the times when operational conditions or control goals (0:00, 2:00 and 4:00) are changed, and the control interval is 10 minutes. Hence it is possible to control the boiler 11 times in each period.

Parameter conditions of learning are shown in Table 6. These conditions are set using prior experimental results. The parameter conditions of reward are shown in Table 7. The parameters $(\varepsilon, \alpha_\phi, \alpha_\theta, \alpha_\rho)$ of the proposed method are also set properly using prior experiments. In the conventional method, the values of ϕ, ρ are fixed to their initial values which are optimal for the first operational condition in Table 5 because their step size parameters $(\alpha_\phi, \alpha_\rho)$ are set to 0.

Objective	Change of Operational Conditions			Change of Goals		
Time	Ope. Cond.	C_1	C_2	Ope. Cond.	C_1	C_2
0:00 - 2:00	A	0.1	0.9	A	0.1	0.9
2:00 - 4:00	B	0.1	0.9	A	0.9	0.1
4:00 - 6:00	C	0.1	0.9	A	0.001	0.999

Table 5. Time table of plant operation simulation

Parameter		Condition
Radius of Gaussian basis	σ	0.2
Max. output of NGnet	m_k^{max}	0.2
Noise ratio	β	0.2
Discount rate	γ	0.9
Learning rate for actor	α_A	0.1
Learning rate for critic	α_C	0.02
Max. basis num of agent	N_L^{max}	100
Min. a_l for basis addition	a_{min}	0.368
Min. δ for basis addition	δ_{min}	0.01
Max. iteration in 1 episode	S	30
Max. episode	T	10000

Table 6. Parameter conditions of learning

Parameter		Prop. Method	Conv. Method
Max. reward	$reward_{max}$	1	1
Smoothing parameter	ε	0.1	0.1
Step size parameter of ϕ	α_ϕ	0.05	0
Step size parameter of ρ	α_ρ	0.05	0
Step size parameter of θ	α_θ	0.05	0
Initial value of ϕ		0.001	3
Initial value of ρ		0.001	0
Initial value of θ		0	186

Table 7. Reward conditions of each method

4.4.2 Results and discussion

Figure 11 shows the time series of normalized f as a result of controls by the two methods, where the initial value at 0:00 is determined as the base. There are four graphs in Fig. 11 with combinations of the two objectives of simulations and λ settings. The optimal f value in each period is shown as well. The computational time of learning in each case was 23[s].

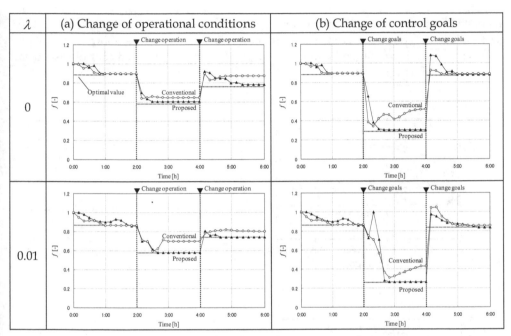

Fig. 11. Time series of normalized f in the boiler operation simulations

To begin with, time series of the normalized f values by the proposed method and conventional method in the case of $\lambda=0.01$ are discussed. The initial f values at 0:00 of these methods have offsets with the optimal values, but they are decreased for control and finally converged near the optimal values. This is because the reward functions used in each method are appropriate to learn the optimal control logic. The RL agent relearns its control logic when the statistical model and its optimal f values are changed at 2:00 by the change of operational conditions or control goals. However, the f values of the conventional method after 11 control times still have offsets from the optimal values, while the proposed method can obtain the optimal values after 11 times. The initial reward setting of the conventional method would be inappropriate for the next operational condition. Similar results of control are obtained for the same reason after changing the statistical model at 4:00. As discussed above, the plant control system by the conventional method has a possibility to deteriorate the control performances in thermal power plants for which operational conditions and control goals are changed frequently. Therefore, the proposed reward adjustment method is effective for the plant control, which can adjust the reward function flexibly for such changes.

Next, the robustness of the proposed control system by weight decay (λ) tuning is discussed. In Fig. 11, every f value of the proposed method can reach nearly the optimal value when λ is 0.01, whereas f converges into the values larger than the optimal values when λ is 0 for 2:00-6:00 in (a) and 2:00~4:00 in (b). The RBF network cannot learn with considered the influences of noise included in the learning data when λ is 0[16]. The response surface is created to fit the noised data closely and many local minimum values are generated in it compared with the response surface of $\lambda = 0.01$. This is because the learned control logic is converged each local minimum. The above results show that the RBF network can avoid overfitting by tuning λ properly and the proposed control system can control thermal power plants robustly.

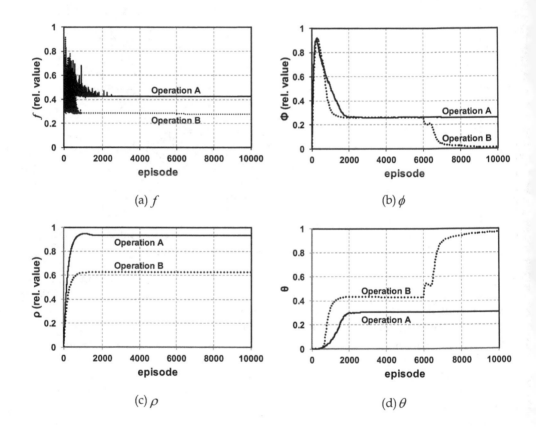

Fig. 12. Learning processes of f and reward parameters (ϕ, ρ, θ) of the proposed method

Finally, the learning processes of f and reward parameters of the proposed method are studied. Fig. 12 shows the f, ϕ, ρ, θ values for episodes in learning at the operational changes at 0:00 and 2:00 when λ is 0.01. In the early stage of learning (episodes 1-500), the ϕ parameter in each case increases nearby 0.9 because the f value does not decrease due to insufficient learning of the RL agent. In the next 1000 episodes, ϕ increases and θ decreases simultaneously as the learning progresses. This behavior can be explained by the Eqs. (29)-(32) which are the updating algorithms of ϕ, θ. On the other hand, ρ value in each case converges to certain values by the 2000th episode. This indicates that the optimal f values are found in the learning process. Then the parameters of each case remain stable during the middle stage of learning (episode 2000-6000), but ϕ, θ change suddenly at the 6000th episode only in the case of operation B. This is because the RL agent can learn the control logic to get a better f value, then ϕ, θ are adjusted flexibly in accordance with the change of f used in Eqs. (29) and (30). As a result, these parameters converge into different values.

These adjustment results of reward parameters for different statistical models can be discussed as follows. By analysis of the characteristics of these statistical models, it seems that the gradient of f in operation A is larger than that of operation B because operation A has a larger difference between the maximum and minimum value of f than operation B. When the gradient of f is larger, f will vary significantly for each control thus it is necessary to set ϕ larger so that the agent can get the reward easily. On the other hand, it is useless to set ϕ larger in the statistical model in operation B for which the gradient of f is small. As for the results of adjustment of ϕ, ρ, θ in Fig. 12, the reward function of operation A certainly becomes easier to give the reward due to the larger ϕ than for operation B. Therefore, the above results show that the proposed method can obtain the appropriate reward function flexibly in accordance with the properties of the statistical models.

5. Conclusions

This chapter presented a plant control system to reduce NOx and CO emissions exhausted by thermal power plants. The proposed control system generates optimal control signals by that the RL agent which learns optimal control logic using the statistical model to estimate the NOx and CO properties. The proposed control system requires flexibility for the change of plant operation conditions and robustness for noise of the measured data. In addition, the statistical model should be able to be tuned by the measured data within a practical computational time. To overcome these problems the authors proposed two novel methods, the adaptive radius adjustment method of the RBF network and the automatic reward adjustment method.

The simulations clarified the proposed methods provided high estimation accuracy of the statistical model within practical computational time, flexible control by RL for various changes of plant properties and robustness for the plant data with noise. These advantages led to the conclusion that the proposed plant control system would be effective for reducing environmental effects.

6. Appendix A. Conventional radius adjustment method

A.1 Cross Validation (CV) method

The cross validation (CV) method is one of the conventional radius adjustment methods for the RBF network with regression and it adjusts radii by error evaluations. In this method, a datum is excluded from the learning data and the estimation error at the excluded datum is evaluated. Iterations are repeated until all data are selected as excluded data to calculate RMSE. After the calculations of RMSE for several radius conditions, the best condition is determined as the radius to use. The algorithm is shown as follows.

Algorithm of Cross Validation Method

Step 1. Initialize the radius is initialized to $r^{\min}$.
Step 2. Select an excluded datum.
Step 3. Learn weight parameters of RBF network using all data except the excluded datum.
Step 4. Calculate the output of the RBF network at the point of the excluded datum.
Step 5. Calculate the error between the output and the excluded datum.
Step 6. Go to **Step 7** if all data have been selected. Otherwise, return to **Step 2**.
Step 7. Calculate RMSE by the estimation errors.
Step 8. Increment the radius by Δr.
Step 9. Select the radius with the best RMSE if the radius is over $r^{\max}$ and terminate the
Step 10. algorithm. Otherwise, return to **Step 2**.

A.2 Radius equation
This method is one of the non-regression methods and it adjusts the radius r by Eq. (34).

$$r = \frac{d_{\max}}{\sqrt{J}\left(\sqrt[J]{N_D} - 1\right)} \tag{34}$$

Here, $d_{\max}$ is the maximum distance among the learning data.

7. References

[1] U.S. Environmental Protection Agency, Available from
      http://www.epa.gov/air/ oaq_caa.html/
[2] Ochi, K., Kiyama, K., Yoshizako, H., Okazaki, H. & Taniguchi, M. (2009), Latest Low-
      NOx Combustion Technology for Pulverized-coal-fired Boilers, *Hitachi Review*, Vol.
      58, No. 5, pp. 187-193.
[3] Jorgensen, K. L., Dudek, S. A. & Hopkins, M. W. (2008), Use of Combustion Modeling in
      the Design and Development of Coal-Fired Furnaces and Boilers, *Proceedings of
      ASME International Mechanical Engineering Congress and Exposition*, Boston.
[4] EPRI (2005), *Power Plant Optimization Industry Experience*, 2005 Update. EPRI, Palo
      Alto.
[5] Rangaswamy, T. R.; Shanmugam J. & Mohammed K. P. (2005), Adaptive Fuzzy Tuned
      PID Controller for Combustion of Utility Boiler, *Control and Intelligent Systems*, Vol.
      33, No. 1, pp. 63-71.
[6] Booth, R. C. & Roland W. B. (1998), Neural Network-Based Combustion Optimization
      Reduces NOx Emissions While Improving Performance, *Proceedings of Dynamic
      Modeling Control Applications for Industry Workshop*, pp.1-6.
[7] Radl B. J. (1999), Neural networks improve performance of coal-fired boilers, CADDET
      Energy Efficiency Newsletter, No.1, pp.4-6.

[8] Winn H. R. & Bolos H. R. (2008), Optimizing the Boiler Combustion Process in Tampa Electric Coal Fired Power Plants Utilizing Fuzzy Neural Model Technology, *Proceedings of Power-Gen International 2008*, Orlando, FL.

[9] Vesel R. (2008), The Million Dollar Annual Payback: Realtime Combustion Optimization with Advanced Multi-Variable Control at PPL Colstrip, *Proceedings of Power-Gen International 2008*, Orlando, FL.

[10] Airikka P. & Nieminen V. (2010), Optimized Combustion through Collaboration of Boiler and Automation Suppliers, *Proceedings of Power-Gen International 2008*, Amsterdam.

[11] Wasserman P. D. (1993), *Advanced Methods in Neural Computing*, Van Nostrand Reinhold.

[12] Rumelhart D. E.; Hinton G. E. & Williams R. J. (1986), Learning Representations of Back-propagation Errors, *Nature*, vol. 323, pp. 533-536.

[13] Camacho, E. F. & Bordons, C. (1999), *Model Predictive Control*. Springer.

[14] Jamshidi, M., Titli, A., Zadeh, L. & Boverie, S. (1997), *Applications of Fuzzy Logic*. Prentice Hall.

[15] Yamamoto K.; Fukuchi T.; Chaki M.; Shimogori Y. & Matsuda J. (2000), Development of Computer Program for Combustion Analysis in Pulverized Coal-fired Boilers, *Hitachi Review*, Vol. 49, No. 2, pp. 76-80.

[16] Orr M. J. L.. Introduction to Radial Basis Function Networks. Available from http://anc.ed.ac.uk/mjo/rbf.html

[17] Maruyama M. (1992), Learning Networks Using Radial Basis Function - New Approach for the Neural Computing. *Trans. of ISCIE*, Vol. 36, No. 5, pp. 322−329. (in Japanese)

[18] Sutton R. S. & Barto A. G. (1998), *Reinforcement Learning-An Introduction*, MIT Press.

[19] Bishop, C., M. (2006). *Pattern Recognition And Machine Learning*. Springer-Verlag.

[20] Kitayama S.; Yasuda K. & Yamazaki K. (2008), The Integrative Optimization by RBF Network and Particle Swarm Optimization, *IEEJ Trans. on EIS*, Vol. 128, No. 4, pp. 636-645. (in Japanese)

[21] Eguchi, T.; Sekiai T.; Yamada, A.; Shimizu S. & Fukai M. (2009), A Plant Control Technology Using Reinforcement Learning Method with Automatic Reward Adjustment, *IEEJ Trans. on EIS*, Vol. 129, No. 7, pp. 1253-1263. (in Japanese)

[22] Eguchi, T.; Sekiai T.; Yamada, A.; Shimizu S. & Fukai M. (2009), An Adaptive Radius Adjusting Method for RBF Networks Considering Data Densities and Its Application to Plant Control Technology, *Proceedings of ICCAS-SICE2009*, pp.4188-4194, Fukuoka, Japan, August 18-21.

[23] Moody J. & Darken C. J. (1989), Fast learning in networks of locally-tuned processing units, *Neural Computation*, Vol.1 , pp. 281-294.

[24] Zhang J.; Yim Y. & Yang J. (1997), Intelligent Selection of Instances for Prediction Function in Lazy Learning Algorithms, *Artificial Intelligence Review*, Vol. 11, pp. 175-191.

[25] Ng. A.; Harada D. & Russell S. (1999), Policy invariance under reward transformations: Theory and application to reward shaping, *Proceedings of 16th International Conference on Machine Learning*, pp.278-287.

[26] Li J. & Chan L. (2006), Reward Adjustment Reinforcement Learning for Risk-averse Asset Allocation, *Proceedings of International Joint Conference on Neural Networks 2006 (IJCNN06)*, pp.534-541.

Part 3

Selected Issues and New Trends in Robust Control Applications

6

Robust Networked Control

Wojciech Grega

Department of Automatics, AGH University of Science and Technology
Poland

1. Introduction

Most of integrated industrial control systems adopt a multilevel, vertical control hierarchy. Logically, such a system (Fig. 1) is structured in three levels: the direct (device) control level, the supervisory level and the management level (Grega, 2010, Tatjewski, 2007, Grega *at al.*, 2009).

The basic task of the direct (device) control level is to maintain the process states at the prescribed set values. The device controller level provides an interface to the hardware, either separate modules or microprocessors incorporated in the equipment to be controlled. Here, mainly PID digital control algorithms are implemented – in some cases these are more advances control methods such as multivariable control or adaptive functions. A number of embedded control nodes and Programmable Logical Controllers (PLC) are used as the front-ends to take the control tasks. High speed networks and fieldbuses are implemented at the direct control level to exchange in real time the information between front-ends and the device controllers and, vertically, with the supervisory control level. This architecture has the advantage of locating the hard real-time activities as near as possible to the equipment.

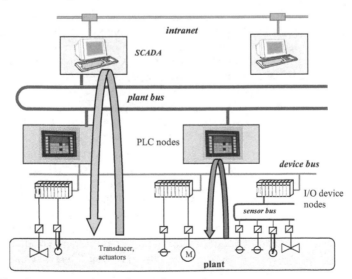

Fig. 1. Multilevel structure of an industrial control system

The supervisory level comprises workstations and industrial PCs providing high-level control support, database support, graphic man-machine interface, network management and general computing resources. Classically, the supervisory level calculates set points for controllers according to the defined criteria. For this purpose more complex mathematical models of the process are employed at this level to find the optimal steady-state, by solving optimisation and identification tasks. Due to the rapid development of control technology, there is growing scope for more advanced close-loop algorithms (predictive control, repetitive control) located at this level. However, increasing computational efficiency of PLCs at the device level supported by high performance networks transferring data and control signals vertically gives more flexibility to the designer. The control loops can be handled by local, device–level controllers, and also by the supervisory controllers (Fig.1). For example, a predictive control algorithm can be handled by a supervisory workstation as well as by a local PLC. It should be noted that upper level loops usually offer shorter computational time due to the higher efficiency of the workstations.

Feedback control systems wherein the control loops are closed through a communication network are referred to as Distributed Control Systems (DSC). They are distributed in the sense that their sensors, actuators and controllers (referred as "nodes") communicate via a shared data transmission network. The behaviour of a networked control system depends on the performance parameters of the underlying network, which include transmission rate and access method to the network transmission medium.

Communication networks were introduced in control in the 1970s. They can be grouped into fieldbuses (e.g. CAN, Profibus, Modbus) and general purpose networks (e.g. IEEE standard LANs), (Zurawski, 2005). Each type of network has its own protocol that is designed for a specific range of applications. Fieldbuses are intended for real-time applications. The most important feature of these industrial networks is that they guarantee bounded transmission delays. More and more popular is application of general-purpose networks, inexpensive and easy to maintain. Ethernet is a solution, which seems to become an industrial standard in the near future (Felsner, 2005).

The advantages of data transmission channels integration into control system are obvious, such as reducing wiring costs and increasing flexibility. Thanks to these important benefits, typical applications of these systems range over various fields, such as automotive, mobile robotics, advanced aircraft, and so on. However, introduction of communication networks in the control loops makes the analysis and synthesis of distributed control systems more complex.

DCS can be considered a special case of digital control systems, as data is sent through the network periodically, in units called packages. Therefore, any signal continuous in time must be sampled to be carried over the network. Real-time assumptions are as important for DCS as for any other computer controlled systems. Hence, there are similarities between DCS and real-time digital control systems due to sampling effects. The most challenging problem with DSC that needs to be properly addressed are time delays. A network induced delays occurs while sending data among nodes connected to the shared data transmission medium of limited throughput. Network-induced delays may vary depending on the network load and Medium Access Protocol (MAC). Lack of access to the communication network is an important constraint compared to lack of computer power or time errors of the real-time operating system. It is well known that time delays can degrade the performance of the control system or even destabilize the system.

Especially, the following effects are observed in DCS:

- variable computation-induced delays,
- variable network induced delays,
- data loss, caused by packet dropouts.

resulting in:

- violation of the assumption that sampling/actuation intervals are evenly spaced,
- violation of the causality principle.

From the point of view of control theory networked control often introduces some additional dynamics and temporal non-determinism. Therefore, novel methodologies should be developed for stability analysis of DCS and optimise the performance. An integrated approach is necessary, that combines data transmission issues (modelling of variable communication delays), sampling theory and control theory.

The notion of robustness of various DCS properties (especially stability) plays an important role in design of control systems, as confirmed by extensive literature discussion (Walsh *et al*, 2002, Gupta and Chow, 2010). Very general formulation of robustness for DCS is illustrated in Fig. 2. As it was mentioned before, DCS can be considered as a special case of digital control systems. Therefore, it is sensitive to the sampling period T_0 variations. For non-networked digital control system the quality of control generally increases while T_0 is getting shorter. This must not be true for DCS. Increasing network traffic results in longer and variable network-induced delays, and leads to the deterioration of control quality. In this case robust design means shifting the DCS quality characteristic as close as possible to the characteristics of digital (non-network) control system.

During last 20 years various methods have been developed to maintain the stability and the performance of DCS with delay problems. In order to enhance robustness of DCS against network induced delays appropriate methods of control theory are supplemented by some methods of network traffic engineering. Therefore, two main research approaches can be distinguished (Gupta and Chow, 2010).

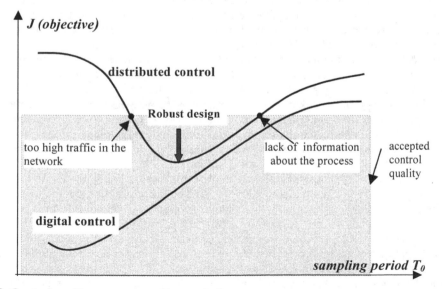

Fig. 2. Control quality versus sampling period

Study and research on communications and networks to make them suitable for real-time DCS, e.g. routing control, real-time protocols, congestion reduction, real-time protocols, codesign of networking and controllers are referred as *Control of network*.

Developing of control strategies and control systems design over the network to minimize the effect of adverse network parameters on DCS performance, such as network delay is referred as *Control over network*. The main advantage of this approach is its simplicity: the designer of DCS can exploit standard control algorithms and make them robust against effects of networking.

Following the *Control of network* approach, effects of the network configuration on the performance of the control system have been studied and different improvements have been proposed. At the physical level the network topology cannot be chosen freely but is subject to many practical constraints such as cost and reliability considerations. For example, the real-time performance of industrial Ethernet network depends strongly on the way the devices are allocated to the individual switches in the network. Therefore, the problem of optimal device allocation in industrial Ethernet networks with real-time constraints remains an important topic (Georges *et al*, 2006).

Another concept was to modify scheduling methods and communication protocols in such a way that data delays are minimized. Several solutions have been proposed. The most interesting of these involve:

- a new scheduling strategies based on a time division (Al-Hammouri *et al*, 2006),
- obtaining a maximum allowable delay bound for DCS scheduling (Walsh *et al*, 2002),
- adjustment of the network parameters (link quality measures) to the control quality,
- measures, by studying impact of frames priorities (Juanole *et al*, 2006).

Desire to incorporate a real-time element into some popular single-network solution has led to the development of different real-time Industrial Ethernet solutions, called *Real-time Ethernet*.

If the second approach is implemented (*Control over network*), the network is considered as a passive component of feedback loop, modeled in a simplified way. In most cases the control theory of delayed systems can be applied to compensate the effects of communication in order to guarantee the Quality of Control (QoC), (Hirai, 1980).

Network delays can be modeled and analyzed in various ways. They can be modeled as a constant delay (timed buffers), independent random delay and delay with known probability distribution, governed by Markov chain model.

One of the first applications taking the randomness of the network into account, either as a constant probability function or as a Markov chain together with time stamping was thesis of Nilson (Nilsson, 1998). Later, the optimal stochastic methods approached the problem as a Linear-Quadratic-Gaussian (LQG) problem where the LQG gain matrix is optimally chosen based on the network delay statistics (Nilsson *et al*, 1998).

One simple idea is that constant delay in the control loop is better than variable delay. Introducing buffers reduces temporal dependency of the individual components of the close-loop model. The data package is delivered as soon as possible, but is hold in the buffer and is implemented to the process in the next sampling intervals. By this way, synchronisation of the control loop is achieved. Constant delay can be compensated using a standard approach, e.g. Smith predictor. It must be noted that constant delay buffer usually creates conservative controller gains. Better solutions give applications of switched or variable delay buffer. The stability analysis of the switched buffer model can be reduced to the problem of stability of the *Asynchronous Dynamical Systems* (ASD) , (Hassibi, 1999).

Smith Predictor-based approach was proposed by several authors (Vatanski *et al.*, 2009) for the control in the case when accurate delay measurements are accessible. In contrast to the robust control-based approach when only the estimate of the upper-bound end-to-end delays are available (Grega, 2002).

Other concept is to increase network utilization by modification of the transmission pattern – by samples grouping. The samples from sensor are transferred through network, however they are grouped together into M-element packages before they enter the network. Grouping effects can be compensated by an approximate model of the process ("observer") at the controller side, and by control signal estimator (output to actuators) for some range of the sampling period and modeling errors (Grega and Tutaj, 2007).

Finally, network observers and state observes can be applied. The idea is that the communication delays between the sensor and the controller can be compensated by an approximate (non-exact) model of the process at the controller side, for some range of the sampling period and modelling errors. The performance of the method greatly depends on the model accuracy (Montestruque *et al.*, 2003).

An intelligent control was proposed using fuzzy logic to adaptively compensate network induced time delay in DCS applications (Cao and Zhang, 2005). The advantage of the fuzzy logic compensator is that the existing PI controller needs not to be redesigned, modified, or interrupted for use on a network environment.

2. Control of the network

2.1 Optimizing protocols

The idea is to implement communication protocols and network topology that minimise data delays. Current communication systems for automation implement different protocols. This is a substantial disadvantage, leading to the need to use vendor-specific hardware and software components, which increase installation and maintenance costs. Moreover, presently used fieldbus technologies make vertical communication across all levels of the automation systems difficult. Gateways need to be used to establish connections between different kinds of fieldbus systems used in the lower levels, and Ethernet used in the upper level.

The evolution of industrial communication has moved to Industrial Ethernet networks replacing the proprietary networks (Larson, 2005, ARC Advisory Group, 2007). Ethernet provides unified data formats and reduces the complexity of installation and maintenance, which, together with the substantial increase in transmission rates and communication reliability over the last few years, results in its popularity in the area of industrial communications.

Ethernet, as defined in IEEE 802.3, is non-deterministic and, thus, is unsuitable for hard real-time applications. The media access control protocol, CSMA/CD can not support real-time communication because back-off algorithm for collision resolution is used. With CSMA/CD it can not be determine in advance how long the collision resolution will take. It was explained before, that delays and irregularities in data transmission can very severely affect real-time system operation. Therefore, various techniques and communication protocol modifications are employed in order to eliminate or minimise these unwanted effects and make the data transmission system time invariant.

To employ Ethernet in an industrial environment, its deterministic operation must first be assured. Coexistence of real-time and non-real time traffic on the same network infrastructure remains the main problem. This conflict can be resolved in several ways by:

- embedding a fieldbus or application protocol on TCP(UDP)/IP – the fieldbus protocol is tunneled over Ethernet, and full openness for "office" traffic is maintained,
- using a special Data Link layer for real-time devices – dedicated protocol is used on the second OSI Layer, implemented in every device. The real-time cycle is divided into slots, one of which is opened for regular TCP/IP traffic, but the bandwidth available is limited,
- using application protocol on TCP/IP, direct MAC addressing with prioritization for real-time, and hardware switching for fast real-time.

All these specific techniques allow a considerable improvement in terms of determinism. Different real-time Industrial Ethernet solutions were proposed, called Real-time Ethernet, such as PROFINET, EtherCAT, Ethernet/IP and many more (CoNet, 2011). The conditions for the industrial use of Ethernet are described by international standard IEC 61 784-2 Real Time Ethernet (See Fig. 3). IEC stands for International Electrotechnical Commission.

The following parameters are covered by the network performance metrics:

- latency (delay) – the amount of time required for a frame to travel from source to destination,
- jitter – a measure of the deviation of the latency from its average value,
- loss rate – the probability that an individual packet is lost (dropped) during the transmission,
- throughput – the amount of digital data transferred per time unit.

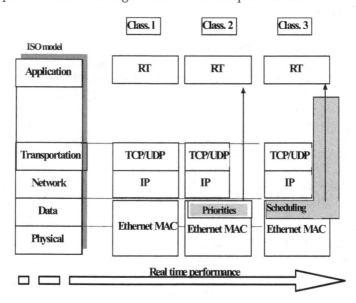

Fig. 3. Classification of industrial Ethernet (IEC 61 784-2)

Class 1 describes the use of standard Ethernet TCP/IP as it is. In this case the different real time protocols and the best-effort protocols, like HTTP, SNMP, FTP etc., uses the services of the TCP/IP protocol suite. This includes examples such as CIP Sync (Ethernet/IP, ModBus/TCP). The class 1 has the largest conformity to the Ethernet TCP/IP standard and can thereby use standard hardware and software components.

Class 2 introduces optimizations, whereby the realtime data bypasses the TCP/IP stack and thus considerably reduces the latency time and increases the achievable packet rate. In Classes 1 and 2, the priority support described by IEEE 802.1Q can also be used depending on the approach. In Class 3 the scheduling on the MAC level is again modified through the introduction of a TDMA method. Class 3 can be used in applications that require maximum latency in the range 1ms and maximum jitter below 1microsec. In this class there are strong restrictions for the use of standard hardware components or the necessity for special components, like dedicated switches. Generally, conformance with the Ethernet standard decreases when ones increase the Class number, while the achievable real-time performance increases.

2.2 Robust codesign
2.2.1 Dynamics of distributed control system
The basic model of the DCS is shown in Fig. 4. The process outputs are measured and control signals are applied through the distance I/O devices. The I/O devices are integrated with A/D and D/A converters.

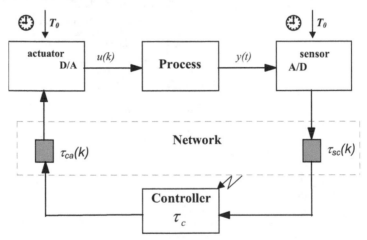

Fig. 4. Basic model of distributed control system

The communication to and from the controller node is supported by a network. From a digital control point of view, it is natural to sample the process with an equal period T_0 and to keep the control delay as short as possible. This suggests that the sensor and actuator (A/D and D/A) converters are time-triggered (sampling period T_0), while the controller is event-triggered, which means that they are triggered by the arrival of the new data. The main complication of this control architecture is the presence of variable time delays. The additional dynamics observed in distributed control system depends on the performance parameters of the underlying network, which include transmission rate and transmission medium access method. Under certain circumstances the network-induced delays can be consider constants, but generally they might be varying from transfer to transfer (Fig.4). Thus, the introduction of a network in the feedback loop violates conventional control theory assumptions such as non-delayed sensing and actuation. This can degrade the performance of the control system or even can destabilise the system.

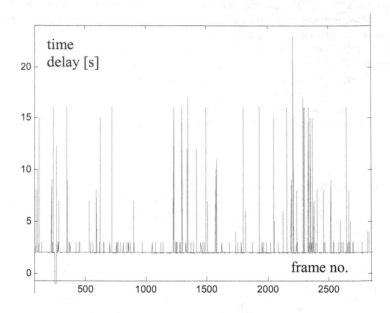

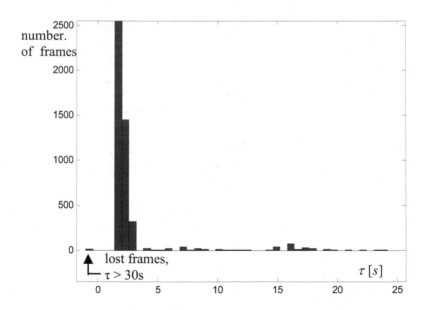

Fig. 5. Example: wireless network data transfer times and histogram of delays ¶

2.2.2 Co-design
Computer implementation of distributed control systems, real-time algorithms, data transmission models and digital control theory methods cannot be developed separately because an unexpected control system performance may occur. Three parameters need particular attention from the distributed control design perspective: sampling and actuation tasks period, controller task period and network parameters (latency and jitter). Due to the close relationships between the network and control parameters the selection of the best sampling period will be a compromise. In this section we will demonstrate the construction of a networked control design chart, which can be used to select proper design parameters.

2.2.3 Sampling and actuation task
We will assume that the control algorithm design is based on correctly identified: model of the process and the model of disturbances (referred to as "nominal models"). We assume that it is possible for the nominal models to estimate a maximal, admissible sampling period, which would guarantee acceptable control performance.

One accepted rule is (Aström and Wittenmark, 1997) that the control task period should be a ($a > 1, a \in N$) times smaller than the period of the cut-off frequency, approximated in some reasonable way for the nominal process model. This upper bound of T_0 is denoted as T_0^u (Fig. 6).

For the design purpose we assume that performance of the closed-loop control system is a strictly monotonic function of T_0: any sampling (actuation) period $T_0 < T_0^u$ improves the control performance. For $T_0 < T_0^l$ improvement is not observed. Finally, the sampling (actuation) task period can be estimated as $T_0 \in [T_0^l, T_0^u]$.

2.2.4 Controller task period
The applied control platforms (processor, peripherals hardware and operating systems) are characterized by a closed - loop execution time, estimated as $\delta_s \in [\delta_s^l, \delta_s^u]$, where δ_s^l - is the lower bound of the execution time for simple control algorithms, δ_s^u - is the execution time of complex control algorithms.

The control algorithm is classified as "simple", if pseudocode of the controller task includes no more than 5-10 operations (loops are excluded). Examples of "simple" algorithms are: incremental PID or state feedback controller. If the pseudocode of the controller includes more than 10 operations or loops are included then the algorithm is classified as "complex".

2.2.5 Network parameters
Presence of networks introduces communication delays and limits the amount of data that can be transferred between nodes. In some cases not all samples from sensor or to actuator (produced with period T_0) can be sent, because the network requires intervals longer than T_0 between the transfers of two consecutive packets. Therefore, constraints on the process data availability, introduced by the communication channel are defined.

The average communication delay between the sensor node and the controller node is denoted as τ^{sc}, τ^{ca} is average communication delay between the controller node and the actuator node, $\Delta(k)$ represents a total jitter in the feedback loop, k – is the number of the control step.

Actually, the communication delays and jitters can be added to the controller execution time creating an estimation of delays and uncertainty in the control loop. The total delay in the control loop is

$$\tau(k) = \tau_{sc} + \tau_{ca} + \delta_s + \Delta(k)$$

It will also be assumed that the jitter is bounded by $0 \le \Delta(k) \le \Delta^u$.

2.2.6 Robust codesign

In the previous section we have introduced a number of parameters that need special attention from the perspective of real-time digital control: T_0 - sampling period defining the temporal granularity related to the process dynamics, δ_s - execution time describing the efficiency of the hardware and software application platform and $\tau_{sc}, \tau_{ca}, \Delta$ - communication delays and jitter. Now, we will demonstrate, how these parameters interacts one to another, how to select the application platforms and how to set closed-loop execution times in such a way, that process dynamics and communication network properties are balanced.

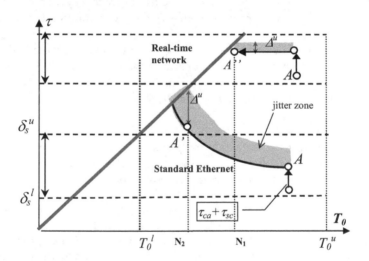

Fig. 6. Distributed control system design chart

The operating point of the distributed control system should be located in the area between T_0^l and T_0^u in Fig. 6. The operating must lie below the line separating "time critical" solution, which simply means that control loop execution time must be less than sampling period. Points A, A' in Fig. 6 also represent a situation where the design is robust against possible variations (jitter) of the task execution and data transfer times (shadowed area in Fig. 6).

Let us assume that Ethernet network is implemented. Computational delay of the controller δ_s is fixed, but for Ethernet network the transmission time delay increases linearly with increasing load - in same case exponentially, when the load on the network exceeds 35 - 40%.

It means, that a faster sampling rate for guaranteeing better control performance will saturate the network traffic load, and eventually increase the data transmission time. For the example given in Fig. 6, the best operating point for Ethernet network is A' and is constrained by the process data availability introduced by transmission time delays of the communication channel.

If communication can be supported by high-speed real-time – network, e.g. ProfiNet, Class 2 (Amiguet *et al.* 2008) the constraint of this kind is not active. However, another constraint becomes active and critical. Control loop execution time can not be longer than the sampling period (A'' in Fig.6), including the jitter $\Delta(k)$. The reason is that cycles of the control loop do not accept intervals between transfers of the two consecutive packets shorter, than N_1. The time diagram for this situation is given in Fig. 7. For the model from Fig.6 we must assume that

$$\tau_{sc} + \tau_c + \tau_{sc} + \Delta(k) \le T_0 = N_1$$

It means, that the operating point (A'') must be located below the line separating "time-critical" zone, including the jitter zone (Fig.6).

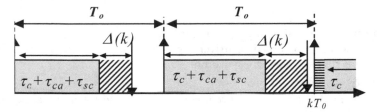

Fig. 7. Timing model that can be used for a regularly sampled process

3. Control over the network: Increasing the robustness

One commonly used approach to increase the robustness of DCS stability with respect to the network effect is extension of the standard control algorithms by new components.

3.1 Buffering

The idea is to reduce temporal dependency of the individual parts of the model from Fig. 4 by introducing buffers at the actuator (Tutaj, 2006). Buffering can be easily implemented using PLCs' or embedded controller at the device level. In digital control this operation can be handled by use of a zero–order holds on the control signal.

First approach presented in this section incorporates one-step buffer introduced at actuator side to compensate variable time delays. Let τ be the overall delay (round trip latency time, $\tau = \tau^{sc} + \tau^{ca} + \tau^{ca}$). The controlled process model is assumed to be linear, in the form

$$\frac{dx}{dt} = Ax(t) + Bu(t - \tau), x(t) \in R^n, \quad u(t) \in R^1 \tag{1}$$

For applied delayed linear control law

$$u(t - \tau) = Kx(t - \tau)$$

the closed loop model takes the form

$$\frac{dx}{dt} = Ax(t) + BKx(t-\tau) = Ax(t) + A_1(t-\tau)$$

The maximum tolerable time delay for given K (or bounds for K under some assumptions on τ) can be computed from the solution of LMI optimisation problem. We should notice, that generally the network induced delays are different from the process delays, because they are time varying and unknown. One solution proposed in (Yi and Hang, 2002) determines condition for exponential stability of system (1) for $\tau(t) \in C_b^0$ - nonnegative, continuous and bounded at $[0,+\infty)$

$$\frac{A^T + A}{2} + \sqrt{\lambda_{\max}(A_1 A_1^T)}I < 0$$

where $\lambda_{\max}$ - is the maximum eigenvalue.

Several authors have pointed out (Fujioka, 2009) that the above stability condition is usually conservative.

Assuming that:

- signal transmission is with a single packet (or frame),
- the sensor and actuator are time driven, the controller is event driven. The clocks operate at time period T_0 and are synchronized,
- the process dynamics is controllable,

then discrete time model can be introduced. For brevity in the ensuing text notation $x(k)$ will be used in place of $x(kT_0)$.

If the actuation period is selected as T_0, than $u(t-\tau)$ is piecewise constant over the actuation period and only changes value at $(kT_0 + \tau)$. Integration of (1) over the sampling period gives a discrete-time, finite dimensional approximation of the delayed model (1)

$$x[k+1] = \Phi_0 x[k] + \Gamma_1 u[k-q-1] + \Gamma_0 u[k-q]$$

where

$$\tau = qT_0 + \gamma, \; q \geq 1, \; \Gamma_1 = \int_{T_0-\gamma}^{T_0} e^{As}B ds, \; \Gamma_0 = \int_0^{T_0-\gamma} e^{As}B ds, \; \Phi_0 = e^{AT_0}$$

We define new state variables

$$z_1[k] = u[k-q-1]$$
$$z_2[k] = u[k-q]$$
$$\vdots$$
$$z_{q+1}[k] = u[k-1]$$

For the assumed considered timing method and the condition on total network delay

$$\tau(k) \leq T_0 \qquad\qquad (2)$$

fulfilled, the model

$$\begin{bmatrix} x(k+1) \\ z(k+1) \end{bmatrix} = \begin{bmatrix} \Phi_0 & \Gamma_1(\tau) \\ 0 & 0 \end{bmatrix} \begin{bmatrix} x(k) \\ z(k) \end{bmatrix} + \begin{bmatrix} \Gamma_0(\tau) \\ 1 \end{bmatrix} u(k) \tag{3}$$

$$y(k) = \begin{bmatrix} 1 & 0 \end{bmatrix} \begin{bmatrix} x(k) \\ z(k) \end{bmatrix}$$

describes behaviour of closed-loop system.

It is known, that for a discrete linear system with time-varying parameters location of the system eigenvalues in a stable region for all admissible values of the parameters does not imply stability of the system. The buffer can be used at actuator side to eliminate the delay variability in the loop, thereby enabling more effective use of delay compensation algorithms (e.g. Smith predictor). Generally, the buffered control loop can take advantage of more deterministic loop delay, and in consequence the controller can be design more "aggressively" - if only a good process model is available.

The augmented state model with one-step, constant length buffer is obtained in the form

$$\begin{bmatrix} x(k+1) \\ z_1(k+1) \end{bmatrix} = \begin{bmatrix} \Phi_0 & \Gamma_1 \\ 0 & 0 \end{bmatrix} \begin{bmatrix} x(k) \\ z_1(k) \end{bmatrix} + \begin{bmatrix} 0 \\ 1 \end{bmatrix} u(k)$$

The data package is delivered as soon as possible to the actuator, but is hold in the buffer and is implemented to the process in the next sampling intervals. As long as (2) is fulfilled, the "buffered" loop delay is constant and is equal to the buffer length ($\tau_B = T_0$).

If the control strategy is assumed as linear feedback

$$u(k) = -\begin{bmatrix} K_x & 0 \end{bmatrix} \begin{bmatrix} x(k) \\ z_1(k) \end{bmatrix}, \quad u(k) \in R^1 \tag{4}$$

the closed-loop system can be written as

$$\begin{bmatrix} x(k+1) \\ z(k+1) \end{bmatrix} = \begin{bmatrix} \Phi_0 - \Gamma_0(\tau)K & \Gamma_1(\tau)) \\ -K & 0 \end{bmatrix} \begin{bmatrix} x(k) \\ z(k) \end{bmatrix} \tag{5}$$

If the condition (2) is not fulfilled for some kT_0, the two-step, constant length buffer can be applied ($\tau \le 2T_0$), Fig.8. For this case the model takes the form ($q = 1$, $\tau_B = 2T_0$).

$$\begin{bmatrix} x(k+1) \\ z_1(k+1) \\ z_2(k+1) \end{bmatrix} = \underbrace{\begin{bmatrix} \Phi_0 & \Gamma_1 & 0 \\ 0 & 0 & 1 \\ -K_x & 0 & 0 \end{bmatrix}}_{\Phi 2} \begin{bmatrix} x(k) \\ z_1(k) \\ z_2(k) \end{bmatrix} \tag{6}$$

If the loop delay $\tau(k)$ is time varying between $[0, 2T_0]$, it is reasonable to switch between T_0 and $2T_0$ buffers. The stability analysis of this model is the problem of stability of the Asynchronous Dynamical Systems (ASD) (Hasibi et al, 1999).

The model (5) can be rewritten in the equivalent form, as

$$\begin{bmatrix} x(k+1) \\ z_1(k+1) \\ z_2(k+1) \end{bmatrix} = \underbrace{\begin{bmatrix} \Phi_0 & 0 & \Gamma_1 \\ 0 & 0 & 0 \\ -K_x & 0 & 0 \end{bmatrix}}_{\Phi 1} \begin{bmatrix} x(k) \\ z_1(k) \\ z_2(k) \end{bmatrix}$$

The following result applies in this case (Zhang, 2001). If for the linear DCS model

$$w((k+1)) = \Phi_{s(k)}w(k), \quad w(k) = \begin{bmatrix} x(k) \\ z_1(k) \\ z_2(k) \end{bmatrix}, \quad s(k) = (1,2)$$

for a given rate r of the frames transmission there exists the Lyapunov function such that

$$V(w(k)) = w^T(k)Pw(k)$$

and scalars α_1, α_2 such that

$$\alpha_1^r \alpha_2^{1-r} > 1$$

$$\Phi_1^T P\Phi_1 \le \alpha_1^{-2}P, \quad \Phi_2^T P\Phi_2 \le \alpha_2^{-2}P \tag{7}$$

than the system is exponentially stable. The rate r represents the fraction of time that each discrete state transition matrix (Φ_1, Φ_2) occurs. Assuming the transmission rate, the problem (7) can be solved as the LMI problem.

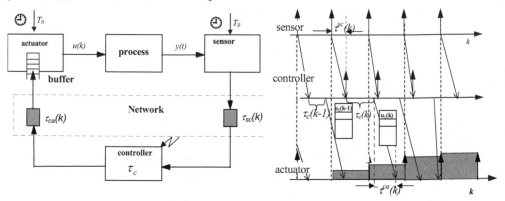

Fig. 8. Time diagram of buffering for $\tau_B = 2T_0$

Clearly, adding any delay to a closed-loop system generally degraders the performance. Therefore, once must investigate:

- proper buffer length for assumed model of delay distribution,
- design of controller that takes advantage of an effectively more deterministic loop delay.

A natural extension of this approach is application of variable length (adaptive) buffers (Tutaj, 2006). It is assumed that frames order can not be changed, frames are not lost or doubled. The initial length of the buffer is T_0. The buffer length is adapted according to the following formula:

$$\tau_B(k) = T_0 + \alpha T_0(p - \varphi(k))$$

where:

α - adaptation parameter, $\alpha > 0$

p - assumed rate of frames delivered to the buffer in time (during the time interval no longer than $\tau_B(k)$), $, 0 < p < 1$

$$\varphi(j) = \begin{cases} 1 & \text{if the frame was delired in time} \\ 0 & \text{otherwise} \end{cases}$$

If the frame is not delivered in time (at $t = kT_0$ the buffer is empty) than $\varphi(k)$ is set to 1. First frame delivered to the buffer is released immediately.

After $k+1$ steps the buffer length can be calculated as (Tutaj, 2006)

$$\tau_B(k+1) = T_0 + \alpha T_0 \sum_{j=0}^{k}(p - \varphi(j))$$

Such a model implements a kind of "filtration" of delays effects (Fig. 9).

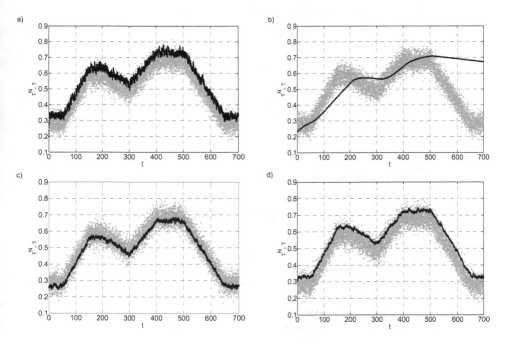

Fig. 9. Example of adaptive filter operation (Tutaj, 2006): a) $\alpha = 0,2$; $p = 0,9$, b) $\alpha = 0{:}002$; $p = 0,9$, c) $\alpha = 0,05$; $p = 0,3$, d) $\alpha = 0,05$; $p = 0,9$ (black – after buffer, grey – before buffer)

3.2 Robust stability of the buffered DCS

Application of variable length buffer simplifies analysis of DCS. It can be assumed that the control delays are constant but not exactly known. In this case the problem of stability analysis of the DCS can be formulated as a parametric robust control problem. This allows using the mapping theorem (Bhattacharyya *et al.* 1995) to develop an effective computational technique to determine robust stability. The advantage of this approach over the stochastic method is that it is not necessary to identify the stochastic model of the delay.

3.2.1 Time-invariant delays in DCS

We assume that the total delay is slowly varying and known only with some precision

$$\tau(k) = \tau, \quad \tau_{min} \leq \tau \leq \tau_{max}$$

In such a case we could design a controller stable for some range of slowly varying delay. The solution of this problem gives answer to the basic question "how much delay can the system tolerate"?
The state matrix of the closed loop system (5) can be next rewritten in the form

$$
M(\Psi) = \begin{bmatrix} \Phi_0 - \Gamma_0(\tau)K & \Gamma_1(\tau)) \\ -K & 0 \end{bmatrix} =
$$
$$
M_0 + M_1(\varphi_1) + M_2(\varphi_2) + .. + M_n(\varphi_n) = \tag{8}
$$
$$
= M_0 + \varphi_1(\tau)\hat{M}_1 + \varphi_2(\tau)\hat{M}_2 + ... + \varphi_n(\tau)\hat{M}_n
$$

where

$$
\Psi^T(\tau) = A^{-1}\Phi_0\Phi(\tau)B = \begin{bmatrix} \varphi_1(\tau) & \varphi_2(\tau) \mid \varphi_n(\tau) \end{bmatrix}
$$

$$
\Phi(\tau) = e^{-A\tau}, \quad M_0 = \begin{bmatrix} \Phi_0 + A^{-1}BK & A^{-1}\Phi_0 B \\ -K & 0 \end{bmatrix}
$$

$$
\hat{M}_i = \begin{bmatrix} 0_1 & 0_2 \\ -K & -1 \\ \hline 0 & 0 \end{bmatrix}, \tag{9}
$$

$$
\dim 0_1 = (i-1) \times n, \dim 0_2 = (i-1) \times 1
$$

The uncertain delay enters affinely into the state matrix of the closed loop system. If $\tau_{min} \leq \tau \leq \tau_{max}$, then we could obtain the boundaries

$$
\Psi_{min} \leq \Psi(\tau) \leq \Psi_{max} \tag{10}
$$

The following stability problem is important for the model formulated above: determine if matrix (9) remains Schur-stable as φ_i parameters ranges over the bounds given by (10)? The structure of the closed loop state matrix (8) is a special case of the interval matrix family and we are free to use results of the robust theory solutions for checking stability (Bhattacharyy *et al.* 1995). Under the assumption $rank(M_i) = 1$ for $i = 1..n$ the coefficients of the characteristics polynomial of $M(\Psi)$ are multilinear function of φ. The following theorem applies in this case:

Let the matrix M_0 be Schur stable. If the $\mathrm{rank}(\hat{M}_i) = 1$ for $i = 1..n$, than the family of the matrices $M(\Psi)$, $\Psi \in \Theta$ defined by (8)-(9) is robust Schur-stable if the testing function

$$F(y) > 0 \quad \forall y \in Y,$$

where the testing function is defined as

$$F(y) = \pi - \alpha(y) \tag{11}$$

$$\alpha(y) = \max\{|\arg(\tilde{p}_r(f(y))) - \arg(\tilde{p}_k(f(y)))|\},$$
$$r, k = 1, 2, \ldots K, \quad r \neq k$$

$$\tilde{p}_k(z) = \frac{p_k(z)}{w_0(z)}, \quad k = 1, 2, \ldots, K$$

$$p_k(z) = \det(zI - M(\varphi_k))$$

$$w_0(z) = \det(zI - M_0) \quad K = 2^n.$$

The function $f(y) = \exp(j\pi y)$, $y \in Y = [0,2]$ is a parametric description of the unit circle, $M(\varphi_k)$ is a vertex matrix calculated for each φ_k - the vertex of the set Θ, K is the number of the vertex matrices. The testing function (11) checks the maximal phase differences of the vertex polynomials over parameter box corresponding to the vertices given by (10).

3.2.2 Example: Distributed control of a tank system

Let us consider a problem of distributed control of a tank system. The process consists of the upper tank having constant cross section and the lower cylindrical tank, so having variable cross section. Liquid is pumped into the top tank by DC motor driven pump. The liquid outflows of the tanks only due to gravity. The orifices C_1 and C_2 determine the outflow of the liquid. The general objective of the control is to reach and stabilise the level in the lower tank by adjustment of the pump operation. The levels in the tanks are measured with pressure transducers (S). The appropriate interfaces (I) enabling distance transmission of the control signals to the pump were installed, creating a distributed control system from Fig.10.

If levels in the tanks are introduced as the states variables, the nonlinear model could be linearized at $H^0 = [H_1^0, H_1^2]^T$ giving finally (Grega, 2002)

$$\frac{d}{dt}\begin{bmatrix} h_1 \\ h_2 \end{bmatrix} = \begin{bmatrix} a_1 & 0 \\ a_3 & a_4 \end{bmatrix}\begin{bmatrix} h_1 \\ h_2 \end{bmatrix} + \begin{bmatrix} b_1 \\ 0 \end{bmatrix} u$$

where: $H_1 = H_1^0 + h_1,$ $H_2 = H_2^0 + h_2,$ $q = q^0 + u,$ $b_1 = \dfrac{1}{S},$ $a_1 = \dfrac{-C_1}{2S\sqrt{H_1^0}},$

$$a_3 = \frac{C_1\sqrt{H_1^0}}{4H_1^0 \cdot w\sqrt{r^2 - (r - H_2^0)^2}}, \quad a_4 = \frac{-C_2\sqrt{H_2^0}}{4H_2^0 \cdot w\sqrt{r^2 - (r - H_2^0)^2}}$$

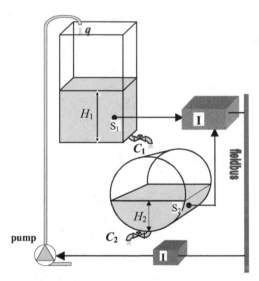

Fig. 10. Distributed control of tank system

For an assumed sampling period T_0 the equivalent discrete model is ($\tau = 0$)

$$\begin{bmatrix} h_1(k+1) \\ h_2(k+1) \end{bmatrix} = \begin{bmatrix} e^{a_1 T_0} & 0 \\ \dfrac{a_3}{a_1 - a_4}(e^{a_1 T_0} - e^{a_4 T_0}) & e^{a_4 T_0} \end{bmatrix} \begin{bmatrix} h_1(k) \\ h_2(k) \end{bmatrix} +$$

$$+ \begin{bmatrix} \dfrac{b_1}{a_1}(e^{a_1 T_0} - 1) \\ \dfrac{b_1 a_3}{a_1 a_4}[\dfrac{a_1(e^{a_1 T_0} - e^{a_4 T_0})}{a_1 - a_4} - (e^{a_1 T_0} - 1)] \end{bmatrix} u(k)$$

Linear feedback control law is in the form

$$u(k) = -K\, h(k)$$

It was assumed that the controller has been design ignoring the network, hence the state matrix of (3) is stable for $\tau = 0$. The assumed parameters of the tank model were: $C_1 = 10$, $C_2 = 15$, $T_0 = 80s$, giving the LQ controller gains: $K_1 = 0.7167$ $K_2 = 3.0950$. Fig. 11 demonstrates the LQ optimal output of the model (simulation). Figure 13 illustrates observed perturbation of data transmission times, when Ethernet protocol was applied and some additional traffic in the network was generated.

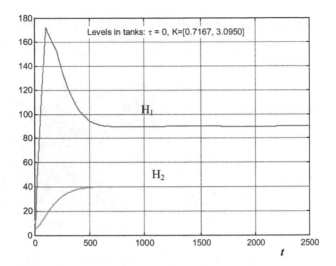

Fig. 11. LQ – optimal control of the tank system

The delay in the control loop reduces the stability margin of the system. Figure 12 shows how the fixed feedback delay ($\tau = 80s$) degrades the performance of the tank system control. Notice that this is equivalent to implementation of the fixed size buffer ($\tau_B = T_0$). So, to increase the stability margin and improve stability it is necessary to tune the feedback gains.

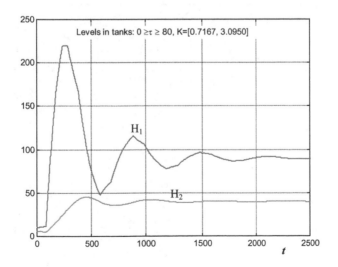

Fig. 12. System performance degradation

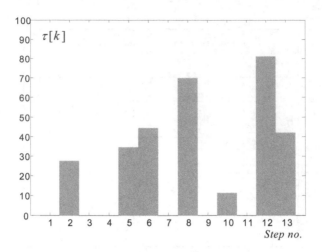

Fig. 13. Network delays – perturbation of data transmission times, $\tau \in [0,100]$s

If the variable-length buffer is introduced, stability of the distributed digital control system for the assumed controller gains and $0 \le \tau \le \tau_{\max}$ can be verified using the methodology described above. It is assumed now, that the control delays are constant but not exactly known. The LQ optimal robust gains (giving the stable matrix M_0) were calculated as: $K_1 = 0.3745 \quad K_2 = 0.3420$.

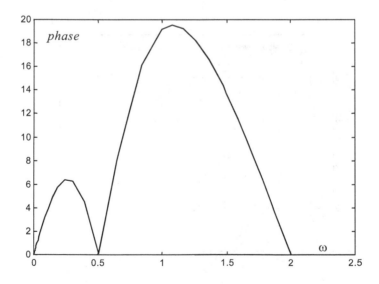

Fig. 14. Maximum phase diffences of vertex matrices

The next step is verification of the testing function $F(y)$. The appropriate testing function is given in Fig. 14. The maximum phase difference over all vertices at each $\omega \in [0, 2\pi)$ is less than 180°. Figure 15 shows operation of the LQ controller for the above set of controller parameters and network delays, as given in Fig.13.

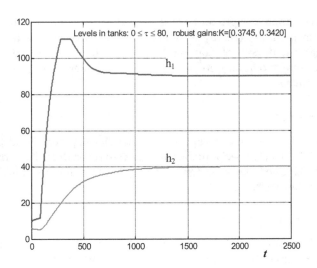

Fig. 15. Robust, LQ – optimal control of the tank system

4. Final remarks

The introduction of networks, limited throughput of data transmission channels, combined with non-optimised hardware and software components introduce non-determinism in the distributed control system. For multilevel industrial systems this problem becomes even more complex. Some control loops can be handle by local, device – level controllers, but also by the supervisory controllers all them implementing data transmission networks. Special care must be taken when the communication channel generates sampling – actuation jitters or other kinds of run time violation of the closed-loop timing assumptions. It means that the introduction of data transmission networks into the feedback loop in many cases violates conventional control theories assumptions such as non-delayed or evenly spaced sampling and actuation. It is now reasonable to redesign controllers improving the temporal robustness of the distributed control system.

Control engineers do not care very much about real-time or distributed control implementations of control algorithms. In many cases they do not understand control timing constraints. The typical solutions proposed are: "buy a faster computer" or "install a more efficient data transmission network". Basic control theory does not advise them on how to redesign controllers to take network limitation into account.

It was demonstrated in this chapter, that robust design it is not only a proper selection and tuning of control algorithms, but also study on communications protocols and networks, to make them suitable for real-time DCS.

We have proposed an integrated design approach combining several components: process dynamics, controller parameters and network constraints, and resulting in better quality of control systems.
Finally, it was shown how the extension of the standard controller with a buffer improves robustness of distributed control system. The model was formulated as variable parameter linear discrete-time model, where variability of parameters was introduced by the time varying delays. The variable length buffer was used at actuator side to eliminate high speed delay variability in the loop, thereby enabling more effective use of delay compensation algorithms. A water tank control example has shown how implementation of variable-length buffer algorithm and application of some results of interval matrices theory increases robustness of the control loop.

5. Acknowledgment

This work was supported by the European Regional Development Fund Grant no. UDA-POIG.01.03.01-12-171/08/00. Special thanks are given to dr Andrzej Tutaj from Department of Automatics, AGH University of Science and Technology for his valuable experiments results included in this work.

6. References

Al-Hammouri, A.T., Branicky, M.S., Liberatore, V. & Phillips, S.M.(2006). Decentralized and dynamic bandwidth allocation in networked control systems, in: *20th International Parallel and Distributed Processing Symposium*, 25-29 April 2006

Amiguet, A., Etienne, L. & Jaggi A. (2008). Performance analysis of PROFINET networks, Available: http://lamspeople.epfl.ch/decotignie/Midterm08_profinet_slides.pdf

ARC Advisory Group (2007). *Industrial Ethernet Infrastructure Worldwide Outlook* (2007), Market Analysis and Forecast through 2011 ed. by Cisco

Aström, K.J. & Wittenmark, B. (1997). *Computer Controlled Systems*, Prentice Hall, London

Bhattacharyya, S.P., Chapellat, H. & Keel, L.H. (1995). *Robust Control: The Parametric Approach*, Prentice Hall, New Jersey, 1995

CoNeT (Cooperative Network Training) project website. (2011). http://www.conet-eu.net/

Felsner, F. (2005). Real-Time Ethernet – Industry Prospective, in: *Proceedings of the IEEE*, Vol. 93, June 2005, pp. 1118- 1129

Fujioka, H. (2009). Stability analysis of systems with aperiodic sample-and-hold devices, *Automatica*, vol. 45, no.3, pp. 771–775

Georges, G.P., Krommenacker, N., Divoux T. & Rondeau, E. (2006). A design process of switched Ethernet architectures according to real-time application constraints, *Engineering Applications of Artificial Intelligence*, vol. 19, no.3, pp. 335-344

Grega, W. (1998). Time-optimal Control of N-tank System, in: *Proceedings of 1998 IEEE International Conference on Control Applications*, Triest, pp. 532-536

Grega, W. (2002). Stability of Distributed Control Systems with Uncertain Delays, in: *8th IEEE International Conference on Methods and Models in Automation and Robotics*, Międzyzdroje 2002, pp. 303 – 307

Grega, W. & Tutaj A. (2007). Network traffic reduction by sample grouping for distributed control systems, in: 3rd *Proceedings International Workshop on: Networked control systems: tolerant to faults,* June 20–21, 2007, Nancy, France, pp. 2-8

Grega, W. (2009). Codesign of distributed and real-time control systems, in: *14th International Conference on Methods and Models in Automation and Robotics,* Międzyzdroje, August 2009, pp. 85-88

Grega, W., Byrski, W. & Duda J. (2009). *InStePro – Integrated Production Control.* Project Description, available from: http://www.InStePro.agh.edu.pl

Grega, W. (2010). Multilevel Control under Communication Constraints, In: *Proceedings of 2010 IEEE International Symposium on Computer-Aided Control System Design,* Yokohama, Japan, September 8-10, 2010, pp. 1176 – 1181, IEEE Xplore Digital Library, Digital Object Identifier: 10.1109/CACSD.2010.5612686

Gupta, R. A. & Chow, M.-Y. (2010). Networked Control System: Overview and Research Trends, *IEEE Transaction on Industrial Electronics,* vol. 57, no.7, pp. 2527-2535

Hassibi A., Boyd, S.P. & How, J.P. (1999). Control of Asynchronous Dynamical Systems with Rate Constraints on Events, in: *Proceedings of 37 IEEE Conference on Decision and Control,* pp. 1345–1351

Hirai, K. & Satoh, Y. (1980). Stability of a System with Variable Time Delay, In: *IEEE Transaction on Automatic Control,* vol. AC-25, pp. 552-554

Juanole, G. & Mouney, M. (2006). Real time distributed systems: QoS and impact on the performance of process control applications. In: *17th International Symposium on Mathematical Theory of Networks and Systems (MTNS'06),* July 2006, Kyoto, Japan, pp. 1739-1746

Larsson, L. (2005). *Fourteen Industrial Ethernet solutions under the spotlight,* The Industrial Ethernet Book, vol.28, Available from: http://ethernet.industrialnetworking.com /articles/articledisplay.asp?id=854

Montestruque, L.A. & Antsaklis, P.J. (2003). On the model-based control of networked systems", *Automatica,* vol. 39, pp. 1837-1843

Nilson, J. (1998). *Real-time Control systems with Delays,* Ph. D. Dissertation, Lund Institute of Technology, Sweden, 1998

Nilsson, J., Bernhardsson, B. & Wittenmark, B. (1998). Stochastic analysis and control of real-time systems with random time delays, *Automatica,* vol. 34, pp. 57-64

Tatjewski, P. (2007). *Advanced Control of Industrial Processes,* Springer-Verlag, London

Tutaj, A. (2009). Packets buffering in network traffic in distributed control systems, in: *Proceedings of 12th IEEE international conference on Methods and Models in Automation and Robotics,* 28–31 August 2006, Międzyzdroje, pp. 27–28

Vatanski, N., Georges, J-P., Aubrun, Ch., Rondeau, E. & Jämsä-Jounela, S-L. (2009). Networked Control with Delay Measurement and Estimation, *Control Engineering Practice* vol.17, no.2, pp. 231-244

Walsh, G.C., Ye, H., & Bushnell, L.G. (2002) Stability analysis of networked control systems, *IEEE Transactions on Control Systems Technology,* vol. 10, no. 3, pp. 438-446

Yi, Z. & Heng, P. A. (2002). Stability of Fuzzy Control Systems with Bounded Uncertain Delays, IEEE *Transactions on Fuzzy Systems,* vol. 10, no. 1 (Feb. 2002), pp. 92-97

Cao, Y. and & Zhang, W. (2005). Modified Fuzzy PID Control for Networked Control Systems with Random Delays, in: *World Academy of Science, Engineering and Technology*, vol. 12, pp. 520-523

Zhang, W. (2001). *Stability Analysis of Networked Control Systems*, PhD Thesis, Case Western Reserve University

Zurawski, R. (2005). *The Industrial Communication Systems. Handbook.* CRC Press, ISBN: 9780849330773

An Application of Robust Control for Force Communication Systems over Inferior Quality Network

Tetsuo Shiotsuki
Tokyo Denki University
Japan

1. Introduction

The developments of computer and network technologies have provided a virtual reality environment and ubiquitous network systems. Especially audio-visual devices play an important role in communication. For example, voice communication by telephone, audio-visual communication, streaming technology, digital television system and so on. However, we know that the human makes communication not only by audio-visual information but also by using all five-senses (touch, taste, hearing, eyesight, and smell). The realization of the five-senses communication system is one of the prospected technologies.

Especially force communication is a hopeful application in the coming e-world. Several kinds of gimmicks can be considered for transmitting or exchanging the sense of touch, haptic, tactile, force and kinesthetic. In the area of the wearable computing technologies some force-like communication system is realized by using pressure, tension, bending, stress sensors and vibration or pressure actuators, which give the illusion of force communication. On the other hand, robotic researchers have discussed on bilateral tele-operation systems, which realizes remote-manipulations with the sense of reaction forces caused by collision or touching of remote objects and environments. An aim of the technology is that the communication channel between two terminals simulates as if a rigid rod or tight rope. In this article, we consider the bilateral tele-operation systems as a force communication device. It is a well-known that the computer network has inevitable time-delay and jitter in the transmission of the data. And in control engineering deterioration of the stability and performance of the closed loop systems is a well-known fact. Control researchers have proposed several kinds of approaches to overcome the problems. The rest of the chapter is composed as follows. In Section 2, a characterization of the computer network from the view point of transmission delay is discussed. In Section 3, control systems of force sensorless bilateral tele-operation system and the problems caused by transmission delay are examined with a brief historical review. Section 4 presents a procedure how to design a robust control system over the uncertain time-delay network. In section 5 a simulation result is introduced, and some discussions are presented. In section 6 experimental results over the real broadband computer network are introduced. And the results of experiments and investigation are explained in detail. Section 6 concludes the article.

2. Communication network and time delay

Fusion of computer and tele-communication technologies has provided the revolution of the computer network such as the Internet. Before the revolution usual tele-communication is established in two steps. Firstly, according to the request from the sender the system searches the receiver and establishes a communication channel by reserving network resources exclusively. Secondly, the session starts on the reserved real communication channel. After the end of the session, the reserved resources are released. In this case, the time-delay over the communication channel is so small as can be ignored.

On the other hand, communication on the computer network between two terminal nodes is realized as a set of the exchange process of datagrams (frame, packet, cell,Ac). For example, the information is converted into digital data and divided into datagrams. These datagrams are put on the node and travel along the path while looking for appropriate next node until they reach to the destination. In general the data exchange process includes the huge number of data processing such as encoding, storing and (route) switching. And the length of the processing time depends on the size of datagram and transmitting rate the busyness of the equipments. Especially the network routers are shared by multi-users. Since the practically implemented algorithm is almost trying and error type, the data buffer sometimes overflowed and fails data(packet loss). In order to ensure the reproducibility of the data several kinds of data processing algorithms are implemented according to transmission protocols. TCP/IP(Transmission Control Protocol/Internet Protocol) provides confirming of receiving data (acknowledge), control of window size, and data retransmission and so on. Because of the complexity of the mechanism and sharing of the resource of the network the time-delay is greater than the circuit channel type communications. And the jitter, variation of the time delay occurs frequently.

Fig.1 shows an example of time delay during a day between two campuses(Kumamoto and Fukuoka) in 1998. The left graph (a) indicates the time series from midnight to midnight, and the right(b) is the histogram of the number of packets with respect to transmission delay. It is too difficult to construct the prediction model of time-delay because of the randomness and chaos. Here we adopt a statistical model as a rectangular distribution as follows.

$$0 < L \leq L_{max} \tag{1}$$

In practice it is possible to set L_{max} such that 95% of packets are travels in the time interval $[0, L_{max}]$.

3. Historical review of tele-operation systems

3.1 Master slave system

Suppose the situation in which an operator manipulates (push/ pull/ lift/ put on and so on) some object through the communication network. Such a kind of system is called a master slave system or *tele-operation system*. Usually the terminals for the operator and the object are called the *master* and the *slave* equipment each other. Operators motion is converted to the motion data by the master mechanism, transmitted to the slave side and realized as a motion of the slave equipment. If the system can transmit the force information caused in the slave side to the master side it called *bilateral tele-operation systems*. Several kind of mechanisms are proposed for the control of bilateral tele-operation systems.

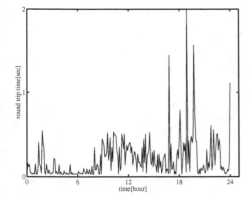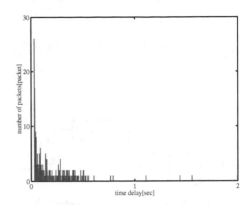

Fig. 1. An example of transmission delay of the Internet: (left)time history(time vs. delay), (right) Histogram (delay vs. frequency)

PE(position error) type is the most simple one. Master and slave exchange the position data each other. Both controllers compensate the deviation of the positions independently. It means that the system is a combination of two position feedback control systems. When the master and the slave equipments have the same characteristics the structure of the system is completely symmetric. In FR(Force reflection) type, master equipment transmits the position data and receives the force data from the slave equipment. On the other hand FRP(Force reflection with passivity) type exchanges the velocity data and the force data respectively.

3.2 Delay and instability
It is well-known that the time delay in the loop deteriorates the stability, performance and robustness of the feedback systems. Fig.2(b) shows a demonstration of the tarde-off of gain K and time-delay L. If (L, K) is chosen in the range of *stable* region the closed loop system depicted in Fig. 2(a) becomes stable, and vice versa. This trade-off curve is identical to the contour of the H_∞ norm of the transfer function

$$\gamma := \left\| \frac{K}{s^2 + K}(1 - e^{-Ls}) \right\|_\infty \tag{2}$$

with $\gamma = 1$. It is easy to calculate that the transfer function matches to one at the cutting point a in Fig.2.
This plot says the following facts.

(1) If $L = 0$ then the gain margin is infinite.

(2) The gain margin decreases rapidly as the time-delay grows, that is, the robustness to time-delay deteriorate as the time-delay grows.

According to the considerations the necessity of careful investigation to time-delay is required.

3.3 Scattering and wave variable method
Anderson and Spong (6) introduced a new communication architecture for tele-operation over the network with time-delay. Their method is based on the passivity and scattering representation of the network. Thus the strictly passivity of master and slave systems

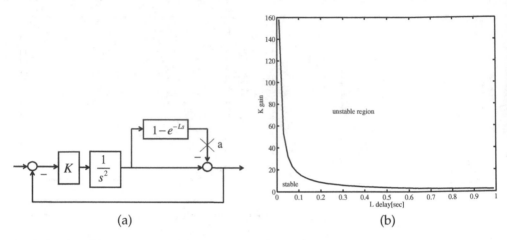

(a)   (b)

Fig. 2. Trade-off between time-delay and loop gain (delay vs. loop gain)

and stationary time-delay are assumed, which are strong constraints for design. Moreover Niemeyer and Slotine (7) extended their method by using wave variables. Since it is a generalization of Anderson-Spong method, it has the same constraints and difficulties in practice. On the other hand Leung, Francis and Apkarian (8) proposed a controller designed via μ−Synthesis. The proposed method based on robust control theory can deal fluctuation of time-delay and has strong practicability. But all the above methods have the same configuration in which the master and slave system exchanges the velocity and the force variables (v, f) through the network. This means that the position, integral of velocity v, of the master and the slave systems are depend on the initial conditions, and the stability is ensured not in the sense of position but velocity. Moreover the necessity of force sensors makes the systems configuration sophisticated. The more simple architecture is prefer for the practical application.

4. Robust control approach

4.1 Paradigm of robust control
There are several kind of strategies to overcome the problem of time delay. Assuming the rectangular (uniform) distribution of time delay H_∞ control theory can be applied as follows. Fig.4 shows the correspondence between time-delay and multiplicative uncertainty. Now let define a 1-st order high-pass filter $W_D(s; L)$ as

$$W_D(s; L) = \frac{As}{s + \dfrac{1}{L}} \tag{3}$$

where $A = 2.102904074495...$ It is easy to verify that the norm of $(e^{-Ls} - 1)$ holds the following inequality for any frequency(on the imaginary axis) and any time delay L with $0 < L \le L_{max}$

$$|1 - e^{-j\omega L}| < W_D(j\omega; L) \le W_D(j\omega; L_{max}), \quad \forall j\omega \in j\mathbf{R}, \tag{4}$$

where L_{max} is the upper bound of the estimated time-delay. This means that the uncertainty caused by the variation of time-delay between $[0, L_{max}]$ can be covered by the weighting function $W_D(s; L_{max})$ as a high-pass filter with cut-off frequency $1/L_{max}$ [rad/sec]

$$W_D(s, L_{max}) = \frac{2.1s}{s + \dfrac{1}{L_{max}}}.$$ (5)

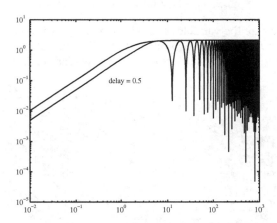

Fig. 3. variation of the gain casued by time delay and inequality in (4)

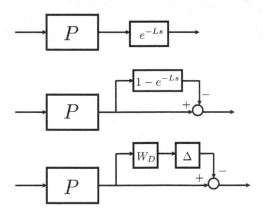

Fig. 4. correspondence between time-delay and multiplicative uncertainty

By using the function $W_D(s; L_{max})$ and uncertain bounded function Δ ($|\Delta| < 1$) the inequality 4 can be replaced as

$$e^{-Ls} = 1 + W_D(s; L_{max})\Delta.$$ (6)

4.2 PE type bilateral tele-operation system
Here we introduce a simple PE type bilateral tele-operation system designed with robust control technique. Two joystick mechanisms, corresponds to master and slave, are considered.

Each joystick has a DC-servo motor for torque generation and a position sensor for measurement of the angle of the joy-stick. Force sensors attached to the joysticks are not for use of the control but for the performance evaluation of force communications. They are controlled by computers which are connected to the computer network (see Fig.5). These joysticks are assumed to be modeled as

$$J_m \ddot{x}_m(t) + D_m \dot{x}_m(t) = K_m u_m(t) + f_m(t) \tag{7}$$

$$J_s \ddot{x}_s(t) + D_s \dot{x}_s(t) = K_s u_s(t) - f_s(t) \tag{8}$$

where x, f and u indicate the variables of position of the joystick, external force and input voltage for motor torque generator each other. J and D indicate the physical parameters of inertia and friction each other. The suffixes m, s indicate the master and the slave respectively.

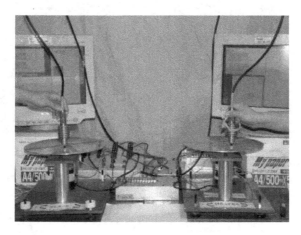

Fig. 5. A view of experimental equipments: Two joysticks controlled by computers connected to the network

J_m	0.0140	[Kgm^2]
J_s	0.0379	[Kgm^2]
D_m	0.0110	[Nms]
D_s	0.0250	[Nms]
K_m	0.2557	[Nm/V]
K_s	0.2557	[Nm/V]

Table 1. Parameters of master and slave joysticks

If there is no time delay between master and slave sides the deviations of the joysticks are evaluated as

$$e_{m0}(t) = x_m(t) - x_s(t) \tag{9}$$

$$e_{s0}(t) = x_s(t) - x_m(t) = -e_{m0}(t). \tag{10}$$

When the master and the slave controllers exchange the information through the network, as stated in the previous section, the time-delay must be considered. Let us assume that the time-delay $L > 0$ exists between master and slave controllers symmetrically. The evaluated deviations (9)(10) at each controller might be computed as follows.

$$e_{mL}(t) = x_m(t) - x_s(t - L) \tag{11}$$

$$e_{sL}(t) = x_s(t) - x_m(t - L) \tag{12}$$

In the rest of the chapter $e_{m0}, e_{s0}(e_{mL}, e_{sL})$ are called as errors in ideal (computed) deviation. The Laplace transform of computed deviation e_{mL} (11) is written as

$$\begin{aligned} E_{mL}(s) &= X_m(s) - e^{-Ls}X_s(s) \\ &= X_m(s) - X_s(s) + X_s(s) - e^{-Ls}X_s(s) \\ &= E_{m0}(s) + (1 - e^{-Ls})X_s(s). \end{aligned} \tag{13}$$

In the same way the Laplace transform of e_{sL} can be written as

$$E_{sL}(s) = E_{s0}(s) + (1 - e^{-Ls})X_m(s). \tag{14}$$

This means that the minimization of computed deviations $(E_{mL}(s), E_{sL}(s))$ is acomplished by the simultaneous minimization of $E_{m0}(s)(= -E_{s0}(s))$, $(1 - e^{-Ls})X_s(s)$ and $(1 - e^{-Ls})X_m(s)$ from the inequality as

$$\begin{aligned} |E_{mL}(j\omega)| &\leq |E_{m0}(j\omega)| + |(1 - e^{-j\omega L})X_s(j\omega)| \\ &\leq |E_{m0}(j\omega)| + |W_D(j\omega; L)X_s(j\omega)|. \\ &\leq |E_{m0}(j\omega)| + |W_D(j\omega; L_{max})X_s(j\omega)|. \end{aligned} \tag{15}$$

$$|E_{sL}(j\omega)| \leq |E_{s0}(j\omega)| + |W_D(j\omega; L_{max})X_m(j\omega)|. \tag{16}$$

As mensioned in previous section the time delay L includes uncertainty. But if the upper bound of L is obtained as L_{max} according to 4and 5 the minimization problem can be acomplished by the minimization of $E_{m0}(s), W_D(s; L_{max})X_s(s)$ and $W_D(s; L_{max})X_m(s)$. H_∞ theory gives a design method to obtain an appropriate feedback gain to keep stability and robustness against the type of model uncertainty.

4.3 Plant model

Let us consider the two joystick mechanisms as a system with two inputs and two outputs plant

$$\begin{bmatrix} X_m(s) \\ X_s(s) \end{bmatrix} = \begin{bmatrix} P_m(s) & 0 \\ 0 & P_s(s) \end{bmatrix} \begin{bmatrix} U_m(s) \\ U_s(s) \end{bmatrix}. \tag{17}$$

where,

$$P_m(s) = \frac{K_m}{s(J_m s + D_m)}, \quad P_s(s) = \frac{K_s}{s(J_s s + D_s)}. \tag{18}$$

The purpose is the design of a controller

$$\begin{bmatrix} U_m(s) \\ U_s(s) \end{bmatrix} = \begin{bmatrix} C_{mm}(s) & C_{ms}(s) \\ C_{sm}(s) & C_{ss}(s) \end{bmatrix} \begin{bmatrix} X_m(s) \\ X_s(s) \end{bmatrix} \tag{19}$$

which satisfies the requirements specified as follows. The schematic diagram is depicted in Fig.6

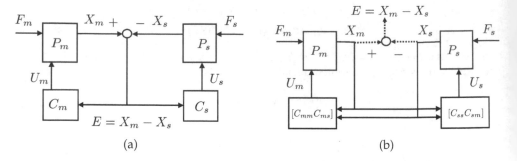

(a)   (b)

Fig. 6. scheme of PE type master-slave system (a)ideal (non time-delay) scheme,(b) practical(implementable) scheme

tracking performance

The closed loop system is a kind of regulator which makes the deviation $e = X_m - X_s \rightarrow 0$ as time goes. For the robust control systems design the deviation e is generalized to a criteria for tracking performance as

$$z_1 = W_{11}e, \quad e = x_m - x_s. \tag{20}$$

In general W_{11} has to be chosen as high gain at low frequency and low gain at high frequency.

stability augmentation

More over in order to obtain a adequate local feedback gain which improves the stability and robustness of closed loop system, the criteria for stability is formulated as

$$z_2 = W_{12}x_m, \quad z_3 = W_{13}x_s. \tag{21}$$

properness of controller

In order to ensure the properness of the controller $C(s)$ in (19) the input variables for the plant are added to the criteria for design as

$$z_4 = W_{21}(w_1 + u_1), \quad z_5 = W_{22}(w_2 + u_2) \tag{22}$$

where w_1, w_2 are exogenous inputs or exerted external forces(torques) as in Fig.7.

robust stability against time-delay

As mentioned in the previous section the robustness corresponds to the minimization of $W_D(s; L_{max})X_s(s)$ and $W_D(s; L_{max})X_m(s)$. Thus we introduce new two output variables

$$z_6 = W_D x_m, \quad z_7 = W_D x_s. \tag{23}$$

with two more variables w_3, w_4 which come from the uncertainty (6) as

$$w_3 = \Delta z_6 , \ w_4 = \Delta z_7. \tag{24}$$

4.4 Construction of generalized plant

Let's define the exogenous input w and evaluated output z as

$$w = \begin{bmatrix} w_1 \ w_2 \ w_3 \ w_4 \end{bmatrix}^T \tag{25}$$

$$z = \begin{bmatrix} z_1 \ z_2 \ z_3 \ z_4 \ z_5 \ z_6 \ z_7 \end{bmatrix}^T . \tag{26}$$

Moreover defining the following vectors

$$U = \begin{bmatrix} U_m \ U_s \end{bmatrix}^T \tag{27}$$

$$X = \begin{bmatrix} X_m \ X_s \end{bmatrix}^T \tag{28}$$

the generalized plant is obtained as follows (see Fig.7).

$$\begin{bmatrix} z \\ X \end{bmatrix} = \begin{bmatrix} G_{11} \ G_{12} \\ G_{21} \ G_{22} \end{bmatrix} \begin{bmatrix} w \\ U \end{bmatrix} \tag{29}$$

$$\begin{bmatrix} G_{11} \ G_{12} \\ G_{21} \ G_{22} \end{bmatrix} = \begin{bmatrix} W_{11}P_m & -W_{11}P_s & W_{11} & -W_{11} & W_{11}P_m & -W_{11}P_s \\ W_{12}P_m & 0 & W_{12} & 0 & W_{12}P_m & 0 \\ 0 & W_{13}P_s & 0 & W_{13} & 0 & W_{13}P_s \\ W_{21} & 0 & 0 & 0 & W_{21} & 0 \\ 0 & W_{22} & 0 & 0 & 0 & W_{22} \\ W_{D1}P_m & 0 & 0 & 0 & W_{D1}P_m & 0 \\ 0 & W_{D2}P_s & 0 & 0 & 0 & W_{D2}P_s \\ \hline P_m & 0 & 0 & 0 & P_m & 0 \\ 0 & P_s & 0 & 0 & 0 & P_s \end{bmatrix} \tag{30}$$

By applying the controller (19) to the above system a transfer function matrix from w to z

$$G_{zw}(s) = G_{11} + G_{12}(I - CG_{22})^{-1}CG_{21} \tag{31}$$

can be obtained. By using the design procedure based on the H_∞ control theory a controller is obtained such that

$$\|G_{zw}(s)\|_\infty < \gamma \tag{32}$$

where γ is a design parameter chosen as small as possible (5).

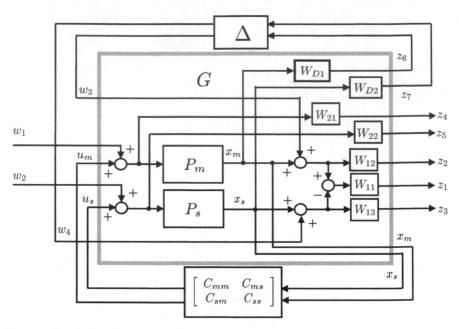

Fig. 7. generalized plant for master-slave systems

5. Simulation and estimates of robustness

In order to demonstrait the robustness w.r.t. time delay computer simulations on the stability and tracking analysis are shown here. The time-delay is assumed as $L_{max} = 0.1[\text{sec}]$. According to the specifications discussed above weighting functions $\{W_i\}, i = 1, 2, 3$ are set as follows.

$$W_{D1}(s) = W_{D2}(s) = \frac{2.1s}{s + 10} \tag{33}$$

$$W_{11}(s) = \frac{1.0 \times 10^5 s + 2.0 \times 10^5}{1.0 \times 10^4 s + 1.0} \tag{34}$$

$$W_{12}(s) = W_{13}(s) = \frac{0.01s + 1}{0.1s + 1} \tag{35}$$

$$W_{21}(s) = W_{22}(s) = 10 \tag{36}$$

Fig.8 shows the bode diagrams of the transfer functions.
Table 2 shows simulation results for analysis of stability and tracking performance.
The values in the left column indicate actual time-delay L_{act} in simulation. When the actual time-delay is not greater than the assumed maximum one, that is $L_{act} \le L_{max}$, the stability and tracking performance are kept well. On the other hand if the time-delay exceeds estimated value , $L_{act} > L_{max}$, the performance of the system becomes worse. It points that the importance of the estimate of maximum time delay L_{max}.

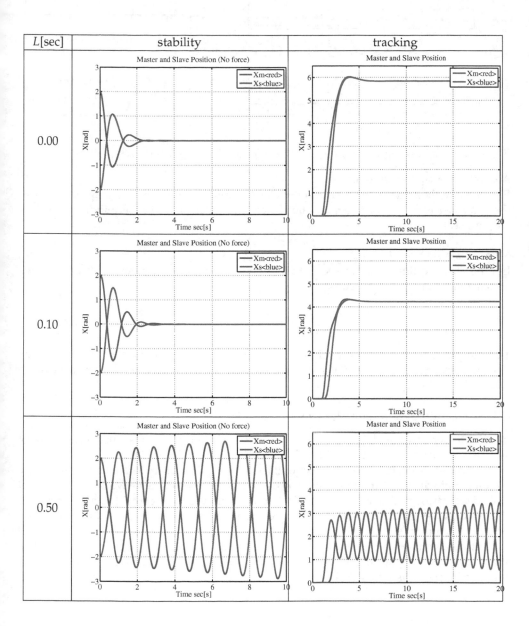

Table 2. Analysis of stability and tracking performance w.r.t. time-delay

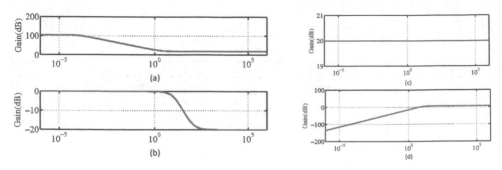

Fig. 8. Bode (gain) diagrams (a) W_{11} ,(b) W_{12}, W_{13}, (c) W_{21}, W_{22}, (d) W_{D1}, W_{D2}

Analysis of designed controller
Fig. 9 shows bode diagrams of controller $C(s)$. It can be observed that roughly seeing of the controller is a kind of integrator, but it works constant gain in the middle range 1 ~ 10^3[rad/sec].

5.1 Analysis via hybrid matrix
In order to investigate the force communication ability and transperency of master-slave system hybrid matrix is defined as

$$\begin{bmatrix} F_s \\ X_m \end{bmatrix} = \begin{bmatrix} h_{11} & h_{12} \\ h_{21} & h_{22} \end{bmatrix} \begin{bmatrix} X_s \\ F_m \end{bmatrix}. \tag{37}$$

Table 10 shows the bode daigram of hybrid matrix. $h_{12} = F_s/F_m$ and $h_{21} = X_m/X_s$ indicate that the tracking ability of position and force communication are expected to work in the range from DC upto 1 rad/sec.

6. Experiments over the network with time-delay

In order to demonstrate the robustness of the proposed control systems a networked control system is constructed as in Figure 11.
Master and slave mechanisms and their local controllers (C_m, C_s) are located on the same cite (at Kumamoto city), and another computer (C_T) is located beyond the network (at Kitakyushu city, 150km far from Kumamoto city). These three computers are connected to the network JGN , which was Japanese broadband network as an experimental testbed administrated by TAO [1]. The controllers C_m and C_s can communicate each other by way of relay computer C_T, but not admitted to communicate directly. The transmission capacity of the network is about 100Mbps. The control period at C_m and C_s is 5[msec] and that of communication period between C_m and C_s is 10[msec]. The communication protocol UDP/IP is adopted.

---

[1] Telecommunications Advancement Organization of Japan; reorganized to NICT(National Institute of Information and Communications Technology) in 2004 (http://www.nict.go.jp/)

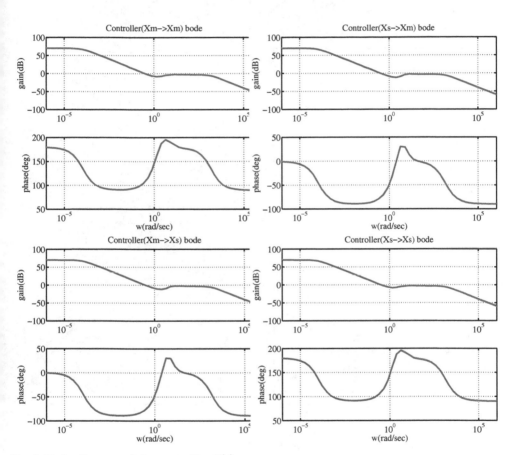

Fig. 9. Bode diagram of the controller $C(s)$

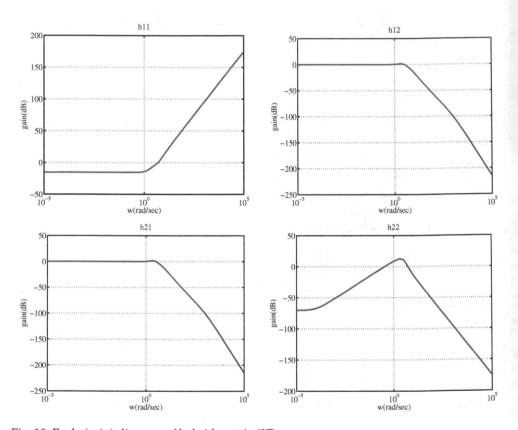

Fig. 10. Bode (gain) diagram of hybrid matrix (37)

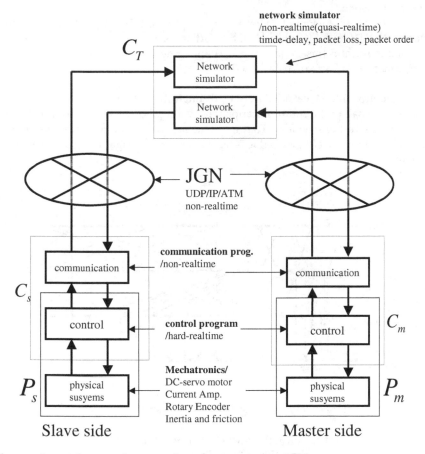

Fig. 11. experimental network system for robust control on JGN

design parameters

Weighting functions in generalized plant (29) are specified as

$$W_{11} = \frac{0.3s + 20 \times 10^7}{3.9 \times 10^6 s + 10^5}, \tag{38}$$

$$W_{12} = W_{13} = \frac{1}{1.5}, \tag{39}$$

$$W_{21} = W_{22} = 0.2, \tag{40}$$

$$W_D = \frac{2.1s + \epsilon}{s + \dfrac{1}{L_{max}}} \tag{41}$$

By specifying the allowable time-delay L_{max} and upper bound of H_∞ norm γ in (32) the controller $C(s)$ is obtained by using MATLAB [2].

---

[2] MATLAB is a product of The MathWorks, Inc.

implementation issues

The controllers are implemented in personal computers. The algorithms are coded by C-language with RT-Linux formats and embedded as a kernel modules of Linux system. The control period is set at 5 [msec] and data exchange rate is set at 10 [msec]. Thus the data processing sequences must be synchronized.

Fig.12 shows a sequence diagram. The time goes from left to right and the datagram travels from master side(top) to slave side(bottom) through the network(middle). Because of the control period is a half of the communication period a copied value of the oposit side is used once every two control calculation. The right half part of the diagram assumes the case of long time-delay. In this case copied value is used over and over again until the new datagram reaches again.

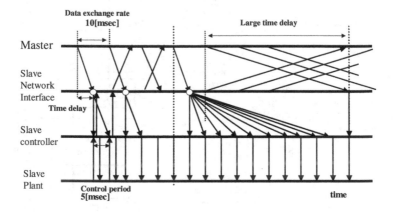

Fig. 12. Sequence diagram of data exchanges between master and slave

MASTER	CPU	AMD Duron 600MHz
	NIC	100/10 Base T
	OS	RT-Linux 3.1 on Linux 2.2.19
SLAVE	CPU	Pentium 75+ 166MHz
	NIC	100/10 Base T
	OS	RT-Linux 2.2 on Linux 2.2.14
RELAY	CPU	Pentium 600MHz
	NIC	100/10 Base T
	OS	Linux 2.2.14

Table 3. Parameters of master and slave controllers

emulation of network with poor quality

C_T is a computer located beyond the network to emulate various kind of qualities. It can emulate various kind of probability distribution of transmission delay, packet loss, packet shuffling and so on. Here we set the maximum time delay 1.0[sec] and the jitter in the Pareto distribution . The design parameter for robustness w.r.t. time-delay is set at $L_{max} = 1.5$[sec] and $\epsilon = 6.6 \times 10^{-3}$ Here the $\epsilon > 0$ is selected to reduce the effects of integrator.

experimental result

Fig. 13 indicates an experimental result for evaluation of tracking performance. In the first half master(solid line) leads to the slave(dashed line). And last half slave leads to the master. This means that the master-slave tele-operation system works symmetricaly well.

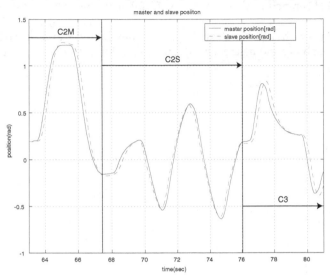

Fig. 13. experimental result of position tracking: master (- slid line), slave(– dashed line)

7. Summary

In this chapter we discussed on an application of robust control for force communication systems over inferior quality network. According to the investigation of the experiments the effectiveness of bilateral tele-operation system for force communication is confirmed. Especially the most important problem of the robustness w.r.t. time-delay is improved by H_∞ control systems theory.

8. References

[1] Shiotsuki,T., Force communication over the computer network, *3rd IFAC Symposium on Mechatronic Systems, Manly Beach, Sydney, Australia*, (2004)353-358
[2] Shiotsuki,T., Nasu,T., A case study of tele-operation system with time-delay, *SICE02* (2002)
[3] Kim,J., Kim,H., Tay,B.K.,Muniyandi, M., Srinivasan,M.A., Jordan, J., Mortensen,J., Oliveira,M. and Slater,M., Transatlantic Touch: A Study of Haptic Collaboration over Long Distance, *PRESENCE*, 13-3, 328-337 (2004)
[4] Yashiro,D., Tian,D., and Ohnishi,K., Centralized Controller based Multilateral Control with Communication Delay, *Proceeding of The IEEE International Conference on Mechatronics*, ICM 2011, Istanbul, Turkey, 13th(2011)
[5] Doyle , Francis and Tannenbaum(1992), *Feedback Control Theory*, Macmillan Publish Company

[6] R. J. Anderson and M. W. Spong, Asymptotic stability for force reflecting teleoperators with time delay *IEEE Trans. Automatic. Contr.* (1988) 1618–1625

[7] Niemeyer,G and Slotine,J.J, Stable adaptive tele-operation, *IEEE Journal of Ocean Eng.* 16-1,(1991)152–162

[8] Leung,G.M.H. Francis,B.A. and Apkarian,J., Bilateral controller for teleoperators with time delay via μ-synthesis, *IEEE Trans.of Robotics and Automation*, RA-11-1,(1995) 105–116

[9] N.L.Johnson A.Kotz and N.Balakrishnan, Continuous uninvariate distributions: Weily series in probability and mathematical statistics, 1, John Weily & Sons, Inc.(1994)

8

Design of Robust Policies for Uncertain Natural Resource Systems: Application to the Classic Gordon-Schaefer Fishery Model

Armando A. Rodriguez[1], Jeffrey J. Dickeson[2],
John M. Anderies[3] and Oguzhan Cifdaloz[4]
Arizona State University
USA

1. Introduction

Introduction. A critical challenge faced by sustainability science is to develop robust strategies to cope with highly uncertain social and ecological dynamics. The increasing intensity with which human societies utilize (limited) natural resources is fueling the global debate and urging the development of resource management methodologies/policies to effectively deal with very demanding socio-bio-economical issues. Unfortunately, despite concerted efforts by governments, many natural resources continue to be poorly managed. The collapse of many fisheries worldwide is the most notable example (Clark, 2006; Clark et al., 2006; Holland, Gudmundsson; Myers, Worm 2003; Sethi et al., 2005) but other examples include forests (Moran, Ostrom), groundwater basins (Shah, 2000), and soils (ISRIC, 1990). The suggested causes are varied but (Clark, 2006) highlights two: (1) lack of consideration of economic incentives actually faced by economic agents and (2) uncertainty associated with the dynamics of biological populations. In the case of fisheries, Clark notes that "complexity and uncertainty will always limit the extent to which the effects of fishing can be understood or predicted" (Clark, 2006, p. 98). This suggests that we need policies capable of effectively managing natural resource systems despite the fact that we understand them poorly at best.

Real-World Management Issues. Real-world resource management must address three components: goal setting, practical (robust) implementation, and learning. Clark and others (Clark, 2007; 2006; Clark et al., 2006) have recently noted that practical implementation issues are frequently at the root of fishery management failures. For most fisheries, the necessary institutional contexts exist (Wilen, Homans) and we know what to do, yet management efforts fail. This suggests a need to focus on the actual *process* of resource management. For example, how can managers make decisions with incomplete information concerning how the resource and the resource users will respond to management actions?

---

[1]Electrical Engineering, Ira A. Fulton School of Engineering
[2]Electrical Engineering, Ira A. Fulton School of Engineering
[3]School of Human Evolution and Social Change, School of Sustainability
[4]ASELSAN, Inc. Microelectronics, Guidance and Electro-Optics Division, Turkey

When managers can't learn fast enough, yet still must make decisions, how should they proceed?

Stochastic Optimization. A common approach to such policy[1] problems is stochastic optimization. Examples include studies of the performance of management instruments in the face of a single source of specific uncertainty such as in the size of the resource stock (Clark, Kirkwood; Koenig, 1984), the number of new recruits (Ludwig, Walters; Weitzman, 2002), or price (Andersen, 1982). Unfortunately, because they require assigning probabilities to possible outcomes, the insights from stochastic optimization techniques can be somewhat restricted. As Weitzman puts it, "The most we can hope to accomplish with such an approach is to develop a better intuition about the direction of the pure effect of the single extra feature being added...when the rest of the model is isolated away from all other forms of fisheries uncertainty" (Weitzman, 2002, p. 330). Such models generate interesting insights regarding how uncertain resources *should* be managed, but they contribute little to improving actual resource management practice. In our presentation, we attempt to provide some guidance through the development and application of a set of tools for practical (robust) policy implementation decisions in situations with multiple sources of uncertainty. While our approach is fundamentally deterministic, we show how probabilistic information can be accommodated within our framework.

Literature Survey. Several different threads concerning practical policy implementation challenges have emerged in the literature. Adaptive management (Walters, 1986) and resilience-based management (Holling, Gunderson; 1986; 1973; Ludwig et al., 1997) are examples from ecology. In parallel, robust control ideas from engineering (Zhou, Doyle) have begun to permeate macroeconomics (Hansen, Sargent; Kendrick, 2005) and there is recent work on resource management problems in the engineering literature (Belmiloudi, 2006; 2005; Dercole et al., 2003). A concept of robust optimization has also been developed in the operations research and management science literature (Ben-Tal, Nemirovski; Ben-Tal et al., 2000; Ben-Tal, Nemirovski) with some specific applications of these ideas to environmental problems (Babonneu et al., 2010; Lempert et al., 2006; 2000). The overarching theme of robust optimization is to select the best solution from those "immunized" against data uncertainty, i.e. solutions that remain feasible for all realizations of the data (Ben-Tal, Nemirovski).

Our Approach: Exploiting Concepts from Robust Control. This chapter presents a sensitivity-based robustness-vulnerability framework for the study of policy implementation in highly uncertain natural resource systems in which uncertainty is characterized by parameter bounds (not probability distributions). This approach is motivated by the fact that probability distributions are often difficult to obtain. Despite this, it is shown how one might exploit distributions for uncertain model parameters within the presented framework. The framework is applied to parametric uncertainty in the classic Gordon-Schaefer fishery model to illustrate how performance (income) can be sacrificed (traded-off) for reduced sensitivity, and hence increased robustness, with respect to model parameter uncertainty. Our robustness-vulnerability approach provides tools to systematically compare policy uncertainty-performance properties so that policy options can be systematically discussed.

More specifically, within this chapter, we exploit concepts from robust control in order to analyze the classic Gordon-Schaefer fishery model (Clark, 1990). Classic maximization of net present revenue is shown to result in an optimal control law that exhibits limit

---

[1] We use the terms "policies" and "control laws" interchangeably in this presentation.

cycle behavior (nonlinear oscillations) when parametric uncertainty is present. As such, it cannot be implemented in practice (because of prohibitively expensive switching costs). This motivates the need for robust policies that (1) do not exhibit limit cycle behavior and (2) offer performance (returns) as close to the optimal perfect information policy as model parameter (and derived fishery biomass target) uncertainty permits. Given the state of most world fisheries, our presentation focuses on a fishery that is nominally (i.e. believed to be) biologically over exploited (BOE); i.e. the optimal equilibrium biomass lies below the maximum sustainable yield biomass (Clark, 2006; Clark et al., 2006; Clark, 1990; Holland, Gudmundsson; Myers, Worm 2003; Sethi et al., 2005). By so doing, we directly address a globally critical renewable resource management problem. As in our prior work (Anderies et al., 2007), (Rodriguez et al., 2010), we do not seek "a best policy." Instead, we seek families of policies that are robust with respect to uncertainties that are likely to occur. Such families can, in principle, be used by a fishery manager to navigate the many tradeoffs (biological, ecological, social, economic, political) that must be confronted. More specifically, our effort to seek robust performance focuses on reducing the worst case downside performance; i.e. maximizing returns when we have the worst case combination of parameters. Such worst case (conservative) planning is critical to avoid/minimize the possibility of major regional/societal economical shortfalls; case in point, the recent "Great Recession." It is important to note that the simplicity of our model (vis-a-vis our performance objective of maximizing the net present value of returns) permits us to readily determine the worst case combination of model parameters (i.e. growth rate, carrying capacity, catchability, discount rate, price, cost of harvesting). Given this, we seek control laws that do not exhibit limit cycle behavior and whose returns are close (modulo limitations imposed by uncertainty) to that of the worst case perfect information optimal control policy - the best we could do in terms of return if we knew the parameters perfectly. Other design strategies are also examined; e.g. designing for the best case set of parameters. "Blended strategies" that attempt to do well for the worst case downside perturbation (i.e. minimize the economic downside) as well as the best case upside perturbation (i.e. maximize the economic upside) are also discussed. Such strategies seek to flatten the return-uncertainty characteristics over a broad range of likely parameters. The above optimal control (derived) policies are used as performance benchmarks/targets for the development of robust control policies. While our focus is on bounded deterministic parametric uncertainty, we also show how probability distributions for uncertain model parameters can be exploited to help in the selection of benchmark (optimal) policies. After targeting a suitable optimal (benchmark) policy, we show how robust policies can be used to approximate the benchmark (as closely as the uncertainty will permit) in order to achieve desired performance-robustness-vulnerability tradeoffs; e.g. have a return that is robust to worst case parameter perturbations.

While the presentation is intended to provide an introduction into how concepts from optimal and robust control may be used to address critical issues associated with renewable resource management, the presentation also attempts to shed light on challenges for the controls community. Although the presentation builds on the prior work presented in (Anderies et al., 2007), (Rodriguez et al., 2010), the focus here is more on defining the problem, describing the many issues, and sufficiently narrowing the scope to permit the presentation of a design methodology (framework) for robust control policies.

Finally, it must be noted that the robust policies that we present are not intended to be viewed as final policies to be implemented. Rather, they should be viewed as policy targets -

providing guidance to resource managers for the development of final implementable policies (based on taxes, quotas, etc. (Clark, 1990, Chapter 8)) that will (in some sense) approximate our robust policies. While our focus has been on parametric uncertainty, it must be noted that robustness to unmodeled dynamics (e.g. lags, time delays) is also important. While some discussion on this is provided, this will be examined in future work.

Contributions of Work. The main contributions of this chapter are as follows:

- *Benefits of Robust Control in Renewable Resource Management.* The chapter shows how robust control laws can be used to eliminate the limit cycle behavior of the optimal control law while increasing robustness to parametric uncertainty and achieving a return that is close (modulo limitations imposed by uncertainty) to the perfect information optimal control law. Special attention is paid to minimizing worst case economic downside. As such, the policies presented shed light on fundamental performance limitations in the presence of (parametric) uncertainty. The policies presented are intended to serve as targets/guidelines that fishery managers may try to approximate using available tools (e.g. taxes, quotas, etc. (Clark, 1990, Chapter 8).

- *Tutorial/Introductory Value.* The chapter serves as an introduction for the controls community to a very important resource management problem in the area of global sustainability. As such, the chapter offers a myriad of challenging problems for the controls community to address in future work.

Organization of Chapter. The remainder of the chapter is organized as follows.

- Section 2 describes the classic Gordon-Schaefer nonlinear fishery model (Clark, 1990) to be used.

- Section 3 describes the optimal control law and its properties. The latter motivates the need for robust control laws for fishery management - laws that try to achieve robust near optimal performance in some sense.

- Section 4 describes a class of robust control laws to be examined.

- Section 5 contains the main results of the work - comparing the properties of the optimal policy to those of the robust policies being considered.

- Finally, Section 6 summarizes the chapter and presents directions for future research.

2. Nonlinear bioeconomic model

In this section, we describe the nonlinear bioeconomic model to be used for control design. The model is then analyzed.

2.1 Description of bioeconomic model

The nonlinear Gordon-Schaefer bioeconomic model (Clark, 1990; Gordon, 1954; Schaefer, 1957) is now described.

Nonlinear Gordon-Schaefer Bioeconomic Model.

The nonlinear model to be used is as follows:

$$\dot{x} = F(x) - qxu_p \qquad x(0) = x_o, \tag{1}$$

where

$$F(x) = rx \left(1 - \frac{x}{k}\right)$$

(2)

represents the natural regeneration rate of the resource and x, x_o, and u_p represent resource biomass, initial resource biomass, and harvesting effort, respectively. The parameters r, k, and q, retain their traditional definitions of intrinsic growth rate, carrying capacity, and catchability, respectively. Table 1 in Section 2.5 summarizes model parameter definitions, units, nominal values, and ranges. Model uncertainty will be addressed in Section 2.6.

Saturating Nonlinearity. Typically, effort is bounded above by some maximum and below by zero, i.e. $u_p \in [0, u_{max}]$. Typically, this physical constraint is implicitly taken into account when the optimal control problem is solved. However, a more general family of controls may generate control signals outside the allowable range, and it is important to be explicit about how these signals are "clipped" by physical constraints. We thus define the saturation function

$$\text{sat}(x; x_{min}, x_{max}) \overset{\text{def}}{=} \begin{cases} x_{min} & -\infty \le x \le x_{min} \\ x & x_{min} \le x \le x_{max} \\ x_{max} & x_{max} < x < \infty. \end{cases}$$

(3)

The feasibility condition can then be written in terms of (3), i.e.

$$u_p \in [0, u_{max}] \Leftrightarrow u_p = \text{sat}(u; 0, u_{max})$$

(4)

where u is the control signal. When there is no risk of confusion, we will write $u_p = \text{sat}(u)$.

Performance Measure. The fishery performance measure to be used, denoted J, is the net present value of future returns:

$$J(u_p) \overset{\text{def}}{=} \int_0^T e^{-\delta\tau}(pqx - c)u_p \, d\tau$$

(5)

where price p, cost per unit effort c, discount rate δ, and planning horizon T are assumed constant. (We will use $T - \infty$ to develop the optimal control law.)

2.2 Equilibrium analysis of bioeconomic model

One of the desired control objectives will be for the fishery to operate at specific equilibrium (set) points. Given this, the set of equilibria for the nonlinear model are as follows:

$$x_e = o \qquad\qquad u_e = 0$$

(6)

$$when \quad u_e \in (0, 1] \qquad\qquad x_e = k\left(1 - \frac{q}{r}u_e\right).$$

(7)

Observe that as the equilibrium effort increases, the equilibrium biomass decreases (as expected).

2.3 LTI small signal model

To further understand the local characteristics of the above nonlinear model, we can linearize it about equilibria. Doing so yields the following small signal linear time invariant (LTI) model:

$$\delta\dot{x} = a\,\delta x + b\,\delta u \tag{8}$$

$$f(x) = rx\left(1 - \frac{x}{k}\right) - qxu \tag{9}$$

$$a = \left[\frac{\partial f}{\partial x}\right]_{(x_e, u_e)} = r - \frac{2rx_e}{k} - qu_e = -\left(\frac{r}{k}\right)x_e \qquad b = \left[\frac{\partial f}{\partial u}\right]_{(x_e, u_e)} = -qx_e \tag{10}$$

$$\delta x(t) = x(t) - x_e \qquad \delta x(0) = x(0) - x_e = x_o - x_e \qquad \delta u(t) = u(t) - u_e \tag{11}$$

The associated transfer function from δu to δx is given by:

$$P(s) = \frac{b}{s - a} \tag{12}$$

Since $a = -\left(\frac{r}{k}\right)x_e < 0$, it follows that the equilibrium point (x_e, u_e) is asymptotically stable with the rate of convergence (pole) being proportional to the equilibrium biomass x_e, the fishery growth rate r, and inversely proportional to the fishery's carrying capacity k. The dc gain associated with P is $P(0) = -\frac{kq}{r}$; the minus sign implying that fishing reduces the equilibrium biomass.

Utility of LTI Small Signal Model. The above LTI model can be used to approximate the response x of the nonlinear model. If the response of the LTI model is denoted

$$\hat{x} = x_e + \delta x \tag{13}$$

then $\hat{x} \approx x$ when $u \approx u_e$ (i.e. $\delta u(t) \approx 0$) and $x_o \approx x_e$ (i.e. $\delta x(0) = x_o - x_e \approx 0$).

2.4 Control objectives

The control objectives for the fishery may be summarized (roughly) as follows:

1. Maximize the net present value of future returns

$$\text{maximize } J \overset{\text{def}}{=} \int_0^\infty e^{-\delta t}(pqx - c)u_p \, dt \tag{14}$$

   Note: We would be willing to give up some return for increased robustness.

2. Closed loop stability
   (a) Limit cycle behavior is not acceptable because it can have an prohibitively expensive implementation cost. While this is not captured in J, it could be addressed by introducing an additional $\dot{u}_p$ term within J.
   (b) Closed loop responses should be "relatively smooth" (continuous) when we have nearly continuous sampling of the biomass x. It is understood that sampling is inevitable in practice; i.e. continuous sampling is prohibitively expensive and hence impossible. As such, closed loop responses should be robust with respect to some discrete sampling.

3. Follow (achievable) step biomass commands issued by the fishery manager in the steady state

4. Reject additive step input and output disturbances in the steady state

5. Attenuate high frequency sensor noise so that it does not significantly impact control action

6. Ensure that the fishery biomass overshoot to step reference biomass commands is suitably bounded

7. Robustness with respect to model parametric uncertainty

2.5 Nominal model parameters

Nominal parameter values to be used are given below in Table 1.

Symbol θ	Description	Unit	Nominal θ_0	Range
Biological Parameters				
x_0	Initial resource biomass	Kilotons, KT	varies	$[0.5x_0, 1.5x_0]$
u_{min}	Minimum harvesting effort	$fleet \cdot power \cdot year / year$	0	-
u_{max}	Maximum harvesting effort	$fleet \cdot power \cdot year / year$	1	-
r	Intrinsic growth rate	$1/year$	0.3	[0.15,0.45]
q	Catchability	$1/fleet \cdot power \cdot year$	0.3	[0.15,0.45]
k	Carrying capacity	KT	100	[50,150]
Economic Parameters				
p	Resource market price	M\$ per kiloton	10	[5,15]
c	Cost of harvesting per effort	M\$ per year	13.24	[6.62, 19.86]
δ	Annual discount rate	$1/year$	0.1	[0.05,0.15]
T	Planning horizon	years	50	N/A

Table 1. Nominal Parameter Values Used

A planning horizon of $T = 50$ years was selected because the nominal discount rate is $\delta = 0.1$ and in roughly $T = \frac{5}{\delta} = 50$ years, the integrand within J is negligible.

Focus of Work: Biologically Exploited (BOE) Fishery. The focus of our presentation will be on a fishery that biologically overly expoilted (BOE) as opposed to biologically under exploited (BUE). This is because most of the world's critical fisheries are overly exploited (Clark, 1990).

- BOE with the 'low cost' $c = 13.24$. BOE occurs when the cost is sufficiently small. For the parameters indicated, it can be shown that:

$$x_e^* = 0.75 \cdot x_{MSY} = 37.5 < x_{MSY} = \frac{k}{2} = 50$$

i.e. the optimal equilibrium biomass is below the maximum sustainable yield biomass.

2.6 Model uncertainty and scope of presentation

Within this presentation, we focus on uncertainty associated with the nominal model parameters: r, k, q, p, c, δ. The following uncertainty will not be addressed in this presentation but it is duly noted:

1. The structure of F may be different than considered above. For example, if F has the form $F(x) geq 0$ for $x \in [k_c, k]$ and $F(x) < 0$ for $x \in (0, k_c)$ where $F(0) = 0$ and $F(k) = 0$, then we say that the fishery exhibits *critical depensation* (Clark, 1990, p. 17). In short, this implies that if x ever drops below the critical depensation parameter $k_c > 0$, then x will decrease toward zero regardless of u; i.e. the fishery will be lost.

2. All plant parameters are uncertain. They may even change with time. Moreover, the plant contains additional dynamics; e.g. it takes time for the fishery workers to mobilize. This can contribute additional lags, time delays, and rate limiters within the plant. One can use a decentralized or distributed model in order to capture the decision making made by individual fisher people (Clark, 1990, Ch. 8 & 9).

3. Input and output disturbances are uncertain.

4. Measurement noise is uncertain.

5. The biomass is not known; it must be estimated

6. The output (biomass) is sampled at some rate; if this rate is not sufficiently high, it could cause aliasing (Ogata, 1995); the sampling rate should be (as a rule-of-thumb)greater than ten times the control system bandwidth.

In contrast to many control applications where the "controller" is implemented with great fidelity, fishery controllers are implemented by an organization. As such, there can be considerable implementation issues/uncertainty. This will be discussed further below.

3. Optimal control law and properties

Within this section, we present the optimal control problem, the associated solution (optimal control law), and the properties of the optimal control law.

3.1 Optimal control law

We begin with a brief derivation of the classical optimal control policy stated in a way that will facilitate comparison to the class of LTI policies described later in this section.
The solution of the traditional optimal control problem:

$$\text{maximize } J \overset{\text{def}}{=} \int_0^\infty e^{-\delta t}(pqx(t) - c)u_p(t) \, dt \tag{15}$$

$$\text{s.t. } \dot{x}(t) = F(x(t)) - qx(t)u_p(t) \qquad x(0) = x_o \tag{16}$$

$$u_{min} = 0 \le u_p(t) \le u_{max} \tag{17}$$

is obtained by forming the Hamiltonian:

$$\mathcal{H}(x, u, \lambda) \overset{\text{def}}{=} e^{-\delta t}(pqx - c)u + \lambda\left[F(x) - qxu\right] = G(x, t)u - \lambda F(x) \tag{18}$$

where $G(x, t) \overset{\text{def}}{=} e^{-\delta t}(pqx - c) - \lambda qx$ and λ is the co-state variable. *Pontryagin's Maximum Principle* then implies that an optimal control policy will satisfy:

$$u(t) = \begin{cases} -\infty \text{ when } G(x, t) < 0 \\ \infty \quad \text{ when } G(x, t) > 0. \end{cases} \tag{19}$$

Because the objective functional is linear, the Maximum Principle says nothing about the case when $G(x, t) = 0$. However, using the co-state variable relationship $\dot{\lambda} = -\frac{\partial \mathcal{H}}{\partial x}$, the well-known implicit formula for the singular control path can be determined (Clark, 1990):

$$F'(x) + \frac{cF(x)}{x(pqx - c)} = \delta \tag{20}$$

Optimal Steady State Equilibrium Biomass. When $F(x) = rx(1 - x/k)$, the above equation can be used to determine the optimal (steady state) equilibrium biomass x_e^*:

$$x_e^* = \frac{\left[\frac{x_\infty}{2} - x_{MSY}\left(\frac{\delta}{r}\right) + x_{MSY}\right] + \sqrt{\left[\frac{x_\infty}{2} - x_{MSY}\left(\frac{\delta}{r}\right) + x_{MSY}\right]^2 + 4x_{MSY}x_\infty\left(\frac{\delta}{r}\right)}}{2}. \quad (21)$$

where

$$x_{MSY} = \frac{k}{2} \quad (22)$$

is the maximum sustainable yield biomass and

$$x_\infty = \frac{c}{pq} \quad (23)$$

is the optimal equilibrium when $\delta = \infty$; i.e. open-access equilibrium (Clark, 1990). The above shows that the optimal biomass x_e^* depends on the three independent parameters x_∞, x_{MSY}, and $\frac{\delta}{r}$. It can be shown that

$$x_\infty \quad \leq \quad x_e^* \quad \leq \quad x_{MSY} + \frac{x_\infty}{2} \quad (24)$$

for all $\delta \in [0, \infty]$ where the quantity $x_{MSY} + \frac{x_\infty}{2}$ is the optimal x_e^* for $\delta = 0$. The associated optimal (steady state) equilibrium control is given by:

$$u_e^* \stackrel{\text{def}}{=} \frac{r}{q}\left(1 - \frac{x_e^*}{k}\right). \quad (25)$$

Optimal Control Policy. Define the *tracking error* as the difference between the desired (reference) state and the actual state, i.e.

$$e \stackrel{\text{def}}{=} x_{ref} - x. \quad (26)$$

Setting $x_{ref} = x_e^*$ and combining (19) with (25) yields following expression for the control law:

$$u(t) = \begin{cases} -\infty & \text{when } e > 0 \\ u_e^* & \text{when } e = 0 \\ \infty & \text{when } e < 0. \end{cases} \quad (27)$$

The saturation function is then applied to this control signal to capture the physical constraints on the system, i.e. $u_p(t) = \text{sat}(u(t))$. This control law implies the following:

- If $e > 0$, set $u_p(t) = u_{min} = 0$, allow $x(t)$ to increase until $x(t) = x_e^*$, then set $u_p(t) = \text{sat}(u_e^*)$.
- If $e < 0$, set $u_p(t) = u_{max}$ until $x(t)$ decreases to x_e^*, then set $u_p(t) = \text{sat}(u_e^*)$.
- If $e = 0$, set $u_p(t) = \text{sat}(u_e^*)$.

Below, we show that this policy (in general) exhibits limit cycle behavior in the presence of parameter uncertainty (see Figure 6).

3.2 Nominal optimal control policy numerics

The numerics for the nominal optimal perfect information control law are summarized in Table 2.

Case	x_e^*	u_e^*	x_∞	u_∞	Optimal Control Law	Optimal Return, J_0^* small IC	large IC
BOE	37.5	0.625	4.41	0.987	$u(t) = \begin{cases} 0 & x(t) < 37.5 \\ u_e^* \overset{\text{def}}{=} \frac{F(x_e^*)}{qx_e^*} = 0.625 & x(t) = 37.5 \\ u_{max} = 1 & x(t) > 37.5 \end{cases}$	451	782

Table 2. Summary of Optimal Control Policy Numerics. BOE corresponds to $c = 13.24$ which yields $x_e^* = 0.75 \cdot x_{\text{MSY}}$. Small IC corresponds to $x_0 = 0.5 \cdot x_e^* < x_e^*$. Large IC corresponds to $x_0 = 1.5 \cdot x_e^* > x_e^*$. $x_\infty = \frac{c}{pq}$ and $u_\infty = \frac{r}{q}(1 - \frac{x_\infty}{k})$ correspond to infinite discounting (open-access); i.e. $\delta = \infty$.

3.3 Properties of the optimal control law

In this section, we describe the properties of the optimal control law assuming perfect information (i.e. model parameters are known with no error) and imperfect information (i.e. model parameters are not perfectly known). Understanding the properties of the optimal policy is very important for several reasons. We wish to understand (1) the fundamental robustness properties (e.g. economic inefficiency) of an optimal policy (e.g. one based on nominal, worst case, or best case parameters); (2) implementation issues associated with the optimal control policy; (3) how the robustness properties for our robust policies compare to those of a particular optimal control policy; (4) how x_e^* depends on parameter perturbations. The latter is important because we will using x_e^* as the reference command x_{ref} for our robust control law policies. This is an issue because the optimal x_e^* (in general) is uncertain; i.e. x_e^* is only known for specific value selections (e.g. nominal, worst case, best case). As such, we will have to address this uncertainty to clearly understand what our robust control policies (with built-in command following) will be driving the state of the fishery to.

In short, we show below that: (1) Since x_e^* is, in general, uncertain, if x_e^* is the desired (reference) state, then we have a major issue in that we will be driving the fishery to the incorrect state. This can have severe economic as well as biological implications (e.g. driving x below the critical depensation parameter k_c, will destroy the fishery). (2) The optimal policy exhibits limit cycle behavior when x_e^* is uncertain. Moreover, it is very sensitive to any discrete sampling. As such, the (imperfect information) optimal policy is prohibitively expensive to implement (see Figure 6).

Optimal Perfect Information Control Law Sensitivity: Single Parameter Results ($x_0 = x_e^*$). The following shows how the the performance of the optimal perfect information control law changes with parameter perturbations. Results for our BOE fishery when $x_0 = x_e^*$ are as follows:

1. (J_e^*, x_e^*, u_e^*) increase with increasing k or increasing r.

2. J_e^* increases while (x_e^*, u_e^*) decrease with increasing q.

3. J_e^* decreases while x_e^* increases and u_e^* decreases with increasing δ.

4. J_e^* increases while x_e^* decreases and u_e^* increases with increasing p.

5. (J_e^*, x_e^*) decrease while u_e^* increases with increasing c.

Robustness with Respect to Parametric Uncertainty: Imperfect Versus Perfect Information.
Figure 1 shows how the optimal control law performs in the presence of parametric
uncertainty. $x_0 = x_e^*$ for the perfect information policy. x_0 is at the unperturbed/nominal
x_e^* for the imperfect information policy. The plots compare the performance of the optimal
control law with imperfect parameter knowledge to that with perfect parameter knowledge.
The perfect information optimal control law (by definition) results in the maximum achievable
return. While it represents a suitable benchmark to compare with, it must be emphasized that
x_e^* is always uncertain. This is particularly crucial when x_e^* is being used as the target biomass
(reference command) for a robust control law (see Sections 4, 5) because an incorrect reference
command x_{ref} will fundamentally limit the achievable performance. Moreover, no (inner
loop) robust policy can address this. To properly address this, one needs some combination of
parameter estimation, system identification, and learning coupled with some adaptive outer
loop policy that adjusts the target based on collected information. While this is challenging
and exciting to pursue, it is beyond the scope of our presentation.

Figure 1 specifically shows the maximum theoretical (perfect information) return on the left
in blue. The return associated with the imperfect information optimal policy (designed for
nominal parameter values) is shown on the left in red. On the right in blue, we see how
much the imperfect information optimal control law under performs the perfect information
optimal control law. When k is perturbed by -30%, the imperfect law under performs the
perfect information law by nearly 10%. Figure 1 shows that for a similar perturbation in r,
the imperfect policy under performs by nearly 2%. It can be shown (figures not provided)
that for a similar perturbation in δ, the imperfect policy under performs by less than 1%. It
can be shown (figures not provided) that for similar perturbations in p, c, or q the imperfect
policy under performs by a very small percentage. Why is it that the biological parameters
k and r matter more in closing the perfect-imperfect information performance gap than δ,
p, c, or q? This is because x_e^* is more sensitive to uncertainty in k and r for the BOE case
under consideration. In short, the plots show that we should be concerned primarily with
uncertainty in k. More generally, we seek (robust) policies that perform closer to the perfect
information optimal policy for likely parametric modeling errors. Imperfect information
obviously limits how close we can get. This and associated issues will be addressed below.

**Impact of Extremal Parameter Uncertainty on Perfect Information (J_e^*, x_e^*, u_e^*) - At Optimal
Equilibrium.** In what follows, x_e^* will be used as a reference command x_{ref} to a robust
control law with good command following properties. Since x_e^* is uncertain, it is important
to understand how commanding an incorrect target will limit achievable performance. Given
this, suppose that $x_0 = x_e^*$.

We now ask, what is the worst case combination of perturbations for the model parameters (r,
k, q, p, c, δ)? While an analytical proof is difficult, it can be shown (numerically) that

J_e^*, in general, decreases when (k, r, p, q) are decreased and/or (c, δ) are increased.

This result is independent of the initial condition x_0 for the BOE case under consideration.
Given uncertainty bounds for each of the model parameters, this observation permits us to
readily determine the worst case set of parameter perturbation - something that, in general, is
very difficult to do.

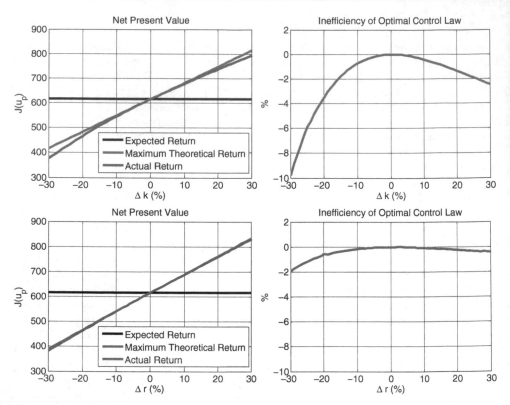

Fig. 1. Economic Inefficiency for Imperfect Information (Nominal) Optimal Control Law: Capacity & Growth Rate Uncertainty

Consider figures 2-3 for (J_e^*, x_e^*, u_e^*), respectively. Within these figures, $x_o = x_e^*$ and perfect information is assumed. The figures show the dependence of the perfect information optimal control law on worst case and best case (extremal) parameter perturbations as defined below.

- *Worst Case Extremal Parameter Perturbations.* Within figures 2-3, negative (worst case extremal) parameter perturbations correspond to

$$\frac{\Delta r}{r_o} = \frac{\Delta k}{k_o} = \frac{\Delta q}{q_o} = \frac{\Delta p}{p_o} < 0 \quad \text{and} \quad \frac{\Delta c}{c_o} = \frac{\Delta \delta}{\delta_o} > 0 \qquad (28)$$

i.e. equal parametric perturbations that result in a smaller return. Here, $\Delta \theta \overset{\text{def}}{=} \theta - \theta_o$ represents a perturbation in the parameter θ with respect to the nominal parameter θ_o.

- *Best Case Extremal Parameter Perturbations.* Within figures 2-3, positive (best case extremal) parameter perturbations correspond to

$$\frac{\Delta r}{r_o} = \frac{\Delta k}{k_o} = \frac{\Delta q}{q_o} = \frac{\Delta p}{p_o} > 0 \quad \text{and} \quad \frac{\Delta c}{c_o} = \frac{\Delta \delta}{\delta_o} < 0 \qquad (29)$$

i.e. equal parametric perturbations that result in a larger return.

The green curves within figures 2-3 represent actual optimal perfect information values. The blue curves give the percent deviation with respect to the nominal value.

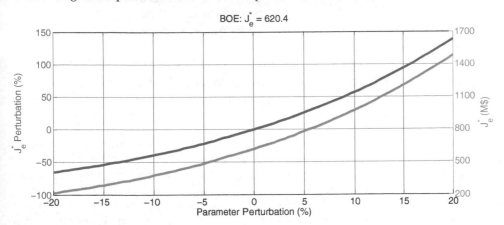

Fig. 2. Perfect Information Optimal Control Law Returns: Extremal Percent Parameter Perturbations, $x_0 = x_e^*$

Assuming $\pm 20\%$ uncertainty for each nominal parameter value, figure 2 shows that the worst case perfect information optimal return is \$215.6 M (65.25% below the nominal of $J_e^* = 620.4M$). In contrast, the best case perfect information optimal return is \$1482M (138.95% above the nominal of $J_e^* = 620.4M$) - a 687% improvement with respect to the worst case perfect information optimal return. Also note from figure 3 that the worst case parameter combination results in a 20% reduction in x_e^* with respect to the nominal. From figure 3, we see that u_e^* is increased by less than 1%.

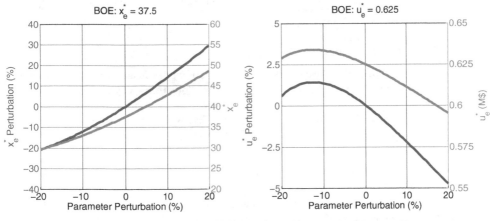

Fig. 3. Perfect Information Optimal Control Law (x_e^*, u_e^*): Extremal Percent Parameter Perturbations, $x_0 = x_e^*$

Dealing with Uncertain x_e^* and J_e^*. Let x_{ref} denote the reference biomass at which the fishery manager wishes to operate the fishery [2]. How does a manager choose the target fishery biomass x_{ref}? A biologically conservative manager may wish to keep the fishery at the maximum sustainable yield $x_{ref} = x_{MSY} = \frac{k}{2}$. A financially aggressive manager may chose to operate the fishery at the infinite discount ($\delta = \infty$)) optimal value $x_{ref} = x_\infty = \frac{c}{pq}$. More generally, a manager could use the optimal value $x_{ref} = x_e^*$ as the point at which to operate. Given that x_e^* is known to within a percentage $\frac{\Delta x_e^*}{x_e^*}$, it follows that a fishery manager might try to operate at (1) $x_e^* - \Delta x_e^*$ if economic aggression is desired, or at (2) $x_e^* + \Delta x_e^*$ if biological conservatism is desired. The x_e^* concept gives the fishery manager a way to systematically think about fishery biomass targets.

Uncertainty In (x_0, x_e^*, x_{ref}): 6 Cases. In general, x_0 and x_e^* are uncertain. How does one choose the target x_{ref}. We'd ideally like $x_{ref} = x_e^*$, but x_e^* is uncertain. What can a manager do? The table below contains the six possible relations that can exist amongst the three scalars (x_0, x_e^*, x_{ref}) - from smallest to biggest. In general, we would (ideally) like the state to move from x_0 toward $x_{ref} = x_e^*$. Since x_e^* is uncertain, it follows that x_{ref} (in general) will differ from x_e^*. As such, it follows that we may issue reference commands x_{ref} that move the state x in an incorrect direction. Since the state moves from x_0 toward x_{ref}, it follows from the table below that in two cases the state moves in the incorrect direction. In the four other cases, the state moves in the correct direction.

Smallest	$\rightarrow$	Biggest	Direction	
x_{ref}	x_0	x_e^*	Incorrect	Way too much fishing (Way Too Aggressive)
x_{ref}	x_e^*	x_0	Correct	Too much fishing (Very Aggressive)
x_0	x_{ref}	x_e^*	Correct	Too much fishing (Moderately Aggressive)
x_0	x_e^*	x_{ref}	Correct	Too little fishing (Moderately Conservative)
x_e^*	x_{ref}	x_0	Correct	Too little fishing (Very Conservative)
x_e^*	x_0	x_{ref}	Incorrect	Way too little fishing (Way Too Conservative)

Table 3. Six Possible Inequality Relations for (x_0, x_e^*, x_{ref})

To select x_{ref}, we offer the following approaches.

1. **Best-Worst Case Approach.** Assume that we have good bounds on parametric uncertainty (not necessarily tight, but encompassing) for the 6 model parameters under consideration: k, r, q, p, c, δ. Suppose that we design for the best worst case scenario; i.e. try to approach the return of the perfect information optimal policy when the worst case parameter perturbations occur; i.e. $\frac{\Delta k}{k_0} = \frac{\Delta r}{r_0} = \frac{\Delta q}{q_0} = \frac{\Delta p}{p_0} < 0$ and $\frac{\Delta c}{c_0} = \frac{\Delta \delta}{\delta_0} > 0$. We assume worst case maximal parameter perturbations. (For simplicity, we assume that all parameters are perturbed by their maximum worst case percentage and that this percentage is the same for all of the parameters.)

One could, for example, pick a worst case percentage which bounds all of the parameters. Doing so can be conservative. Parameter estimation can be used to narrow tighten this worst case percentage. If we have fixed percentage bounds for each of the parameters, our approach remains the same. (Recall: Determining the worst case perturbation in our problem is easy. This is not true in most practical scenarios.)

---

[2] It is understood that x_{ref} can change with time. For now, we assume x_{ref} is fixed.

Now choose x_{ref} equal to the associated worst case x_e^*; i.e. the x_e^* that results from choosing the worst case parameters. By so doing, the actual x_e^* will be greater than x_{ref}. As such, only cases 1-3 can occur; i.e. cases 4-6 cannot occur. The only way, cases 4-6 can occur is if our uncertainty bounds were not truly encompassing.

2. **Best-Best Case Approach.** Assume that we have good bounds on parametric uncertainty (not necessarily tight, but encompassing)for the 6 model parameters under consideration: k, r, q, p, c, δ. Suppose that we design for the best best case scenario; i.e. try to approach the return of the perfect information optimal policy when the best case parameter perturbations occur; i.e. $\frac{\Delta k}{k_o} = \frac{\Delta r}{r_o} = \frac{\Delta q}{q_o} = \frac{\Delta p}{p_o} > 0$ and $\frac{\Delta c}{c_o} = \frac{\Delta \delta}{\delta_o} < 0$. We assume best case maximal parameter perturbations. (For simplicity, we assume that all parameters are perturbed by their maximum best case percentage and that this percentage is the same for all of the parameters.)

Now choose x_{ref} equal to the associated best case x_e^*; i.e. the x_e^* that results from choosing the best case parameters. By so doing, the actual x_e^* will be smaller than x_{ref}. As such, only cases 4-6 can occur; i.e. cases 1-3 cannot occur. The only way, cases 1-3 can occur is if our uncertainty bounds were not truly encompassing.

3. **Blended Best-Worst-Best-Best Approach.** One can also try to offer a blended approach that attempts to offer decent returns when either worse case or best case parameter perturbations occur. We shall illustrate this below.

4. **Probabilistic Approach.** If a probability density function for the parameter percentage θ is available, it can be used to determine where to operate. Let f_θ denote a density function for θ. This can be used to derive the density function f_J for J. Given this, the expected value for J is given by $E[J] = \int_J J \, f_J(J) \, dJ = \int_\theta J(\theta) \, f_J(J(\theta)) \, J'(\theta) \, d\theta$. The density function for θ can be used to reflect what parameter perturbations are most likely to occur. The above expectation can then be used to choose x_{ref} to maximize the expectation.

To illustrate the above ideas, consider figures 4-5 for small and large initial conditions, respectively under extremal parameter perturbations. The figures show results for the perfect information designs (black), best worst case design (blue), best best case design (red), and the nominal design (green).

To summarize, the following specific optimal control laws were implemented:

1. Perfect Information Optimal Designs: $\quad x_{ref} = x_e^*, u_{ref} = u_e^*$

2. A Best-Worst Case Design: $\quad x_{ref} = 29.7, u_{ref} = 0.629$

3. A Nominal Design Based on the Nominal Parameters: $\quad x_{ref} = 37.5, u_{ref} = 0.625$

4. A Best-Best Case Design: $\quad x_{ref} = 48.6, u_{ref} = 0.595$

The performance of the perfect information designs are always best (by definition). The performance of the best-worst case design (blue) duplicates that of the perfect information design for 20% worst case perturbations since it is based on the worst case parameter model and x_e^*. The performance of the best-best case design (blue) duplicates that of the perfect information design for 20% best case perturbations since it is based on the best case parameter model and x_e^*. The following key observations are in order within figure 4 (small IC case):

1. The best-worst case design does better than the best-best case design when its parameter assumptions are maximally incorrect; falling by less than 20% (with respect to perfect information optimal return) while the best best falls by more than 40% (with respect

to perfect information optimal return) when its parameter assumptions are maximally incorrect.

2. The nominal design can be viewed as a nice compromise or blend between the two prior policies. It is based on the nominal parameter model and x_e^*. Its returns deteriorates by a little more than 10% for worst case parameter uncertainty and by a little more than 5% for best case parameter uncertainty. In short, the returns associated with this nominal (blended) policy offers flatter returns over a wider range of extremal parameter perturbations.

Each of the above three approaches offer a specific design model (to base the control design upon) and a specific x_e^* to use as a target. Control laws are always evaluated with the true (nonlinear) plant. In what follows, we will use the above as benchmarks whose performance we shall target via robust control laws. Similar patterns are observed for the large IC case in figure 5.

Sensitivity Analysis: Extremal Perturbations, Small Initial Condition. The expected value for each of the design cases considered are as follows:

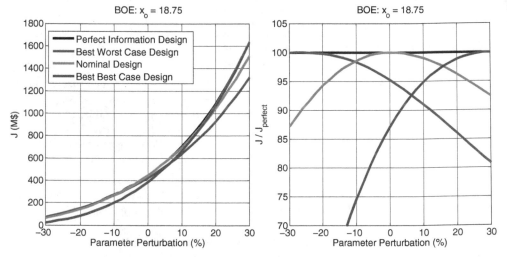

Fig. 4. Economic Inefficiencies for Various Optimal Control Laws: Extremal Perturbations (Small IC)

- $E[J] = 867.8$ for the Perfect Information Optimal Designs
- $E[J] = 772.0$ for the Best-Worst Case Design
- $E[J] = 838.0$ for the Nominal Design
- $E[J] = 800.4$ for the Best-Best Case Design

A uniform distribution has been assumed for the parameter uncertainty. The optimal perfect information control law is included for comparison purposes. Its performance can only be approximated over a range of parameter perturbations. This is because the (1) design plant parameters differ from those of the true plant and the desired target x_{ref} differs from the perfect information target x_e^*.

The following additional points are in order:

- Although the best-best case design appears worse in terms of percentages at off design conditions, it has a higher expected return across all cases versus the best-worst case design.

- A manager could readily design a policy that limited the worst case downside return to a certain percentage of the maximum possible. For example, if the manager wanted a worst case downside return no worse than 5% of the maximum possible, a policy should be designed around roughly a -2% parameter perturbation.

- A manager may also be interested in implementing the following policy: $\max_\theta E[J(\theta)]$.

Sensitivity Analysis: Extremal Perturbation, Large Initial Condition. The expected value for each of the design cases considered are as follows:

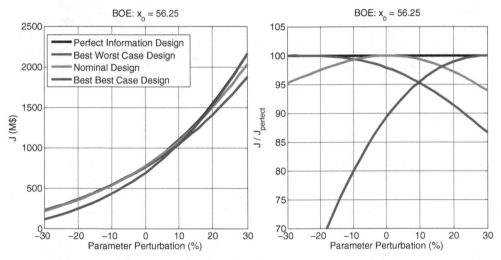

Fig. 5. Economic Inefficiencies for Various Optimal Control Laws: Extremal Perturbations (Large IC)

- $E[J] = 1368.2$ for the Perfect Information Optimal Designs
- $E[J] = 1284.5$ for the Best-Worst Case Design
- $E[J] = 1336.8$ for the Nominal Design
- $E[J] = 1259.3$ for the Best-Best Case Design

Finally, it should be noted that in contrast to the low initial condition study conducted, the Best-Best Case Design performs worse both in terms of the percentage possible and the expected return when compared to the Best-Worst Case Design.

Limit Cycles In the Presence of Uncertainty. Finally, consider figure 6. The optimal control law is based on the nominal BOE parameters. The initial condition is above the uncertain x_e^*. The simulation is conducted with a truth plant possessing a 10% reduction in k - hence the limit cycle behavior. The figure shows that: (1) The optimal control policy (in general) will exhibit limit cycle behavior when we have imperfect information; i.e. model parameters are not known exactly. (2) The optimal control policy (in general) will be very sensitive to finer sampling (ΔT smaller) under imperfect information; i.e. more oscillations (switching) will be exhibited as our x time samples are spaced closer together. The figure also shows that low pass filtering the optimal with a lag can be used to smooth oscillations a bit. To significantly reduce the oscillations, however, there is no easy fix. We either need a penalized $\dot{u}_p$ term within J to penalize switching or we need policies that are inherently more robust (like the ones we will describe subsequently). As such, this implies that, in practice, the optimal control policy is prohibitively expensive to implement in the presence of parametric uncertainty because of the inherent limit cycle behavior and the associated switching costs.

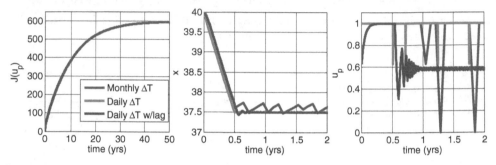

Fig. 6. Optimal Control Law Robustness: Limit Cycles In Presence of (-10% Capacity) Uncertainty

Motivation for Robust Control Laws. The above motivates the need for more robust control laws; i.e. control laws that (1) exhibit an acceptable return (i.e. return robustness) in the presence of anticipated (likely) parametric uncertainty; (2) do not exhibit limit cycle behavior in the presence of anticipated (likely) parametric uncertainty. As such, the above motivates the robust control laws to be considered in our presentation.

Control Law Implementation Issues. Unlike many control applications where controllers are implemented with great fidelity (within state-of-the-art digital computing units), controllers within a resource management system are implemented by an organization by setting rules for the fishery worker community (e.g. quotas, taxes (Clark, 1990, Chapter 8). As such, many types of uncertainties can be introduced by the organization. These could include any of the following: (1) parameter uncertainty, (2) additional uncertain actuation/sensing dynamics (e.g. lags, time delays, rate limiters, etc.), (3) nonlinearities (e.g. rate limiters, saturations, quantization, dead zones), (4) actuation/incentive errors (e.g. quota/tax miscalculations), (5) sensing, measurement, and estimation errors (e.g. sensor dynamics, biomass sampling/aliasing/quntization errors, noise, disturbances).

4. Robust control laws

The model under consideration is very simple. Many tools from the controls literature may be applied (e.g. classical control (Rodriguez, 2003), H-infinity (Rodriguez, 2004), feedback linearization, SDRE's, etc.). Given the introductory/tutorial nature of the paper, the simplicity of the model being used, as well as the fact that this text covers advanced control methodologies, we shall focus on simple control strategies from classical control theory. We will show that such control laws can be used to avoid limit cycles, increase robustness with respect to parametric uncertainty, and achieve returns that are close to those of the perfect information optimal control law.

Control System Structure. The structure of the control system may be visualized as shown in Figure 7.

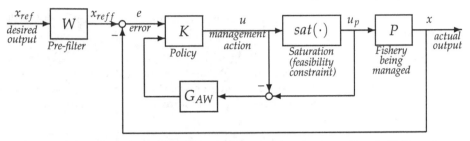

Fig. 7. Renewable Resource Management Problem Represented as a Standard Negative Feedback System with a Pre-Filter and Anti-Windup Logic

1. *Plant.* Here, P represents the plant under control. We shall use an LTI small signal model to approximate our nonlinear plant.

2. *Reference State or Command.* x_{ref} is the desired reference biomass state. Ideally, we would like to use $x_{ref} = x_e^*$. Parameter uncertainty prevents us from commanding the desired state. As such, we are forced to choose x_{ref} more judiciously. Given this, we will give special attention to maximizing our return under the worst case parameter uncertainty.

3. *PI Controller.* K is a proportional-plus-integral (PI) controller possessing the structure:

$$K(s) = \frac{g(s+z)}{s}\left[\frac{p_{ro}}{s+p_{ro}}\right] \tag{30}$$

where $g > 0$, $z > 0$, and $p_{ro} > 0$. The integrator within the controller will ensure that step biomass commands are followed in the steady state while step input/output disturbances are rejected in the steady state. The $(s+z)$ term will ensure that the LTI plant-integrator pair will be stabilized. The term $\left[\frac{p_{ro}}{s+p_{ro}}\right]$ provides high frequency roll-off to ensure that high frequency sensor noise n is suitably attenuated.

4. *Command Pre-Filter.* W is a reference command pre-filter possessing the structure:

$$W(s) = \left[\frac{z}{s+z}\right] \tag{31}$$

This pre-filter can be used to ensure that the overshoot to step reference commands is suitably bounded.

5. *Observer-Based Integrator Anti-Windup Logic.* Anti-windup logic is included so that the integrator in the PI controller does not windup. That is, the integrator is turned off so that it does not integrate constant errors which occur when the input to the plant is saturated (Aström, Hägglund). The structure of the anti-windup logic is as follows $\dot{x}_k = A_k x_k + B_k e + L(sat(u) - u)$ where L is an observer gain matrix. The PI controller with the anti-windup logic may be described by the following equations:

$$\dot{x}_1 = e + G_{AW}(sat(u) - u) \qquad \dot{x}_2 = gzx_1 - p_{ro}x_2 + ge \qquad u = p_{ro}x_2 \quad (32)$$

where G_{AW} is the anti-windup gain.

Nominal Design Methodology. The nominal design methodology can be described as follows (Rodriguez, 2003):

1. *Plant Approximant.* The following small signal LTI model $P \approx P_d \overset{\text{def}}{=} \frac{b}{s-a}$ will be used to approximate our nonlinear plant. Here, P_d is referred to as the *design plant*; i.e. the plant upon which we will base our control law design. While any design we obtain can be evaluated using plant approximants such as P_d, control designs must be evaluated with the actual nonlinear plant model.

2. *Controller Approximant.* Use the controller approximant $K \approx \frac{g(s+z)}{s}$ where $g > 0$ and $z > 0$.

3. *Nominal Open Loop Approximant.* Form the open loop transfer function approximant

$$L = P_d K \approx \frac{bg(s+z)}{s(s-a)} = \frac{n(s)}{d(s)}. \quad (33)$$

4. *Nominal Closed Loop Characteristic Equation.* Form the nominal closed loop characteristic equation

$$\Phi_{cl}(s) = d(s) + n(s) = s^2 + (bg - a)s + bgz = 0 \quad (34)$$

This polynomial has the "standard second order form"

$$\Phi_{cl}(s) = s^2 + 2\zeta\omega_n s + \omega_n^2 \quad (35)$$

where $\zeta = \frac{bg-a}{2\sqrt{bgz}}$ is the damping factor and $\omega_n = \sqrt{gz}$ is the undamped natural frequency. For stable nominal complex closed loop poles, we require $0 < \zeta < 1$.

5. *Closed Loop Poles.* Determine the nominal closed loop poles (assumed complex for rapid transient response):

$$s = -\zeta\omega_n \pm j\omega_n\sqrt{1 - \zeta^2} \quad (36)$$

Given this, we will have nominal (local) closed loop exponential stability with an associated time constant $\tau = \frac{1}{\zeta\omega_n}$. The associated (approximate 1%) settling time is $t_s = 5\tau$.

6. *Standard Second Order Closed Loop Transfer Function and Percent Overshoot.* With the command pre-filter W, the associated closed loop transfer function takes the standard second order form:

$$T_{x_{ref}x} = \frac{WPK}{1 + PK} \approx \frac{\omega_n^2}{s^2 + 2\zeta\omega_n s + \omega_n^2} \quad (37)$$

As such, the associated percent overshoot to a step reference command is given by

$$M_p = e^{-\zeta\omega_n t_p} = e^{-\left(\frac{\zeta\pi}{1-\zeta^2}\right)} \quad (38)$$

where $t_p = \frac{\pi}{\omega_n\sqrt{1-\zeta^2}}$ is the time at which the peak overshoot occurs.

7. *Damping Factor from Percent Overshoot Specification.* Determine ζ from the overshoot
specification:

$$\zeta = \frac{|lnM_p|}{\sqrt{\pi^2 + |lnM_p|^2}} \tag{39}$$

8. *Undamped Natural Frequency from Settling Time Specification.* Determine ω_n from the settling
time specification:

$$\omega_n = \frac{5}{\zeta t_s} \tag{40}$$

9. *PI Controller Parameters.* Determine the PI controller gain g and zero z from:

$$g = \frac{2\zeta\omega_n + a}{b} \qquad\qquad z = \frac{\omega_n^2}{bg} \tag{41}$$

10. *Controller Roll-Of Parameter.* Choose the roll-off parameter p_{ro} as follows:

$$p_{ro} = 10\omega_n \tag{42}$$

so that the added high frequency roll-off does not significantly degrade the nominal phase
margin within the loop. It could also be selected in order to satisfy a specific sinusoidal
steady state noise attenuation specification.

11. *Anti-Windup Gain.* Choose the anti-windup gain $G_{AW} > 0$ to be sufficiently large so that
the integrator suitably shuts down in order to "maximally recapture" the dominant second
order response characteristics described above. A family of gains is examined below.

5. Control law comparisons

In this section, we compare the properties of the nominal optimal control law with those for
the robust policies based upon the nominal LTI plant model $P_d = \frac{b}{s-a}$.

5.1 Sample control law time responses
Within this section, sample time responses are provided for families of robust control laws
(based upon the nominal LTI plant model) - families that approximate the performance of the
nominal optimal control law. (Note: There will be an approximation gap when uncertainty is
considered.)

Reference Biomass Tracking: Anti-Windup Gain Study. Figure 8 shows closed loop biomass
tracking time responses for a family of robust control law designs where $\zeta = 1$, $t_s = 1$. The
anti-windup gain G_{AW} is varied to control how well the responses approximate that of the
optimal with no limit cycle behavior. As the anti-windup gain G_{AW} is increased, the responses
come closer to the (nominal) optimal control law (with no limit cycle behavior). The limit cycle
behavior of the (nominal) optimal has been cleaned up in order to improve the readability of
the figure (see Figure 6).

A Note On Robustness with Respect to High Frequency Unmodeled Dynamics. It should be
noted that as the speed of a policy is increased, the significance of unmodeled high frequency
dynamics within the fishery or within the policy implementing organization/evironment
(e.g. lags, time delays, rate limiters) becomes an issue to consider in final policy evaluation.

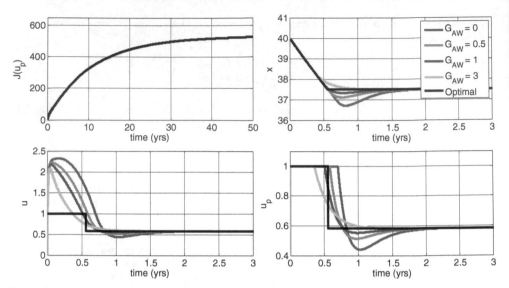

Fig. 8. Reference Biomass Tracking: Anti-Windup Gain Study ($\zeta = 1$, $t_s = 1$)

It is well known from fundamental robustness theory (Rodriguez, 2004; 2003) that fast control laws can result in closed loop oscillatory responses or instability when high frequency unmodeled dynamics are "significantly excited." This issue will be examined in future work.
Reference Biomass Tracking: Damping Factor Study. Figure 9 shows shows closed loop biomass tracking time responses for a family of robust control law designs where $t_s = 1$, $G_{AW} = 3$. The damping factor ζ is varied in order to control the speed of the response as

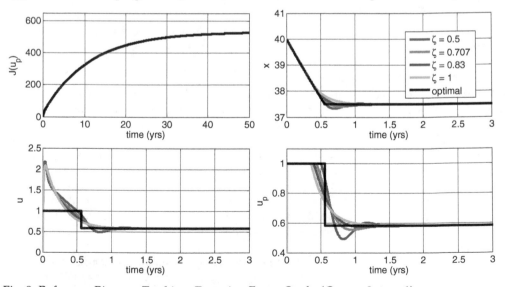

Fig. 9. Reference Biomass Tracking: Damping Factor Study ($G_{AW} = 3$, $t_s = 1$)

well as the undershoot. As the damping factor ζ is reduced, the response speeds up (getting closer to that of the (nominal) optimal with no limit cycle behavior), although the observed undershoot increases. The limit cycle behavior of the (nominal) optimal has been cleaned up in order to improve the readability of the figure (see Figure 6).

Reference Biomass Tracking: Settling Time Study. Figure 10 shows closed loop biomass tracking time responses for a family of robust control law designs where $\zeta = 1$ (critically damped, $M_p = 0$) and $G_{AW} = 3$. As the settling time t_s of the closed loop system is reduced, the responses come closer to the (nominal) optimal (with no limit cycle behavior). The limit cycle behavior of the (nominal) optimal has been cleaned up in order to improve the readability of the figure.

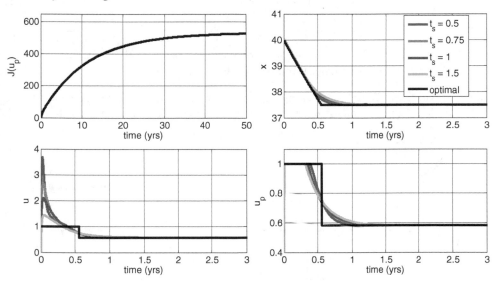

Fig. 10. Reference Biomass Tracking: Settling Time Study ($G_{AW} = 3, \zeta = 1$)

5.2 Utility of linear design methodology

In this section, we try to shed light on the utility of our linear time invariant (LTI) based robust control system design methodology and how linear simulation can be used to approximate/predict the behavior of the nonlinear simulations. All designs are based upon nominal parameter values.

Linear vs Nonlinear Biomass Tracking: x_0 Near x_{ref}. Figure 11 compares linear and nonlinear closed loop biomass tracking simulations where the the initial condition (IC) is near the desired set point (target biomass). Four responses are shown for x and u_p: (1) purely linear; i.e. linear plant model, linear controller, and no saturation, (2) linear with plant saturation; i.e. linear plant model, linear controller, and plant saturation, (3) linear with anti-windup logic; i.e. linear plant model, linear controller, plant saturation, and anti-windup logic, (4) nonlinear; i.e. nonlinear plant model, linear controller, plant saturation, and anti-windup logic. Here, the reference command is very small ($x_{ref} = 0.375$), the control does not saturate, and all of the responses match one another. This shows that the "pure linear theory" suffices under small signal conditions (as expected).

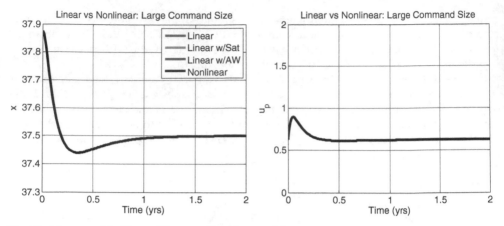

Fig. 11. Linear vs Nonlinear Biomass Tracking: x_0 Near x_{ref}

Linear vs Nonlinear Biomass Tracking: x_0 Far From x_{ref}. Figure 12 compares linear and nonlinear closed loop biomass tracking simulations where the the initial condition (IC) is

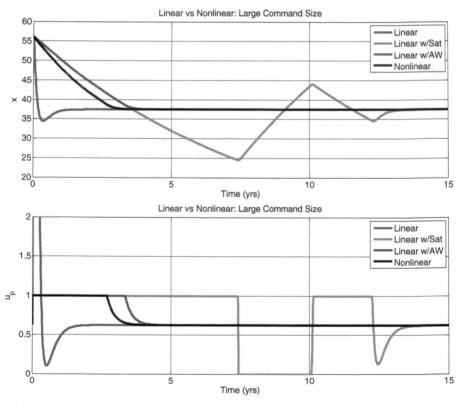

Fig. 12. Linear vs Nonlinear Biomass Tracking: x_0 Far From x_{ref}

far from the desired set point (target biomass). Here, the reference command is large (x_{ref} = 18.75), the controls saturate, windup is exhibited in the linear w/Sat case, and we observe relatively good agreement between the linear (particularly linear w/AW) and nonlinear responses.

Biomass Tracking Robustness In Presence Of Capacity Uncertainty: Anti-Windup Gain Study. Figure 13 shows how our robust control laws can be adjusted to achieve the "flatter" economic inefficiency of the nominal optimal control law (see Figures 4-5). We observe the following:

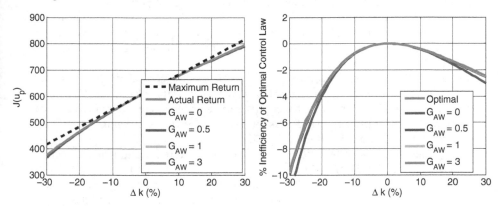

Fig. 13. PI Biomass Tracking Robustness (Capacity Uncertainty): Anti-Windup Gain Study ($\zeta = 1, t_s = 1$)

- With an anti-windup implementation, a PI control law can come arbitrarily close to matching the performance of the nominal optimal control law with imperfect information.

- Improving upon the nominal optimal control law with imperfect information requires some outer loop control logic as well as system identification to more appropriately select the reference/target biomass.

The observed performance gap (or inefficiency) is fundamentally because the target x_{ref} differs from the perfect information x_e^*; not because the nominal design plant differs from the truth plant. Closing the observed performance gap further requires an outer loop controller and/or parameter estimation techniques in order to get a more accurate target x_{ref} that is closer to the perfect information target x_e^*.

6. Summary and future directions

Summary. This chapter has shown how ideas from robust control may be applied to a fishery. It has been specifically shown how some small amount of income may be sacrificed for increased robustness with respect to uncertain fishery parameters.

Directions for Future Research. Future work will examine more complex models (e.g. decentralized, distributed), pros/cons associated with parameter estimation schemes, more complex robust control laws (e.g. use of receding horizon control for long-term management), robustness with respect to plant and controller uncertainty (parametric and dynamic).

7. References

Anderies, J.M., Rodriguez, A., Janssen, M. & Cifdaloz, O. (2007). Panaceas, uncertainty, and the robust control framework in sustainability science. *Proceedings of the National Academy of Sciences USA 104*, 15,194–15,199

Andersen, P. (1982). Commercial fisheries under price uncertainty. *Journal of Environmental Economics and Management 9*(1), 11–28

Aström, K. & Hägglund, T. (1995). PID Controllers: Theory, Design, and Tuning. *Int. Society for Measurement and Control*, (2nd Ed.), Research Triangle Park, N.C.

Babonneau, F., Vial, J.P. & Apparigliato, R.: Robust optimization for environmental and energy planning. *In: J.A. Filar, A. Haurie (eds.) Uncertainty and Environmental Decision Making, International Series in Operations Research & Management Science*, vol. 138, chap. 3, pp. 79–126. Springer (2010)

Belmiloudi, A. (2006). Minimax control problems of periodic competing parabolic systems with logistic growth terms. *International Journal of Control 79*(2), 150–161

Belmiloudi, A. (2005). Nonlinear optimal control problems of degenerate parabolic equations with logistic time-varying delays of convolution type. *Nonlinear Analysis-theory Methods & Applications 63*(8), 1126–1152

Ben-Tal, A., Nemirovski, A. (2008). Selected topics in robust convex optimization. *Mathematical Programming 112*(1), 125–158

Ben-Tal, A., Nemirovski, A. (2002). Robust optimization—methodology and applications. *Mathematical Programming 92*(3, Ser. B), 453–480. ISMP 2000, Part 2 (Atlanta, GA)

Ben-Tal, A., El-Ghaoui L. & Nemirovski, A. (2000) Robust semidefinite programming. *In: R. Saigal, L. Vandenberghe, H. Wolkowicz (eds.) Semidefinite Programming and Applications. Kluwer Dordrecht*

Ben-Tal, A., Nemirovski, A.(1998). Robust convex optimization. *Mathematics of Operations Research 23*(4), 769–805

Clark, C. (2007) The Worldwide Crisis in Fisheries: Economic Models and Human Behavior. *Cambridge University Press, Cambridge*, UK

Clark, C. (2006). Fisheries bioeconomics: why is it so misunderstood?, In: *Population Ecology 48*, 95-98

Clark, C., Munro, G. & U.R., S. (2006). Subsidies, buybacks, and sustainable fisheries. *Journal of Environmental Economics and Management 50*, 47–58

Clark, C.W. (1990). Mathematical Bioeconomics: The Optimal Management of Renewable Resources, 2 edn. *J. Wiley*, N.Y., U.S.A.

Clark, C. & Kirkwood, G.: On uncertain renewable resource stocks - optimal harvest policies and the value of stock surveys. *Journal of Environmental Economics and Management 13*(3), 235–244 (1986)

Dercole, F., Gragnani, A., Kuznetsov, Y.A. & Rinaldi, S. (2003) Numerical sliding bifurcation analysis: an application to a relay control system. *Ieee Transactions on Circuits and Systems I-Fundamental Theory and Applications 50*(8), 1058–1063

Gordon, H. (1954) The economic theory of a common property resource: the fishery. *Journal of Political Economy 62*, 124–142

Hansen, L.P. & Sargent, T.J. (2007) Robustness. *Princeton University Press*, Princeton, NJ

Holland, D. & Gudmundsson, E., J., G. (1999) Do fishing vessel buyback programs work? a survey of the evidence. *Marine Policy 23*, 47–69

Holling, C.S., Gunderson, L.H. (2002). Resilience and adaptive cycles. *In: L.H. Gunderson, C.S. Holling (eds.) Panarchy: Understanding Transformations in Systems of Humans and Nature,* chap. 2. Island Press

Holling, C.S. (1986) The resilience of terrestrial ecosystems, local surprise and global change. *In: C.W. C., R.E. Munn (eds.) Sustainable development of the biosphere,* pp. 292–317. Cambridge University Press, Cambridge

Holling, C.S.(1973). Resilience and stability of ecological systems. *Annual Review of Ecology and Systematics 4,* 1–23

ISRIC. (1990). Global assessment of the status of human induced soil degradation (glasdod). *dataset, International Soil Reference and Information Centre,* Wageningen, The Netherlands

Kendrick, D.A. (2005). Stochastic control for economic models: past, present and the paths ahead. *Journal of Economic Dynamics and Control 29,* 3–30

Koenig, E.F. (1984). Controlling stock externalities in a common property fishery subject to uncertainty. *Journal of Environmental Economics and Management 11*(2), 124–138

Lempert, R.J., Groves, D.G., Popper, S.W. & Bankes, S.C. (2006) A general, analytic method for generating robust strategies and narrative scenarios. *Management Science 52*(4), 514–528

Lempert, R.J., Schlesinger, M.E. (2000). Robust strategies for abating climate change - an editorial essay. *Climatic Change 45*(3-4), 387–401

Ludwig, D., Walker, B. & Holling, C.S. (1997). Sustainability, stability, and resilience. *Conservation Ecology 1*(1), (online) URL: http://www.consecol.org/vol1/iss1/art7/

Ludwig, D. & Walters, C. (1982). Optimal harvesting with imprecise parameter estimates. *Ecological Modelling 14,* 273–292

Moran, E.F., Ostrom, E. (eds.) (2006). Seeing the Forest and the Trees: Human-Environment Interactions in Forest Ecosystems. *MIT Press,* Cambridge, MA

Myers, R. & Worm, B. (2003). Rapid worldwide depletion of predatory fish communities. *Nature 423,* 280–283

Ogata, K. (1995). Discrete-Time Control Systems. *Prentice Hall,* (2nd Ed.), N.J.

Rodriguez, A.A., Cifdaloz, O., Anderies, J.M., Janssen, J. & Dickeson, J., (2010). Confronting Management Challenges in Highly Uncertain Natural REsource Systems: a Robustness-Vulnerability Trade-off Approach," *Environmental Modeling & Assessment,* Volume 16, Issue 1 (2011), Page 15.

Rodriguez, A.A. (2004). Analysis and Design of Multivariable Feedback Control Systems. *Control3D, LLC.,* Tempe, AZ

Rodriguez, A.A. (2003). Analysis and Design of Feedback Control Systems. *Control3D, LLC.,* Tempe, AZ

Schaefer, M. (1957). Some considerations of population dynamics and economics in relation to the management of the commercial marine fisheries. *Journal of the Fisheries Research Board of Canada 14*(5), 669–681

Sethi, G., Costello, C., Fisher, A., Hanemann, M. & Karp, L. (2005). Fishery management under multiple uncertainty. *Journal of Environmental Economics and Management 50*(2), 300–318

Shah, T., Molden, D., Sakthivadivel, R., Seckler. (2000). The global groundwater situation: Overview of opportunities and challenges. *Tech. rep., International Water Management Institute, Colombo, Sri Lanka*

Walters, C. (1986). Adaptive Management of Renewable Resources. *MacMillan Publishing Co.*

Weitzman, M. (2002). Landing fees vs harvest quotas with uncertain fish stocks. *Journal of environmental economics and management* 43(2), 325–338

Wilen, J., Homans, F. (1998). What do regulators do? Dynamic behavior of resource managers in the North Pacific Halibut Fishery 1935-1978. *Ecological Economics* 24(2-3), 289–298

Zhou, K., Doyle, J. (1998). Essentials of Robust Control. *Prentice Hall*

9

Robust Control for Single Unit Resource Allocation Systems

Shengyong Wang, Song Foh Chew and Mark Lawley

University of Akron, Southern Illinois University Edwardsville, and Purdue University

USA

1. Introduction

Supervisory control for deadlock-free resource allocation has been an active area of manufacturing systems research. Most work, however, assumes that allocated resources do not fail. Little research has addressed allocating resources that may fail. Automated manufacturing systems have many types of components that may fail unexpectedly. We develop robust controllers for single unit resource allocation systems with unreliable resources (Chew et al., 2008; Chew et al., 2011; Chew & Lawley, 2006; Lawley, 2002; Lawley & Sulistyono, 2002; Wang et al., 2008; Wang et al., 2009). These controllers guarantee that when unreliable resources fail, parts requiring failed resources do not block the production of parts not requiring failed resources. Further, while resources are down, the system is controlled so that when repair events occur, the system is in a safe and admissible state.

There is little manufacturing research literature on robust supervision. Reveliotis (1999) considers the case where parts requiring a failed resource can be re-routed or removed from the system through human intervention. Park & Lim (1999) address existence questions for robust supervisors. Hsieh (2004) develops methods that determine the feasibility of production given a set of resource failures modelled as the extraction of tokens from a Petri net. In contrast, our work models the failure of the workstation server while assuming that buffer space remains accessible after the failure event. We assume that when the server of a workstation fails, we can continue allocating its buffer space up to capacity, but that none of the waiting parts can be processed and thus cannot proceed along their routes until the server is repaired. We further assume that server failure does not prevent finished parts occupying the workstation's buffer space from being moved away from the workstation and proceeding along their routes. Finally, we assume that server failure does not damage or destroy the part being processed and that failure can only occur when the server is working. The last two assumptions are made for notational efficiency and presentation clarity. They can be easily relaxed by adding appropriate events and state variables to our treatment.

Our objective is to control the system so that failure of an unreliable resource does not prevent processing of parts not requiring the failed resource. When a resource fails, all parts in the system requiring the failed resource for future processing are unable to complete until the failed resource is repaired. Because these parts occupy buffer space, they can block production of parts not requiring the failed resource. Thus, we want to assure that, when unreliable resources fail, the buffer space allocation can evolve under normal operation so that parts not requiring failed resources can continue production. Operation must continue to obey part routings and must assure that when a failed resource is repaired, the system is not in an unsafe state. We refer to supervisors guaranteeing this as *robust*.

The remainder of the chapter comprises the following sections. Most briefly, Section 2 discusses the way we model our systems. An example system is presented in this section to motivate properties that robust controllers must possess. In Section 3, we develop robust controllers for systems with multiple unreliable resources where each part type requires at most one unreliable resource. Specifically, Subsection 3.1 develops two robust controllers using a neighbourhood policy, a modified version of banker's algorithm, and a single step look ahead policy. Subsection 3.2 uses a resource order policy to construct another robust controller; Subsection 3.3 employs a notion of shared buffer capacity to develop a robust controller. Relaxing the restriction, Section 4 builds robust controllers for systems for which part types may require multiple unreliable resources. Finally, Section 5 concludes the chapter and discusses future research directions.

2. Modelling of robust control

There are two subsections in this section. Specifically, we will discuss the way we model our systems in Subsection 2.1. Subsection 2.2 will provide examples to motivate properties that robust controllers must possess.

2.1 The discrete event system

We model our systems using the approach of Ramadge & Wonham (1987). This is necessary to define the properties that we want our supervisors to enforce. The following model is similar to that developed by Lawley & Sulistyono (2002), but differs in that now we have more complex failure scenarios and thus some of the underlying formalism has to be generalized. Figure 1 provides an example for the following development.

The system is defined as a 9–tuple vector $S = \langle R, C, P, \rho, Q, Q_0, \Sigma, \xi, \delta \rangle$. In S, R is the set of system resource types, with $R = R^R \cup R^U$, $R^R \cap R^U = \varnothing$, where R^R is the set of reliable resource types, not subject to failure and R^U is the set of unreliable resource types, subject to failure. Let $C = \langle C_i : i=1 \ldots |R| \rangle$ where C_i is the capacity of the buffer space associated with system resource type $r_i \in R$.

The set P of part types is produced by the system with each part type $P_j \in P$ representing an ordered set of processing stages, $P_j = \langle P_{j1} \ldots P_{j|P_j|} \rangle$, where P_{jk} represents the kth processing stage of P_j. Also, let $RP_{jk} = \langle P_{jk} \ldots P_{j|P_j|} \rangle$ be the *residual* part stages. We will use p_{jk} to represent a part instance of P_{jk}. Let $\rho : P_j \rightarrow R$ such that $\rho(P_{jk})$ returns the resource type required by P_{jk}. Thus, the route of P_j is $T_j = \langle \rho(P_{j1}) \ldots \rho(P_{j|P_j|}) \rangle$, and the residual route $RT_{jk} = \langle \rho(P_{jk}) \ldots \rho(P_{j|P_j|}) \rangle$. Finally, let $\Omega_i = \{P_{jk} : \rho(P_{jk}) = r_i \in R\}$, the set of part type stages associated with resource $r_i \in R$.

We will suppose that our resource types are workstations with buffer space for staging and storing parts and a processor or server for operating on parts. We will use the standard assumption from queuing theory that the server is not idle so long as there are unfinished parts in a workstation's buffer space. The resource units that we are concerned with allocating are instances of the workstation's buffer space. The controllers that we design are not intended to allocate the server among parts waiting at the workstation. We assume this to be done by some local queuing discipline.

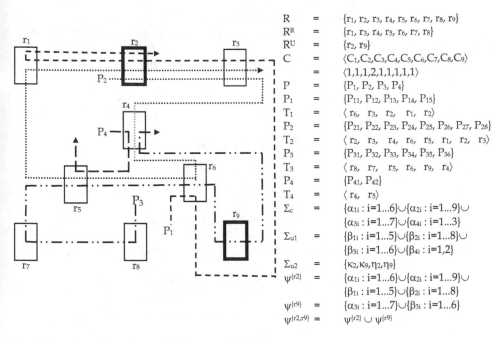

$$
\begin{aligned}
R &= \{r_1, r_2, r_3, r_4, r_5, r_6, r_7, r_8, r_9\} \\
R^R &= \{r_1, r_3, r_4, r_5, r_6, r_7, r_8\} \\
R^U &= \{r_2, r_9\} \\
C &= \langle C_1, C_2, C_3, C_4, C_5, C_6, C_7, C_8, C_9 \rangle \\
&= \langle 1,1,1,2,1,1,1,1,1 \rangle \\
P &= \{P_1, P_2, P_3, P_4\} \\
P_1 &= \{P_{11}, P_{12}, P_{13}, P_{14}, P_{15}\} \\
T_1 &= \langle r_6, r_3, r_2, r_1, r_2 \rangle \\
P_2 &= \{P_{21}, P_{22}, P_{23}, P_{24}, P_{25}, P_{26}, P_{27}, P_{28}\} \\
T_2 &= \langle r_2, r_3, r_4, r_6, r_5, r_1, r_2, r_3 \rangle \\
P_3 &= \{P_{31}, P_{32}, P_{33}, P_{34}, P_{35}, P_{36}\} \\
T_3 &= \langle r_8, r_7, r_5, r_6, r_9, r_4 \rangle \\
P_4 &= \{P_{41}, P_{42}\} \\
T_4 &= \langle r_4, r_5 \rangle \\
\Sigma_c &= \{\alpha_{1i} : i=1...6\} \cup \{\alpha_{2i} : i=1...9\} \cup \\
&\quad \{\alpha_{3i} : i=1...7\} \cup \{\alpha_{4i} : i=1...3\} \\
\Sigma_{u1} &= \{\beta_{1i} : i=1...5\} \cup \{\beta_{2i} : i=1...8\} \cup \\
&\quad \{\beta_{3i} : i=1...6\} \cup \{\beta_{4i} : i=1,2\} \\
\Sigma_{u2} &= \{\kappa_2, \kappa_9, \eta_2, \eta_9\} \\
\psi^{\{r2\}} &= \{\alpha_{1i} : i=1...6\} \cup \{\alpha_{2i} : i=1...9\} \cup \\
&\quad \{\beta_{1i} : i=1...5\} \cup \{\beta_{2i} : i=1...8\} \\
\psi^{\{r9\}} &= \{\alpha_{3i} : i=1...7\} \cup \{\beta_{3i} : i=1...6\} \\
\psi^{\{r2,r9\}} &= \psi^{\{r2\}} \cup \psi^{\{r9\}}
\end{aligned}
$$

Fig. 1. An example system with two unreliable resources

Workstation *failure* will imply the failure of the workstation's server, not any of its buffer space. We will assume that when the server of a workstation fails, we can continue to allocate its buffer space up to capacity, but that none of the waiting parts can be processed and thus cannot proceed along their respective routes until the server is repaired. We further assume that server failure does not prevent finished parts occupying the workstation's buffer space from being moved away from the workstation and proceeding along their respective routes. Finally, we assume that server failure does not damage or destroy the part being processed and that failure can only occur when the server is working.

We are now in a position to define the system states and events. Let Q represent the set of system states, where $Q \ni q = \langle sv_i, y_{jk}, x_{jk} : i=1...|R|, j=1...|P| \text{ and } k=1...|P_j|\rangle$, with sv_i being the status of the server of workstation i (0 if failed, 1 if operational), y_{jk} being the number of unfinished units of P_{jk} (parts waiting or in-process) located in the buffer space of $\rho(P_{jk})$, and x_{jk} being the number of finished units of P_{jk} located in the buffer space of $\rho(P_{jk})$. Q_0 is the set of initial states with $q_0 \in Q_0$ being the state in which no resources are allocated and all servers are operational. The dimension of q is $\sum_{j=1}^{|P|} 2|P_j| + |R|$.

Let $\Sigma = \Sigma_c \cup \Sigma_u$, where $\Sigma_c = \{\alpha_{jk} : j=1...|P| \text{ and } k=1...|P_j|+1\}$ is the set of controllable events with α_{jk} representing the allocation of $\rho(P_{jk})$ to a part instance of P_{jk}; that is, α_{jk} is the event that a part instance of a part type P_j advances into the buffer space of a workstation that will perform its kth operation. Then, $\alpha_{j,|P_j|+1}$ represents a finished part of type P_j leaving the system. We assume that the supervisor controls the occurrences of these events through resource allocation decisions.

We have $\Sigma_u = \Sigma_{u1} \cup \Sigma_{u2}$ being the set of uncontrollable events where $\Sigma_{u1} = \{\beta_{jk} : j=1\ldots|P|$ and $k=1\ldots|P_j|\}$ represents the completion of service for P_{jk}. Then, $\Sigma_{u2} = \{\kappa_i, \eta_i : r_i \in R^U\}$ represents the failure (κ_i) and repair (η_i) of the server of unreliable resource $r_i \in R^U$. Service completions, failures and repairs are assumed to be beyond the controller's influence.

Let $\xi: Q \to 2^\Sigma$ be a function that, for a given state, returns the set of enabled events. This function is defined for a state, $q \in Q$, as follows:

1. For $P_{j1} \in \Omega_i$, if $C_i - \sum_{P_{jk} \in \Omega_i} (y_{jk} + x_{jk}) > 0$, then $\alpha_{j1} \in \xi(q)$.

    Events that release new parts into the system are enabled when space is available on the first required workstation in the route.

2. For $P_{jk} \in \Omega_i$, if $y_{jk} > 0$ and $sv_i = 1$, then $\beta_{jk} \in \xi(q)$.
    If a part is at service, then the corresponding service completion event is enabled.

3. For $r_i \in R^U$, $P_{jk} \in \Omega_i$ and $\beta_{jk} \in \xi(q) \Rightarrow \kappa_i \in \xi(q)$.
    If the server is busy with a part, then the corresponding failure event is enabled.

4. For $r_i \in R^U$, if $sv_i = 0$, then $\eta_i \in \xi(q)$ and $\beta_{jk} \notin \xi(q) \ \forall P_{jk} \in \Omega_i$.
    If the server is failed, the corresponding repair event is enabled and the corresponding service completion events are disabled.

5. For $P_{jk} \in \Omega_i$, $1 < k \leq |P_j|$, if $x_{j,k-1} > 0$ and $C_i - \sum_{P_{jk} \in \Omega_i} (y_{jk} + x_{jk}) > 0$, then $\alpha_{jk} \in \xi(q)$.

    When a part finishes its current operation and buffer space becomes available at the next required workstation in its route, the event corresponding to advancing the part is enabled.

6. For $P_{j,|P_j|} \in \Omega_i$, if $x_{j,|P_j|} > 0$, then $\alpha_{j,|P_j|+1} \in \xi(q)$.
    If a part has finished all of its operations, the event corresponding to unloading it from the system is enabled.

The state transition function is now defined as follows. The transition function, δ, is a partial function from the cross product $Q \times \Sigma$ to the set Q of system states. Specifically, let $\delta: Q \times \Sigma \to Q$ such that

$\delta(q, \alpha_{jk}) = q - e_{x_{j,k-1}} + e_{y_{jk}}$, advancing a part $p_{j,k-1}$;

$\delta(q, \beta_{jk}) = q - e_{y_{jk}} + e_{x_{jk}}$, service completion of a part p_{jk};

$\delta(q, \kappa_i) = q - e_{sv_i}$, failure of server i;

$\delta(q, \eta_i) = q + e_{sv_i}$, repair of server i;

where $e_{x_{j,k-1}}$, $e_{y_{jk}}$, $e_{x_{jk}}$, and e_{sv_i} are the standard unit vectors with components corresponding to $x_{j,k-1}$, y_{jk}, x_{jk} and sv_i being 1, respectively. Note that, $e_{y_{j,|P_j|+1}} = e_{x_{j0}} = 0$, the zero vector with the same dimension, and that p_{j0} represents a raw part of P_j waiting to be released into the system.

We assume that $|R^U| \geq 1$. In this case, any subset of the unreliable resources can be simultaneously in a failed state. Thus, if one of the $\binom{|R^U|}{i}$ subsets of size i, $i=1\ldots|R^U|$, is down, we want the remaining resources to continue producing parts not requiring any of the failed resources without human intervention to remove or rearrange the parts requiring failed resources. Further, when one of the failed resources is repaired, we want production of parts requiring that resource to resume. A robust controller must possess certain properties in order to accomplish the above-mentioned characteristics.

2.2 Motivating examples for properties of robust supervisory control

This subsection motivates a set of desired properties for a robust controller based upon an example production system. Figure 1 presents an example manufacturing system with two unreliable resources. The stages, routes, and resource capacities are given, as is the complete discrete event model. This model enumerates the resources, capacities, events, and so forth. For now, we will constrain our discussion to the system states presented in Figures 2-4. We recall that, by definition, a resource allocation state is safe if, starting from that state, there exists a sequence of resource allocations/deallocations that completes all parts and takes the system to the empty and idle state, the state in which no resources are allocated and no servers are busy. Our underlying assumption is that if a resource allocation state is safe, then, under correct supervision and starting from that state, it is possible to produce all part types indefinitely.

We have several control objectives for the system of Figure 1. First, we desire that the controller guarantee deadlock-free operation, i.e., that it keeps the system producing all part types. Second, in the event that r_2 fails, we want to continue producing part types not requiring r_2, $\{P_3,P_4\}$, without having to intervene by clearing the system of parts requiring r_2. Similarly, in the event that r_9 fails, we want to continue producing part types not requiring r_9, $\{P_1,P_2,P_4\}$, again without having to intervene by clearing the system of parts requiring r_9. Further, if both r_2 and r_9 are in the failed state, we want to continue producing part types not requiring r_2 or r_9, $\{P_4\}$, again without explicit intervention.

Consider for example the state given in Figure 2. This state is safe; however, if r_2 fails while processing part p_{27} in this state, the production of both P_3 and P_4 will be blocked by two p_{23}'s at r_4. Note that if we advance a p_{23} from r_4 to r_6, then production of P_4 can proceed. However, production of P_3 will now be blocked. Thus, this state does not satisfy our condition that after the failure of r_2, we should be able to continue producing both P_3 and P_4. As another example, consider the state of Figure 3. Again, we see that this state is safe. However, if r_9 fails while processing part p_{35} in this state, production of part types P_1 and P_2 will be blocked by p_{34} at r_6, although the production of P_4 is unaffected.

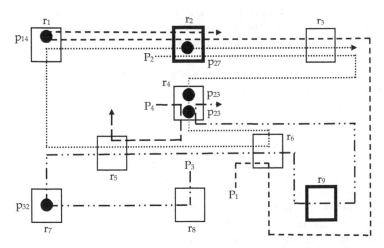

Fig. 2. An undesirable system state since unreliable resource r_2 may fail while processing part p_{27}

Thus, these examples illustrate that parts requiring a failed resource can prevent the system from producing parts not requiring the failed resource through propagation of blocking. Our objective is to develop supervisory controllers that avoid this by guaranteeing that if an unreliable resource fails, it is possible to redistribute the parts requiring that resource so that part types not requiring that resource can continue to produce.

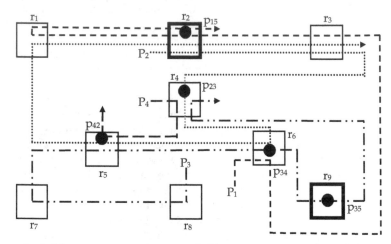

Fig. 3. An undesirable system state since unreliable resource r_9 may fail while processing part p_{35}

For the third objective, consider the state of Figure 4. Again, we see that the state is safe. If r_2 fails, production of P_3 is blocked by p_{11} at r_6. Further, production of P_4 is blocked by p_{33} at r_5. We note that by advancing p_{11} from r_6 to its next required resource, r_3, the blockages of P_3 and P_4 can now be resolved and thus the system can continue producing both P_3 and P_4, as desired. However, when r_2 is repaired, the system is no longer safe since resources r_2 and r_3 are now involved in deadlock. This illustrates that our controller must guarantee that any redistribution of parts requiring the failed resource does not result in system deadlock when the resource is repaired.

The above discussion lays a foundation for a robust supervisory controller. In summary, a supervisory controller is said to be robust to resource failures of R^U if the supervisory controller satisfies Property 2.2.

Property 2.2:

2.2.1:   The supervisory controller ensures continuing production of part types not requiring failed resources, given that additional failures/repairs do not occur.

2.2.2:   The supervisory controller allows only those states that serve as feasible initial states if an additional resource failure occurs.

2.2.3:   The supervisory controller allows only those states that serve as feasible initial states if a failed resource is repaired and becomes operational.

We say that a state is a *feasible initial state* if, starting from that state, it is possible to produce all part types not requiring failed resources. The formal development and definition of this property using language theory is presented in Chew and Lawley (2006).

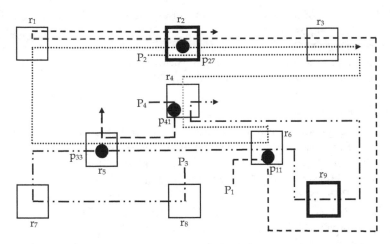

Fig. 4. An undesirable system state since r_2 may fail while processing part p_{27}

3. Robust control for systems with multiple unreliable resources

This section endeavours to delve into robust control for single unit resource allocation systems with unreliable resources.

3.1 Robust control using a neighbourhood policy

This subsection develops controllers that satisfy Property 2.2 above, while maintaining polynomial complexity. Each controller is a conjunction of a modified deadlock avoidance policy and a set of neighbourhood constraints. The deadlock avoidance policy guarantees deadlock-free operation, while the neighbourhood constraints control the distribution of parts that require unreliable resources. Subsection 3.1.1 develops the neighbourhood constraints, NHC. Subsection 3.1.2 constructs a supervisor based on a modified Banker's Algorithm and NHC, while subsection 3.1.3 develops a supervisor based on single-step look-head (SSL) and NHC. The complete proofs can be found in Chew and Lawley (2006).

3.1.1 A neighbourhood policy

In this subsection, we discuss neighbourhood constraints based on the notion of *failure dependency*. Informally, a resource is failure-dependent if every part that enters its buffer space requires some future processing on an unreliable workstation. Thus, all unreliable resources are failure-dependent. Some reliable resources may also be failure-dependent if they only process parts that require future processing on an unreliable resource. This is defined more precisely later. For each failure-dependent resource, we generate a neighbourhood. The neighbourhood of a failure-dependent resource is a virtual space of finite capacity that is used to control the distribution of parts requiring that failure-dependent resource. Again, this is formalized in the following, where we extend the neighbourhood concepts presented by Lawley & Sulistyono (2002) for systems with multiple unreliable resources. We first discuss and illustrate neighbourhood concepts, and then illustrate how neighbourhood constraints are constructed for failure-dependent resources.

Recall that R^U is the set of unreliable resources in the system S, and that $\Omega_i=\{P_{jk}:\rho(P_{jk})=r_i\in R\}$ is the set of part type stages supported by resource r_i. If $r_i\in R^U$, then $r_v\in R$ is said to be *failure-dependent* on r_i if $\forall P_{jk}\in\Omega_v$, $\exists P_{j,k+c}\in\Omega_i$ with $c\geq0$. In other words, r_v is failure-dependent on r_i if every part that enters the buffer of r_v requires future processing on unreliable resource r_i (note that r_i is failure-dependent on itself). For $r_i\in R^U$, let $R_i^{FD} = \{r_v : r_v\in R$ and $\forall P_{jk}\in\Omega_v$, $\exists P_{j,k+c}\in\Omega_i$ with $c\geq0\}$ be the set of failure-dependent resources on r_i, and let $R^{FD} = \bigcup_{r_i\in R^u} R_i^{FD}$ and $R^{NFD} = R \setminus R^{FD}$.

For each failure-dependent resource of R_i^{FD}, we construct a neighbourhood. The neighbourhood of $r_v \in R_i^{FD}$, NH_v^i, is defined as the set of part type stages that require r_v now or later in their processing and have no intervening failure-dependent resources of R_i^{FD}. Formally, $NH_v^i = \Omega_v \cup \{P_{jk}: \exists c>0$ with $P_{j,k+c}\in\Omega_v$ and $\forall d\in[0,c), \rho(P_{j,k+d}) \notin R_i^{FD}\}$. Thus, if $\rho(P_{j,k+c}) = r_v \in R_i^{FD}$, $\rho(P_{j,k-1}) = r_w \in R_i^{FD}$, with $r_v\neq r_w$, and $\{\rho(P_{jk}), \rho(P_{j,k+1})...\rho(P_{j,k+c-1})\} \cap R_i^{FD} = \varnothing$, then $\{P_{jk},P_{j,k+1} ... P_{j,k+c-1},P_{j,k+c}\} \subseteq NH_v^i$, and $P_{j,k-1} \notin NH_v^i$. Let $NH^i = \{NH_v^i : r_v\in R_i^{FD}\}$ be the neighbourhood set for $r_i\in R^U$, and let $NH=\{NH^i : r_i\in R^U\}$.

For example, the system of Figure 1 has two unreliable resources, $R^U=\{r_2,r_9\}$. Note that anytime r_1 appears in a route, r_2 appears later in the route, and thus, $R_2^{FD} = \{r_1,r_2\}$. Also, anytime r_7 or r_8 appear in a route, r_9 appears later in the route, so, $R_9^{FD} = \{r_7,r_8,r_9\}$. Thus, $NH^2 = \{NH_1^2, NH_2^2\}$ and $NH^9 =\{NH_7^9, NH_8^9, NH_9^9\}$, where the neighbourhoods are as follows: $NH_1^2 =\{P_{14},P_{22},P_{23},P_{24},P_{25},P_{26}\}$, $NH_2^2 = \{P_{11},P_{12},P_{13},P_{15},P_{21},P_{27}\}$, $NH_7^9 = \{P_{32}\}$, $NH_8^9 = \{P_{31}\}$, $NH_9^9 = \{P_{33},P_{34},P_{35}\}$.

To understand this construction, consider NH_1^2 and NH_2^2. Note that $\Omega_1= \{P_{14},P_{26}\}$ and $\Omega_2=\{P_{13},P_{15},P_{21},P_{27}\}$. Since $\Omega_v \subseteq NH_v^i$, $\{P_{14},P_{26}\} \subseteq NH_1^2$, and $\{P_{13},P_{15},P_{21},P_{27}\} \subseteq NH_2^2$. Now consider $T_1 = \{\rho(P_{11}),\rho(P_{12}),\rho(P_{13}),\rho(P_{14}),\rho(P_{15})\} = \{r_6,r_3,r_2,r_1,r_2\}$. Since $\{r_6,r_3\} \cap R_2^{FD} = \varnothing$, $\{P_{11},P_{12}\} \subseteq NH_2^2$. Similarly, $T_2 = \{\rho(P_{21}),\rho(P_{22}),\rho(P_{23}),\rho(P_{24}),\rho(P_{25}),\rho(P_{26}),\rho(P_{27}),\rho(P_{28})\} = \{r_2,r_3,r_4,r_6,r_5,r_1,r_2,r_3\}$. Since $\{r_3,r_4,r_6,r_5\} \cap R_2^{FD} = \varnothing$, $\{P_{22},P_{23},P_{24},P_{25}\} \subseteq NH_1^2$. Thus, we get $NH_1^2 = \{P_{14},P_{22},P_{23},P_{24},P_{25},P_{26}\}$ and $NH_2^2 = \{P_{11},P_{12},P_{13},P_{15},P_{21}, P_{27}\}$.

Although all parts supported by r_6 later need an unreliable resource, r_6 is shared by r_2 and r_9, and thus it is not failure-dependent on either. This implies that failure-dependent sets are disjoint, i.e., $R_2^{FD} \cap R_9^{FD} = \varnothing$. Furthermore, we observe that no part stage is in more than one neighbourhood, i.e., $NH_1^2 \cap NH_2^2 \cap NH_7^9 \cap NH_8^9 \cap NH_9^9 = \varnothing$. These and other important neighbourhood properties are established in Chew and Lawley (2006).

We restrict the number of parts allowed in a neighbourhood. Our intention is to guarantee that every part in the neighbourhood of a failure-dependent resource has capacity reserved at that resource. That is, we want to be able to advance every part requiring an unreliable resource into its associated failure-dependent resource in the event of a resource failure so that it will not block production of parts not requiring the failed resource. In the example, for a permissible state, we want, for example, every part in $NH_9^9 = \{P_{33},P_{34},P_{35}\}$ to have a reserved unit of buffer at r_9. As a consequence, we will reject a state if this constraint is violated. For instance, a state is not admissible if, at this state, the sum of parts in $NH_9^9 > 1$; recall that r_9 has a single unit of capacity. To see this, at this inadmissible state, if r_9 fails, at least one part of NH_9^9 must reside at r_5 or r_6. Although P_1, P_2, and P_4 do not require failed r_9 in their processing, this distribution of parts may in turn block production of some of these part types. Our objective is to develop supervisory controllers capable of rejecting these undesirable states.

We now construct neighbourhood constraints to enforce the above intention. The constraint for a neighbourhood, say NH_v^i, is an inequality of the form $Z_v^i \leq C_v$ where $Z_v^i = \sum_{P_{jk} \in NH_v^i} (x_{jk} + y_{jk})$. Recall that x_{jk} is the number of finished instances, and y_{jk} is the number of unfinished instances, of P_{jk} located in the buffer of $\rho(P_{jk})$; and that the right hand side C_v is the capacity of r_v. NH_v^i is said to be *capacitated* if $Z_v^i = C_v$ and *over-capacitated* if $Z_v^i > C_v$. Define the set of all possible neighbourhood constraints with respect to $r_i \in R^U$ as:

$$NHC_1^i = \{ Z_v^i \leq C_v : NH_v^i \in NH^i \}.$$

In the example, we have

$$NHC_1^1 = \{ Z_1^1 = \sum_{P_{jk} \in NH_1^1} (x_{jk} + y_{jk}) \leq C_1, \ Z_2^1 = \sum_{P_{jk} \in NH_2^1} (x_{jk} + y_{jk}) \leq C_2 \};$$

$$NHC_1^9 = \{ Z_7^9 = \sum_{P_{jk} \in NH_7^9} (x_{jk} + y_{jk}) \leq C_7, \ Z_8^9 = \sum_{P_{jk} \in NH_8^9} (x_{jk} + y_{jk}) \leq C_8,$$

$$Z_9^9 = \sum_{P_{jk} \in NH_9^9} (x_{jk} + y_{jk}) \leq C_9 \}.$$

Constraints of NHC_1^i assure that no neighbourhood of NH^i becomes over-capacitated. As Lawley & Sulistyono (2002) discuss, NHC_1^i may induce deadlock among failure-dependent resources of R_i^{FD}, since if all neighbourhoods are capacitated, parts cannot move from one neighbourhood to another without over-capacitating a neighbourhood. In the example, a state may satisfy both 1= $Z_1^1 \leq C_1 = 1$ and 1= $Z_2^1 \leq C_2 = 1$. But, a part moves from one of these associated neighbourhoods to another must over-capacitate the other neighbourhood. To resolve this dilemma, we develop an additional set of constraints, NHC_2^i.

It is first necessary to compute the set of strongly connected neighbourhoods for NHC_2^i. To do this, for each $r_i \in R^U$, we construct a directed graph (NH^i, A^i) where $A^i = \{(NH_g^i, NH_h^i) : \exists P_{jk} \in NH_g^i$ with $P_{j,k+1} \in NH_h^i \}$. Thus, in operation, there will be part flow from NH_g^i to NH_h^i. We then compute the set of strong components of (NH^i, A^i) using standard polynomial graph algorithms (Cormen et at., 2002). For example, we see that NH_1^1 and NH_2^1 are strongly connected, since $\{P_{14}, P_{26}\} \subseteq NH_1^1$ and $\{P_{13}, P_{27}\} \subseteq NH_2^1$. Therefore, in operation, there is flow from NH_1^1 to NH_2^1 and from NH_2^1 to NH_1^1. Let SC^i be the set of strongly connected components of (NH^i, A^i). Then, $SC^2 = \{SC_1^2 = \{NH_1^1, NH_2^1\}\}$, and $SC^9 = \{SC_1^9 = \{NH_7^9\}, SC_2^9 = \{NH_8^9\}, SC_3^9 = \{NH_9^9\}\}$. Then, NHC_2^i is stated as follows:

$$NHC_2^i = \{ Z_g^i + Z_h^i < C_g + C_h : \{NH_g^i, NH_h^i\} \subseteq SC_m^i \in SC^i, \ m=1 \ldots |SC^i| \}.$$

Hence, for every strongly connected component of (NH^i, A^i), NHC_2^i guarantees that at most one neighbourhood can be capacitated at a time. In the example, we have the following:

$$NHC^2 = \{ Z_1^1 + Z_2^1 < C_1 + C_2 \}, \ NHC_3^2 = \varnothing.$$

NHC^2 guarantees that NH_1^2 and NH_2^2 are not simultaneously capacitated.

To summarize, $NHC^i = NHC_1^i \cup NHC_2^i$ guarantees that no neighbourhood is over capacitated, and that neighbourhoods with mutual flow dependencies are not simultaneously capacitated. The complete set of neighbourhood constraints is defined as:

$$NHC = \{ NHC^i : r_i \in R^U \}.$$

Note that in the worst case, we generate one constraint for each pair of resources and thus the size of NHC is of $O(|R|^2)$.

Chew and Lawley (2006) establish several important properties of NHC. These properties are required to establish robustness of the two supervisors that we develop later. We next modify two deadlock avoidance policies that we use in conjunction with NHC to develop robust supervisors.

3.1.2 Banker's algorithm

In this subsection, we configure Banker's Algorithm (BA) (Habermann, 1969) to work with NHC. BA is perhaps the most widely known deadlock avoidance policy (DAP), and its underlying concepts have influenced the thinking of numerous researchers. BA is a suboptimal DAP in the sense that it achieves computational tractability by sacrificing some safe states. BA avoids deadlock by allowing an allocation only if the requesting processes can be ordered so that the terminal resource needs for the ith process, P_i, in the ordering can be met by pooling available resources and those released by completed processes $P_1, P_2 \ldots$ P_{i-1}. The ordering is essentially a sequence in which all processes in the system can complete successfully. BA is of $O(mn\log n)$ where m is the number of resource types and n is the number of requests. Other manufacturing related work also uses BA (Ezpeleta et al., 2002; Lawley et al., 1998; Reveliotis, 2000).

Our modifications are straightforward and are a generalization of those undertaken by Lawley & Sulistyono (2002). Our objective is to search for an ordering of parts that advances failure-dependent parts (those requiring unreliable resources) into the resource of their current neighbourhood, and non-failure-dependent parts (those not requiring unreliable resources) out of the system. Again, the ordering is such that the resources required by the first part are all available, those required by the second part are all available after the first part has finished and released the resources held by the part, and so forth. If the system can be cleared in this way (all failure-dependent parts are advanced into failure-dependent resources and all non-failure-dependent parts are advanced out of the system), then we can guarantee that if any unreliable resource fails, the system can continue producing parts that do not require this failed resource.

In the following, let $\Lambda = \Lambda^{NFD} \cup \Lambda^{FD}$ be the set of part type stages instantiated in q *whose parts hold non-failure-dependent resources*, where Λ^{NFD} is the set of non-failure-dependent part type stages (those that do not require failure-dependent resources in the residual route) and Λ^{FD} is the set of failure-dependent part type stages (those that do require failure-dependent resources in the residual route). We now present our modified version of BA as Algorithm A1 as follows.

Algorithm A1:

Query: Is state q admissible?
Input: state q;
Output: ACCEPT / REJECT
Step 1: Initialization
For P(u)
  For r_v R
    ALLOCATION[u][v]=0
    NEED[u][v]=0
    AVAILABLE[v]=C_V
  End For
End For
For P(u)=P_{jk} and r_v = (P_{jk})
  ALLOCATION[u][v]=x_{jk}+y_{jk}
End For
For P(u)=P_{jk} NFD
  For r_v RT_{jk}\{ (P_{jk})}
    NEED[u][v]=1
  End For
End For
For P(u)=P_{jk} FD
  For r_v RT_{jk}
    NEED[u][v]=1
  End For
  For r_v RT_{jk} R^{FD}
    NEED[u][v]=0
  End For
  For r_s= (P_{jc}) and r_t= $(P_{j,c+1})$, c=k....$|P_j|$ 1

NEED[u][t]=NEED[u][s]*NEED[u][t]

End For
For r_v RT_{jk}
  If r_v= (P_{jk})
    NEED[u][v]=0
  End If
End For
End For
For r_v R^{NFD}
  AVAILABLE[v]=C_V $_u$ALLOCATION[u][v]
End For
=

Step 2: Test and Evaluation
While
  Find   P(u)   such   that NEED[u][v] AVAILABLE[v] for all r_v R^{NFD}
  If no such P(u) exists
    Return REJECT
  Else
    = \{P(u)}

    AVAILABLE[v]=AVAILABLE[v]+ALLOCATION[u][v] for r_v= $(P(u))$
  End If
End While
Return ACCEPT

Step 1 of the algorithm configures the data structures required. For every part type stage represented in the system, these capture the current resource holding and the future processing need. These structures also capture the resource availability of resources in the state being tested. Three additional comments regarding the algorithm are in order. First, the need for every failure-dependent resource is explicitly set to zero, so this version looks only at the availability of non-failure-dependent resources. Second, for non-failure-dependent part type stages (those not requiring unreliable resources), the need for every resource in the residual route (except the one held) is set to one. Finally, for failure-dependent part type stages (those requiring unreliable resources), the need for every resource in the residual route (except the one held) up to the one immediately preceding the first encountered failure-dependent resource is set to one, all others are set to zero. Note that these are the resources such a part will need to advance into the failure-dependent resource of its current neighbourhood. Step 2 then executes the usual Banker's logic.

Algorithm A1 is not correct by itself, since it does not handle allocation of failure-dependent resources (for detailed examples the reader is referred to the work by Lawley & Sulistyono

(2002)). However, A1 and NHC together form a robust controller, that is, if we allow the system to visit only those states acceptable to both A1 and NHC, then the system operation will satisfy the requirements of Property 2.2. The detailed proofs for this are given in Chew and Lawley (2006). The supervisor is defined as follows:

Definition 3.1.1: Supervisor Δ_1 = A1 $\wedge$ NHC.

Supervisor Δ_1 permits a system state that satisfies both A1 and NHC in runtime. Consider Figure 5, which illustrates a state, say q, in which r_4 holds p_{23} and p_{14}; and r_5 holds p_{33}. It is clear, at q, that there exists an admissible sequence by A1; that is, p_{33} can advance into failure-dependent resource r_9; p_{23} can advance into failure-dependent resource r_1; and finally, p_{41} can be advanced out of the system. In addition, q satisfies NHC since

$$\text{NHC}_1^2 = \{\ Z_1^4 = 1 \le 1, \text{(there is one } P_{23}) \quad Z_2^4 = 0 \le 1\};$$

$$\text{NHC}_1^9 = \{\ Z_7^9 = 0 \le 1, \quad Z_8^9 = 0 \le 1, \quad Z_9^9 = 1 \le 1 \text{ (there is one } P_{33})\};$$

$$\text{NHC}^2 = \{1 + 0 < 1 + 1 = 2\}; \ \text{NHC}^9 = \varnothing.$$

Therefore, q is an admissible state by Δ_1. Supervisor Δ_1 will prohibit, at q, advancing p_{23} into r_6 (where it becomes p_{24}) because p_{24} and p_{33} will block, causing the resulting state to violate A1 although not NHC. Loading a p_{11} into r_6 at q is also precluded by Δ_1 since the resulting state violates NHC^2 , although not A1. However, advancing p_{33} one step into r_6 or loading a p_{31} into r_8 will result in an admissible state.

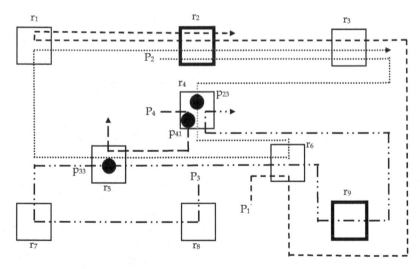

Fig. 5. An admissible system state by supervisor Δ_1

Supervisor Δ_1 is of polynomial complexity since both A1 and NHC require polynomial time for runtime implementation. Chew and Lawley (2006) formally establish that Δ_1 yields a robust supervisor for systems where every part type requires in its route at most one unreliable resource.

3.1.3 A Single step look ahead policy

It is well known that certain system structures, such as a central buffer, input/output bins, and non-unit buffer capacities, eliminate the possibility of deadlock-free unsafe states (Lawley & Reveliotis, 2001). In these systems, every state is either deadlock or safe, and therefore, a single-step look-ahead policy (SSL) is a correct and optimal deadlock avoidance policy. Further, it is of polynomial complexity, and thus ideal for runtime applications in real systems. In the following, we will modify the SSL presented by Lawley (1999) so that it works with systems with multiple unreliable resources.

A resource allocation graph (RAG) is a digraph that encodes the resource requests and allocations of parts (Lawley, 1999). For our purposes, let RAG=$(R\backslash R^{FD},E)$ where $R\backslash R^{FD}$ is the set of system non-failure-dependent resource types and E=$\{(r_u,r_v): r_u,r_v \in R\backslash R^{FD}$ and r_u is holding a part p_{jk} with $\rho(p_{j,k+1})=r_v\}$. A subdigraph of RAG, say (R,E), is *induced* when R $\subseteq R\backslash R^{FD}$ and E =$\{(r_u,r_v):(r_u,r_v) \in E$ and $r_u,r_v \in R\}$. A subdigraph, (R,E), forms a *knot* in RAG if $\forall r_u \in R$, $\Gamma(r_u)= R$, where $\Gamma(r_u)$ is the set of all nodes reachable from r_u in RAG. In other words, a set of nodes, R, forms a knot in RAG when, for every node in R, the set of nodes reachable along arcs in RAG is exactly R. Further, we define a *capacitated knot* to be a knot in which every resource in the knot is filled to capacity with parts requesting other resources in the knot. It is commonly known that a capacitated knot in RAG is a necessary and sufficient condition for deadlock in these types of sequential resource allocation systems. We now provide an algorithm, Algorithm A2, below to detect a capacitated knot in RAG = $(R\backslash R^{FD},E)$. This algorithm has the same polynomial complexity as that given by Lawley (1999).

Algorithm A2:

Input: RAG=$(R\backslash R^{FD},E)$

Output: DEADLOCK, NO DEADLOCK

Step 1: Compute the set of strongly connected components of RAG: C=$\{C_1...C_q\}$

Step 2: Construct digraph (C,E_c) such that C=$\{C_1...C_q\}$ and $E_c=\{(C_i,C_j):(r_u,r_v) \in E$ with $r_u \in C_i$ and $r_v \in C_j$ for $i \neq j\}$

Step 3: For every strongly connected component $C_i \in C$ such that $(C_i,C_j) \notin E_c$ $\forall j=1...q$

        If C_i is a capacitated knot

           Return DEADLOCK

        End If

    End For

Step 4: Return NO DEADLOCK

We note that, for our present work, this version of deadlock detection algorithm operates only on non-failure-dependent resources and parts held by these resources. In A2, Step 1 computes the set of strongly connected components in RAG. As mentioned earlier, this is a standard digraph operation. Step 2 constructs a digraph that defines the reachability relationship between these components. Step 3 looks for a component with no outgoing arc. If such a component is filled to capacity with parts requesting other resources in the component, then it is a capacitated knot, and deadlock exists. If no such capacitated knot exists then the RAG is deadlock-free.

Note that A2 is not correct by itself since it considers only the non-failure-dependent resources. Failure-dependent resources can easily deadlock themselves. However, when A2 is taken in conjunction with NHC, it guarantees Property 2.2 and thus assures that the system will continue to operate even when multiple unreliable resources are down.

Definition 3.1.2: Supervisor Δ_2 = A2 $\wedge$ NHC.

Supervisor Δ_2 accepts a system state that contains no deadlock and satisfies NHC. For example, in Figure 1, suppose that every non-failure-dependent resource has non-unit capacity; that is, $C_i>1$, $\forall r_i \in R \backslash R^{FD}= \{r_3,r_4,r_5,r_6\}$. Then, A2 permits any state in which no subset of parts residing on $\{r_3,r_4,r_5,r_6\}$ is deadlocked on $\{r_3,r_4,r_5,r_6\}$. If the state also satisfies NHC, then Property 2.2 is guaranteed.

Note that Δ_2 = A2 $\wedge$ NHC is suited for real-time implementation since both A2 and NHC are of polynomial complexity. Chew and Lawley (2006) formally establishes that Δ_2 yields a robust supervisor for systems where every part type requires in its route at most one unreliable resource.

3.2 Robust control using a resource order policy

This subsection configures a deadlock avoidance policy, resource order policy (RO). We will employ this configured resource order policy in conjunction with the neighbourhood constraints of Subsection 3.1 to develop a robust controller. Consider, for configuration purposes, Figure 1. Define RCO = $R \backslash R^{FD}_i$ as the set of non-failure-dependent resources. Since $R^{FD}_2 = \{r_1,r_2\}$ and $R^{FD}_9 = \{r_7,r_8,r_9\}$, thus RCO = $\{r_3,r_4,r_5,r_6\}$. Let ω : RCO $\rightarrow \aleph$ (the set of natural numbers) be a one to one mapping of non-failure-dependent resources (ω orders the non-failure-dependent resources so that RO can be applied); $P^{FD}=\{P_j: \rho(P_{jk}) \in R^U$ for some k$\}$ (P^{FD} is the set of part types requiring unreliable resources; thus, in Figure 1, $P^{FD} = \{P_1,P_2,P_3\}$); and $P^{NFD}=P \backslash P^{FD}$ (P^{NFD} is the set of part types not requiring any unreliable resources; hence, in Figure 1, $P^{NFD} = \{P_4\}$). For each $P_j \in P^{FD}$, determine all maximal subsequences in the route of P_j that do not contain failure-dependent resources. For instance, in Figure 1, $P_3 \in P^{FD}$ where $P_3=\langle P_{31}, P_{32}, P_{33}, P_{34}, P_{35}, P_{36}\rangle$ with route $\langle r_8,r_7,r_5,r_6,r_9,r_4\rangle$, the maximal subsequences in $\langle r_8,r_7,r_5,r_6,r_9,r_4\rangle$ that do not contain failure-dependent resources are $\langle r_5,r_6\rangle$ and $\langle r_4\rangle$.

To express this formally, for each $P_j \in P^{FD}$, break the route of P_j into subroutes as follows: for $P_j=\langle P_{j1} \dots P_{j,k_1-1},P_{jk_1},P_{j,k_1+1} \dots P_{j,k_2-1},P_{jk_2},P_{j,k_2+1} \dots P_{j,k_{hj}-1},P_{jk_{hj}},P_{j,k_{hj}+1} \dots\rangle$, $\{P_{jk_1},P_{jk_2} \dots P_{jk_{hj}}\}$ being precisely the set of part type stages of P_j that is processed on failure-dependent resources (that is, $\{\rho(P_{jk}) : k=k_1,k_2 \dots k_{hj}\} \subseteq R^{FD}$ and $\{\rho(P_{jk}) : k\neq k_1,k_2 \dots k_{hj}\} \cap R^{FD} = \varnothing)$, let $P^1_j =\langle P_{j1} \dots P_{j,k_1-1}\rangle$, $P^2_j = \langle P_{j,k_1+1} \dots P_{j,k_2-1}\rangle$, $P^3_j = \langle P_{j,k_2+1} \dots P_{j,k_3-1}\rangle,\dots,$ $P^{hj}_j = \langle P_{j,k_{(hj-1)}+1} \dots P_{j,(k_{hj}-1)}\rangle$ and $P^{hj+1}_j = \langle P_{j,(k_{hj}+1)} \dots P_{j|P_j|}\rangle$. For each $P_j \in P^{NFD}$, rename P_j P^0_j. Finally, let $P' = \{P^0_j : P_j \in P^{NFD}\} \cup \{P^k_j : k =1 \dots h_j$ and $P_j \in P^{FD}\}$. Note that in P', a part type $P_j \in P^{FD}$ is replaced by a set of part types $\{P^1_j, P^2_j \dots P^{hj}_j\}$ each having a route that is a maximal segment of the route of P_j not containing a failure-dependent resource.

In Figure 1, for example, P_3 is replaced by $P^3_3 = \langle P_{33},P_{34}\rangle$ with route $\langle r_5,r_6\rangle$ and $P^3_3=\langle P_{36}\rangle$ with route $\langle r_4\rangle$, and P_4 is renamed P^0_4. Thus, the revised set of part types is $P'=\{P^0_4\} \cup \{P^1_1, P^1_2, P^2_2, P^3_3, P^3_3\}$. Note that none of the routes of part types in P' contains any failure-dependent resources.

We now use P' and RCO to construct a set of RO constraints as follows. For each $P^i_j = \langle P_{j,k_{(i-1)}+1} \dots P_{j,(k_i-1)}\rangle \in P'$ and for each $P_{jk} \in P^i_j$, consider the inclusive remaining route, $\langle \rho(P_{jk}) \dots \rho(P_{j,(k_i-1)})\rangle$, and its mapping, $\langle \omega(\rho(P_{jk})) \dots \omega(\rho(P_{j,(k_i-1)}))\rangle$. (Recall that to implement RO, the resources must be ordered. ω represents the ordering function.) If the mapping of the inclusive remaining route is strictly increasing (decreasing), then P_{jk} is classified as 'right' ('left'); if the mapping of the inclusive remaining route switches direction at some point, then P_{jk} is classified as 'undirected.' If P_{jk} is terminal, it is ignored. For $r_m \in RCO$, let Π_m^{RU} represent the set of right and undirected part type stages associated with r_m; and Π_m^{LU}, the set of left and undirected part type stages associated with r_m. In the example, consider that $\omega(r_1)=1$, $\omega(r_2)=2$, $\omega(r_3)=3$ $\omega(r_4)=4$, $\omega(r_5)=5$, $\omega(r_6)=6$, $\omega(r_7)=7$, $\omega(r_8)=8$ and $\omega(r_9)=9$. We now have that the inclusive remaining route of P_{33}, $\langle r_5, r_6 \rangle$ supporting $\langle P_{33}, P_{34} \rangle \subseteq P_3^1$, is strictly increasing for ω, thus P_{33} is classified as 'right' and hence $\Pi_5^{RU} = \{P_{33}\}$. In the meantime, since $P_{25} \in P_2^1$ is the terminal part type stage for P_2^1, P_{25} is ignored. Clearly, $\Pi_5^{RU} = \varnothing$. On the other hand, the inclusive remaining route of P_{11}, $\langle r_6, r_3 \rangle$ supporting $\langle P_{11}, P_{12} \rangle \subseteq P_1^1$, is strictly decreasing for ω, hence P_{11} is classified as 'left.' The inclusive remaining route of P_{24} is $\langle r_6, r_5 \rangle$ supporting $\langle P_{24}, P_{25} \rangle \subseteq P_2^1$, which is strictly decreasing for ω, hence P_{24} is classified as 'left.' Therefore, $\Pi_6^{LU} = \{P_{11}, P_{24}\}$. Meanwhile, since $P_{34} \in P_3^1$ is the terminal part type stage for P_3^1, P_{34} is ignored. It is obvious that $\Pi_6^{LU} = \varnothing$. After all the part type stages are classified in this way, a constraint is generated for each pair of non-failure-dependent resources, yielding RO constraints. We now define RO constraints formally as follows.

Definition 3.2.1: RO^{RCO} is the set of constraints:

$$\forall r_m, r_n \in RCO \text{ such that } \omega(r_m) < \omega(r_n), \sum_{P_{jk} \in \Pi_m^{RU}} (x_{jk} + y_{jk}) + \sum_{P_{jk} \in \Pi_n^{LU}} (x_{jk} + y_{jk}) < C_m + C_n$$

where C_m and C_n are the respective buffer capacities of r_m and r_n.

In the example, for r_5, $r_6 \in RCO$, we have $(x_{33} + y_{33}) + (x_{11} + y_{11} + x_{24} + y_{24}) < 2$, recalling that $C_5 = C_6 = 1$. This constraint assures that for every resource allocation state that the system is allowed to visit, the number of 'right' and 'undirected' parts occupying buffer space at r_5 plus the number of 'left' and 'undirected' parts occupying buffer space at r_6 will be less than the combined capacity of the two resources. Similar constraints are generated for the resource pairs $\{r_3, r_4\}$, $\{r_3, r_5\}$, $\{r_3, r_6\}$, $\{r_4, r_5\}$ and $\{r_4, r_6\}$.

We are now in the position to establish that the conjunction of RO^{RCO} and NHC, call it supervisor Δ_3, satisfies Property 2.2. Supervisor Δ_3 is a control policy such that it disables $\alpha_{jk} \in \xi(q)$ if $\delta(q, \alpha_{jk})$ violates either RO^{RCO} or NHC. Formally, it is stated as follows.

Definition 3.2.2: Supervisor $\Delta_3 = RO^{RCO} \wedge NHC$.

Chew et al. (2011) establish that Δ_3 is a robust controller for systems where every part type requires at most one unreliable resource.

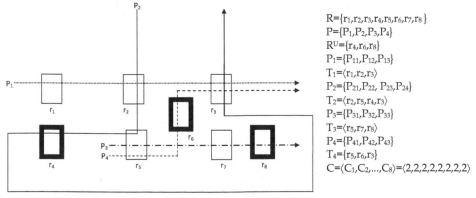

Fig. 6. An example production system with three unreliable resources

3.3 Robust control using shared resource capacity

The robust supervisory control policies presented in sections 3.1-3.2 assume that that parts requiring failed resources can be advanced into FD buffer. We refer this type of control policies as "absorbing" policies. This subsection relaxes this assumption because, in some systems, providing FD buffer space might be too expensive or it might be desirable to load the system more heavily with FD parts. A "distributing" type of control policy is developed and presented in this subsection. This policy distributes parts requiring failed resources throughout the buffer space of shared resources so that these distributed parts do not block the production of part types that are not requiring failed resources.

Now, the development of the "distributing" control policy, namely, RO⁴ policy is discussed in details. First, based on the definitions of resource sets in the previous sections, we further define three resource regions: (1) the region of continuous operation, $RCO = R^{PFD} \cup R^{NFD}$, (2) the region of failure dependency, $RFD = R^{FD}$, and (3) the region of distribution, $ROD = RFD \setminus R^U = R^{FD} \setminus R^U = R^R \setminus R^{NFD}$. In the example system in Figure 6, we have $RCO = \{r_1, r_2, r_3\}$; $RFD = \{r_2, r_4, r_5, r_6, r_7, r_8\}$; $ROD = \{r_2, r_5, r_7\}$. RO⁴ policy is the conjunction of four modified RO policies applied to different resource regions. We now define the RO constraints as follows.

Definition 3.3.1: RO^{RCO} is the set of constraints:

$$\sum_{P_{jk} \in \Omega_g} z_{jk} + \sum_{P_{uv} \in \Omega_h} z_{uv} < C_g + C_h$$

$$where \quad z_{st} = x_{st} + y_{st}, \quad r_g, r_h \in RCO \ and \ g \neq h.$$

RO^{RCO} admits states that exhibit at most one capacitated resource in RCO.

Definition 3.3.2: RO^{RFD} is the set of constraints

$$\sum_{P_{jk} \in \Omega_g \cap P_i^{FD}} z_{jk} + \sum_{P_{uv} \in \Omega_h \cap P_i^{FD}} z_{uv} < C_g + C_h \quad for \quad r_i \in R^U$$

$$where \quad z_{st} = x_{st} + y_{st}, \quad r_g, r_h \in RFD, \quad and \quad g \neq h.$$

RO^{RFD} admits states for which at most one resource of RFD is capacitated with P_i^{FD} parts for each $r_i \in R^U$. Note that it does not place any constraint on the total number of RFD resources capacitated.

Definition 3.3.3: RO^{RFD^2} is the set of constraints

$$\sum_{P_{jk} \in \Omega_g \cap P^{FD}} z_{jk} + \sum_{P_{mn} \in \Omega_h \cap P^{FD}} z_{mn} + \sum_{P_{uv} \in \Omega_j \cap P^{FD}} z_{uv} < C_g + C_h + C_j$$

$$where \quad z_{st} = x_{st} + y_{st}, \quad r_g, r_h, r_j \in RFD \ and \ g \neq h \neq j.$$

RO^{RFD^2} admits states for which at most two resources of RFD are capacitated with FD parts, but does not place any constraint on the total number of RFD resources capacitated.

Definition 3.3.4: RO^{ROD} is the set of constraints

$$\sum_{P_{jk} \in \Omega_g \cap P^{FD}} z_{jk} + \sum_{P_{uv} \in \Omega_h \cap P^{FD}} z_{uv} < C_g + C_h$$

$$where \quad z_{st} = x_{st} + y_{st}, \quad r_g, r_h \in ROD \ and \ g \neq h.$$

RO^{ROD} admits states for which at most one resource of $ROD=RFD \backslash R^U$ is capacitated with FD parts, although it places no constraint on the number of unreliable resources that are capacitated.

As in the example system in Figure 6, the set of constrains are as follows.

RO^{RCO}

r_1r_2:	$z_{11}+z_{12}+z_{21}<4$	r_2r_3:	$z_{12}+z_{21}+z_{13}+z_{24}+z_{43}<4$
r_1r_3:	$z_{11}+z_{13}+z_{24}+z_{43}<4$		

RO^{RFD}

r_2r_4:	$z_{21}+z_{23}<4$	r_5r_7:	$z_{31}+z_{32}<4$
r_2r_5:	$z_{21}+z_{22}<4$	r_5r_8:	$z_{31}+z_{33}<4$
r_4r_5:	$z_{23}+z_{22}<4$	r_7r_8:	$z_{32}+z_{33}<4$
r_5r_6:	$z_{41}+z_{42}<4$		

RO^{RFD^2}

$r_2r_4r_5$:	$z_{21}+z_{23}+z_{22}+z_{31}+z_{41}<6$	$r_4r_5r_6$:	$z_{23}+z_{22}+z_{31}+z_{41}+z_{42}<6$
$r_2r_4r_6$:	$z_{21}+z_{23}+z_{42}<6$	$r_4r_5r_7$:	$z_{23}+z_{22}+z_{31}+z_{41}+z_{32}<6$
$r_2r_4r_7$:	$z_{21}+z_{23}+z_{32}<6$	$r_4r_5r_8$:	$z_{23}+z_{22}+z_{31}+z_{41}+z_{33}<6$
$r_2r_4r_8$:	$z_{21}+z_{23}+z_{33}<6$	$r_4r_6r_7$:	$z_{23}+z_{42}+z_{32}<6$
$r_2r_5r_6$:	$z_{21}+z_{22}+z_{31}+z_{41}+z_{42}<6$	$r_4r_6r_8$:	$z_{23}+z_{42}+z_{33}<6$
$r_2r_5r_7$:	$z_{21}+z_{22}+z_{31}+z_{41}+z_{32}<6$	$r_4r_7r_8$:	$z_{23}+z_{32}+z_{33}<6$
$r_2r_5r_8$:	$z_{21}+z_{22}+z_{31}+z_{41}+z_{33}<6$	$r_5r_6r_7$:	$z_{22}+z_{31}+z_{41}+z_{42}+z_{32}<6$
$r_2r_6r_7$:	$z_{21}+z_{42}+z_{32}<6$	$r_5r_6r_8$:	$z_{22}+z_{31}+z_{41}+z_{42}+z_{33}<6$
$r_2r_6r_8$:	$z_{21}+z_{42}+z_{33}<6$	$r_5r_7r_8$:	$z_{22}+z_{31}+z_{41}+z_{32}+z_{33}<6$
$r_2r_7r_8$:	$z_{21}+z_{32}+z_{33}<6$	$r_6r_7r_8$:	$z_{42}+z_{32}+z_{33}<6$

RO^{ROD}

r_2r_5:	$z_{21}+z_{22}+z_{31}+z_{41}<4$ r_5r_7: $z_{22}+z_{31}+z_{41}+z_{32}<4$
r_2r_7:	$z_{21}+z_{32}<4$

We are now in the position to establish that RO^4 policy (the conjunction of RO^{RCO}, RO^{RFD}, RO^{RFD^2}, and RO^{ROD}), call it supervisor Δ_4, satisfies Property 2.2. Supervisor Δ_4 is a control policy such that it admits the enabled controllable event α if and only if $\delta(q,a)$ satisfies $RO^{RCO} \wedge RO^{RFD} \wedge RO^{RFD^2} \wedge RO^{ROD}$. Formally, it is stated as follows.

Definition 3.3.5: Supervisor $\Delta_4 = RO^{RCO} \wedge RO^{RFD} \wedge RO^{RFD^2} \wedge RO^{ROD}$.

The intuition behind this control policy is that it ensures that if a shared resource (i.e., a PFD resource) is filled with FD parts, at least one can be advanced out of the shared resources and, thus, out of RCO, which can then operate under RORCO. Furthermore, clearing RCO of this part will not create problems in the FD resources. To summarize, RO^{RFD} allows states with at most one FD resource filled with parts that are FD on the same unreliable resource. RO^{RFD2} allows states for which at most two FD resources are capacitated with FD parts. RO^{ROD} admits states for which at most one resource of ROD is capacitated with FD parts. Wang et al. (2008) establish that Δ_4 is a robust controller for systems where every part type requires at most one unreliable resource.

4. Robust control for product routings with multiple unreliable resources

In Section 3, we develop robust controllers for the single unit resource allocation systems with multiple unreliable resources. These guarantee that if any subset of resources fails, parts in the system requiring failed resources do not block production of parts not requiring failed resources. To establish supervisor correctness, we assume that each part type requires at most one unreliable resource in its route. We now relax this assumption using a central buffer and present robust controllers that guarantee robust operation without assumptions on route structure. To this end, we will construct new robust controllers in conjunction with the robust controllers, Δ_1 and Δ_2, developed in Subsection 3.1. The following three subsections will demonstrate the way we use a central buffer to extend Δ_1 and Δ_2 for systems where parts may require multiple unreliable resources.

4.1 Route partitioning algorithm

We now show how to use a central buffer to extend Δ_1 and Δ_2 for systems where parts may require multiple unreliable resources. We partition routes with multiple unreliable resources into subroutes, each of which contains one unreliable resource. A part in the last stage of a subroute can move to the first resource of the succeeding subroute or into the central buffer. With this partition, the system resembles one with at most one unreliable resource per route, allowing us to apply Δ_1 and Δ_2.

The route partitioning algorithm (RPA) performs this operation. It starts with the last stage and builds the subroute backwards. A subroute is extended until two unique unreliable resources are detected. Then, a new subroute is begun. We demonstrate below on P_1 of Figure 7.

Route Partitioning Algorithm (RPA)

Algorithm Notation: j, q, u are indices and counters; ε is the empty list; Ψ is a temporary set.
for j=1... $|P|$
    let u= $|P_j|$, q=1, $SP_{j1}=\varepsilon$, $\Psi=\varnothing$
    while u≠0
        (a) if $\rho(P_{ju})\in R^U\backslash\Psi$, $\Psi=\Psi\cup\{\rho(P_{ju})\}$
            (b) if $|\Psi|<2$, $SP_{jq}=push(P_{ju},SP_{jq})$, u=u–1
            (Note: The function 'push' takes two parameters, an object and an ordered list of objects, and inserts the object into the head of the list.)
        (c) else $\Psi=\varnothing$, q=q+1, $SP_{jq}=\varepsilon$
    end while
    NS_j = q *(Number of Segments for P_j)*

For j=1, u= $|P_1|$=8, q=1, $SP_{11}=\varepsilon$, $\Psi=\varnothing$. Then, $\rho(P_{18})=r_1\notin R^U\backslash\Psi$ ={r_2,r_4,r_5,r_7}, execute (b): $SP_{11}=\langle P_{18}\rangle$, u = 7.

Next, $\rho(P_{17})=r_7\in R^U\backslash\Psi=\{r_2,r_4,r_5,r_7\}$, execute first if: $\Psi=\Psi\cup\{r_7\}=\{r_7\}$. Since $|\Psi|<2$, execute (b) $SP_{11}=\langle P_{17},P_{18}\rangle$, u=6.

Next, $\rho(P_{16})=r_6\notin R^U\backslash\Psi=\{r_2,r_4,r_5\}$, execute (b): $SP_{11}=\langle P_{16},P_{17},P_{18}\rangle$ and u=5.

Next, $\rho(P_{15})=r_5\in R^U\backslash\Psi=\{r_2,r_4,r_5\}$, execute (a): $\Psi=\Psi\cup\{r_5\}=\{r_5,r_7\}$. Since $|\Psi|=2$, execute (c): $\Psi=\varnothing$, q=2, $SP_{12}=\varepsilon$. This completes the first subroute $SP_{11}=\langle P_{16},P_{17},P_{18}\rangle$.

Next, u=5, $\rho(P_{15})=r_5\in R^U\backslash\Psi=\{r_2,r_4,r_5,r_7\}$, execute (a): $\Psi=\Psi\cup\{r_5\}=\{r_5\}$. Since $|\Psi|<2$, execute (b): $SP_{12}=\langle P_{15}\rangle$, u = 4.

Next, $\rho(P_{14})=r_4\in R^U\backslash\Psi=\{r_2,r_4,r_7\}$, execute (a): $\Psi=\Psi\cup\{r_4\}=\{r_4,r_5\}$. Since $|\Psi|=2$, execute (c): $\Psi=\varnothing$, q=3, $SP_{13}=\varepsilon$. This completes the second subroute $SP_{12}=\langle P_{15}\rangle$.

Continuing as shown, RPA partitions P_1 into four subpart types (the remaining two are $SP_{13}=\langle P_{13},P_{14}\rangle$ and $SP_{14}=\langle P_{11}, P_{12}\rangle$) with subroutes $TS_{11}=\langle r_6,r_7,r_8\rangle$, $TS_{12}=\langle r_5\rangle$, $TS_{13}=\langle r_3,r_4\rangle$, and $TS_{14}=\langle r_1,r_2\rangle$. Note that each subroute requires at most one unreliable resource, although the frequency of that resource is not limited. RPA does not affect part types whose routes require at most one unreliable resource.

The maximum number of iterations of the RPA while loop is bounded by the number of part type stages, and thus RPA is no worse than $O(CRL = \sum_{P_j \in P} |P_j|)$, which is polynomial in cumulative route length (CRL).

4.2 Central buffer constraints

The central buffer (CB) will be used to clear workstation buffer space of failure-dependent parts that have finished a subroute. If such parts have completely finished their original routes, they exit the system. Otherwise, they must have available space in the CB. This will ensure that they do not block the production of other part types.

For example, suppose the system of Figure 7 is in a state as follows: r_7 is failed with p_{17} waiting for processing; r_5 is holding a completed p_{15}; and r_4 is holding a completed p_{14}. Because of the blocking effect of p_{14} and p_{15}, it is not possible to produce all other part types. However, if we relocate p_{14} and p_{15} to the CB, the system can continue producing P_2, P_3, and P_4. CB constraints are necessary to achieve this. For P_1, we state the linear inequality: $(x_{11}+y_{11})+(x_{12}+x'_{12}+y_{12})+(x_{13}+y_{13})+(x_{14}+x'_{14}+y_{14})+(x_{15}+x'_{15}+y_{15}) \le B_1$, where x_{jk} and y_{jk} are the number of finished and unfinished p_{jk}'s at $\rho(P_{jk})$, x'_{jk} is the number of finished p_{jk}'s relocated to the CB, and B_j the CB space reserved for P_j.

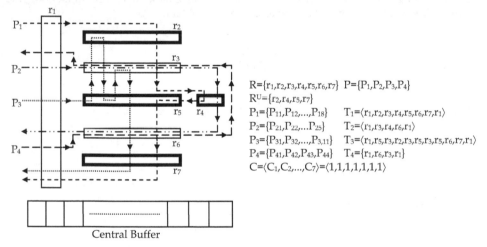

$R=\{r_1,r_2,r_3,r_4,r_5,r_6,r_7\}$ $P=\{P_1,P_2,P_3,P_4\}$
$R^U=\{r_2,r_4,r_5,r_7\}$
$P_1=\{P_{11},P_{12},...,P_{18}\}$ $T_1=\langle r_1,r_2,r_3,r_4,r_5,r_6,r_7,r_1\rangle$
$P_2=\{P_{21},P_{22},...P_{25}\}$ $T_2=\langle r_1,r_3,r_4,r_6,r_1\rangle$
$P_3=\{P_{31},P_{32},...,P_{3,11}\}$ $T_3=\langle r_1,r_5,r_3,r_2,r_3,r_5,r_3,r_5,r_6,r_7,r_1\rangle$
$P_4=\{P_{41},P_{42},P_{43},P_{44}\}$ $T_4=\{r_1,r_6,r_3,r_1\}$
$C=\langle C_1,C_2,...,C_7\rangle=\langle 1,1,1,1,1,1,1\rangle$

Central Buffer

Fig. 7. Example with four unreliable resources

With this constraint, finished parts p_{12}, p_{14}, and p_{15}, for subpart types SP_{14}, SP_{13}, and SP_{12}, respectively, can be moved to the CB. Thus, in the example, we can transfer the finished p_{14} and p_{15} to the CB, allowing P_2, P_3, and P_4 to continue production. In the meantime, we decrement x_{14} and x_{15} by 1, and increment x'_{14} and x'_{15} by 1. As an aside, we decrement x'_{14} by 1 and increment y_{15} by 1 when p_{14} advances from the CB into the buffer of r_5.

We now state the CB constraint, CBC. Let $P^*=\{P_j:P_j\in P \wedge |T_j\cap R^U| > 1\}$ be the set of part types that require multiple unreliable resources, and B the total capacity of the CB. For a part type $P_j\in P^*$, let

$$Z_j = \sum_{P_{jk} \in P_j \setminus SP_{j1}} (x_{jk} + y_{jk}) + \sum_{P_{jk} \in LP_j} x'_{jk}$$

where LP_j is the set of "last" part type stages in the subparts of P_j (except SP_{j1}, the final stage of P_j). For example, $LP_1=\{P_{12},P_{14},P_{15}\}$ and $LP_3 = \{P_{32},P_{34},P_{36},P_{38}\}$. In general,

$$LP_j = \left\{ P_{j, |SP_{j,NS_j}|}, P_{j, |SP_{j,NS_j}|+|SP_{j,NS_j-1}|}, \cdots, P_{j, |SP_{j,NS_j}|+\ldots+|SP_{j2}|} \right\} .$$

Z_j keeps track of the total number of instances of part type stages of $P_j \in P^*$ that are in the system. CBC is defined as:

$$\text{(i)} \ \ Z_j \leq B_j, \ \ P_j \in P^* \qquad \text{(ii)} \ \sum_{P_j \in P^*} B_j \leq B$$

CBC ensures that every part in the system requiring multiple unreliable resources has capacity reserved on the CB. CBC has no more than $CRL^*|P|$ constraints and thus checking CBC computation is no worse than $O(CRL^*|P|)$, which is polynomial in stable measures of system size.

The level of B_j for $P_j \in P^*$ can be fixed, in which case B_j does not change; or state-based, where we periodically reallocate CB across all $P_j \in P^*$. Although we cannot preempt CB space from parts that have it reserved, we can reallocate CB space that is not reserved. One simple approach is to let $B_j=Z_j$ as long as (ii) holds. This represents a first-come-first-serve rule. Alternatively, we can solve the following assignment problem:

$$\min \ \sum_{i=1}^{B} \sum_{j=1}^{|P^*|} C_{ij} X_{ij} \tag{1}$$

$$\text{st.} \ \ \ B_j = \sum_{i=1}^{B} X_{ij}, \ \ \ j=1\ldots|P^*| \tag{2}$$

$$Z_j \leq \sum_{i=1}^{B} X_{ij}, \ \ \ j=1\ldots|P^*| \tag{3}$$

$$\sum_{i=1}^{B} \sum_{j=1}^{|P^*|} X_{ij} \leq B \tag{4}$$

$$X_{ij} \in \{0,1\} \ , \ i=1\ldots B, j=1\ldots|P^*| \tag{5}$$

Here, X_{ij} is 1 if the ith unit of CB is assigned to $P_j \in P^*$, 0 otherwise. The objective (1) minimizes assignment cost; (2) counts the assignment to each $P_j \in P^*$; (3) assures no preemption from parts in the system; and (4) assures the CB is not over allocated. C_{ij} is the cost of assigning CB space to $P_j \in P^*$. This cost could reflect production priorities or failure probabilities. This problem can be solved in polynomial time using the Hungarian Algorithm (Papadimitriou, 1982). The solution frequency is a topic for future research.

4.3 Robust controllers with CBC

We now define two supervisory controllers. The first is the conjunction of Δ_1 and CBC; and the second is the conjunction of Δ_2 and CBC. Recall that Δ_1 and Δ_2 are the controllers of Subsection 3.1. Formally, the extended supervisors are stated as follows.

Definition 4.3.1: Supervisor $\Delta_5 = \Delta_1 \wedge CBC$.
Definition 4.3.2: Supervisor $\Delta_6 = \Delta_2 \wedge CBC$.
The following theorems establish that these supervisors ensure robust operation.
Theorem 4.3.1: Δ_5 is robust to failure of R^U.
Proof: The structure of the proof is as follows. We assume the system to be in an admissible state with parts requiring multiple unreliable resources, with some failed. We show that these parts can advance into the CB or into the buffer space of failure-dependent resources, where they do not block production of parts not requiring failed resources. Let $P_j \in P^*$. The subpart types of P_j constructed by RPA are $\{SP_{j,NS_j}, SP_{j,(NS_j-1)}, \ldots, SP_{j1}\}$. Assume that in the current state, q, unreliable resources in the subroutes of P_j have failed and that q satisfies Δ_5. In the following, we want to show that under Δ_5 parts of type P_j do not block other part types from producing. We ignore parts of type P_j in the final subroute since it is covered by Δ_1. That is, Δ_1 guarantees that parts in the final subroute can be advanced into the buffer space of the last resource and completed and removed from the system if the resource is operational or stored there, out of the way of part types not requiring failed resources, if it is not.

Let $\zeta_{qj} = \{p_{jk} \mid P_{jk} \in SP_{jq}, q = NS_j, (NS_j-1), \ldots, 2\}$ be the set of parts of P_j in the state q. Let $\wp_{qj} = \{p_{jk} \mid P_{jk} \in LP_j\}$ be the set of parts of P_j in the final stage of a subroute. By the definition of LP_j, $\wp_{qj} \subseteq \zeta_{qj}$. Now, Δ_1 guarantees that all parts in $\zeta_{qj} \setminus \wp_{qj}$ can be advanced, perhaps through several processing steps, into the buffer spaces of resources required by stages of LP_j. That is, Δ_1 guarantees a sequence of part movements such that the system reaches a new state, say t, where $\zeta_{tj} = \wp_{tj}$. In state t, all instances of P_j are at the end of a subroute.

The left hand side of CBC does not change in moving from state q to state t. To see this, note that CBC is only affected by parts in P^*. Since we allow no new parts to be admitted and no part of P^* is required to move from one subroute to another (only to the end of the current subroute), the left-hand-side of CBC does not change magnitude. Thus, the part advancement under Δ_1 does not violate CBC. Now, CBC guarantees that every part of ζ_{tj} has capacity reserved on the CB, and any finished part of this set can be moved to the CB. Further, any unfinished part of ζ_{tj} can be finished and moved to the CB if its resource is operational. If the associated resource is not operational, the part can be stored at its failed resource where it will not block the production of part types not requiring failed resources. Thus, all operational resources can be cleared of parts of type P_j. Under Δ_1, the resulting state is a feasible initial state if resource repairs or additional failures occur.

Theorem 4.3.2: Δ_6 is robust to failure of R^U.
Proof: The proof follows the same construction as Theorem 4.3.1. The main difference is in how BA and SSLA operate. Thus, Δ_5 and Δ_6 guarantee robust operation for systems where parts can require multiple unreliable resources. Note that if every resource is unreliable, both theorems continue to hold.

5. Conclusion and future research

Supervisory control for manufacturing systems resource allocation has been an active area of research. Significant amount of theories and algorithms have been developed to allocate resources effectively and efficiently, and to guarantee important system properties, such as system liveness, traceability, deadlock-free operations. However, a major assumption these research works are based on is that resources never fail. While resource failures in automated

manufacturing systems are inevitable, we investigate such system behaviours and control dynamics. First, we developed the notion of robust supervisory control for automated manufacturing systems with unreliable resources. Our objective is to allocate system buffer space so that when an unreliable resource fails the system can continue to produce all part types not requiring the failed resource. We established properties that such a controller must satisfy, namely, that it ensure safety for the system given no resource failure; that it constrain the system to feasible initial states in case of resource failure; that it ensure safety for the system while the unreliable resource is failed; and that during resource repair it constrain the system to states that will be feasible initial states when the repair is completed.
We then developed a variety of control policies that satisfy these robust properties.

Taxonomy for Future Research Directions		
System Structure	S1	at most one unreliable resource for each part type
	S2	random number of unreliable resources for each part type
Central Buffer Capacity	C1	without central buffer
	C2	with central buffer
Flexible Routing	FR1	every part type stage can be performed by exactly one resource
	FR2	every part type stage can be performed by exactly two resources
	...	
	FRj	every part type stage can be performed by exactly j resources
Robustness Level	RB1	no resource failures
	RB2	at most one resource failure at any time
	RB3	at most two resource failures at any time
	...	
	RBi	at most i resource failures at any time
Unreliable Resource Condition	RC1	unreliable resources fail at any time
	RC2	unreliable resource failure characteristics can be estimated
Application Areas	AA1	Manufacturing Systems
	AA2	Business Processes and Workflow Management
	AA3	E-Commerce
	AA4	Supply Chain Management
	AA5	Internet Resource Mangement
	AA6	Transporation Systems
	AA7	Healthcare Systems

Table 1. Taxonomy for future research directions

Specifically, supervisory controllers Δ_1-Δ_4 are for systems with multiple unreliable resources where each part type requires at most one unreliable resource. Supervisory controllers Δ_5-Δ_6 control systems for which part types may require multiple unreliable resources. Another classification of the controllers is based on the underlying control mechanism: controllers Δ_1-Δ_3 'absorb' all parts requiring failed resources into the buffer space of failure-dependent resources, controller Δ_4 distribute' parts requiring failed resources among the buffer space of shared resources, and controllers Δ_5-Δ_6 utilize central buffer to achieve robust operations. These robust controllers assure different levels of robust system operation and impose very different operating dynamics on the system, thus affecting system performance in different ways. An extensive simulation study has been conducted and a set of implementation guidelines for choosing the best robust controller based on manufacturing system characteristics and performance objectives are developed in Wang et al. (2009).

A taxonomy is developed and presented in Table 1 to help guide future research in the area of robust supervisory control. By combining the different system structures, the presence/absence of central buffer, flexible routing capability, system robust level requirements, and unreliable resource failure characteristics, a significant amount of future research and development need to be done to address a variety of system control and performance requirements. And, although automated manufacturing systems are the context in which we develop the robust supervisory control research. We expect to expand our research to other application areas due to the similarity in resource allocation requirement and complexity in workflow management. The robust controllers we developed so far only address a small subset of the research taxonomy. For example, controller Δ_1 falls in the category in the taxonomy of (S1, C1, FR1, RB2, RC1, AA1). Especially, it would be interesting and challenging to develop supervisory control policies for systems with flexible routing and for systems where the failure characteristics of resources are dynamically evolving and can be estimated through sensor monitoring and degradation modelling.

6. References

Chew, S. & Lawley, M. (2006). Robust Supervisory Control for Production Systems with Multiple Resource Failures. *IEEE Transactions on Automation Science and Engineering,* Vol.3, No.3, (July 2006), pp. 309-323, ISSN 1545-5955

Chew, S.; Wang, S. & Lawley, M. (2008). Robust Supervisory Control for Product Routings with Multiple Unreliable Resources. *IEEE Transactions on Automation Science and Engineering,* Vol.6, No.1, (January 2009), pp. 195-200, ISSN 1545-5955

Chew, S.; Wang, S. & Lawley, M. (2011). Resource Failure and Blockage Control for Production Systems. *International Journal of Computer Integrated Manufacturing,* Vol.24, No.3, (March 2011), pp. 229-241, ISSN 0951-192X

Cormen, T.; Leiserson, C. & Rivest, R. (2002). *Introduction to Algorithms* (Second Edition), McGraw-Hill, ISBN 0072970545, New York, USA

Ezpeleta, J.; Tricas, F.; Garcia-Valles, F. & Colom, J. (2002). A Banker's Solution for Deadlock Avoidance in FMS with Flexible Routing and Multiresource States. *IEEE Transactions on Robotics and Automation,* Vol.18, No.4, (August 2002), pp. 621–625, ISSN 1042-296X

Habermann, A. (1969). Prevention of System Deadlocks. *Communications of the ACM,* Vol.12, No.7, (July 1969), pp. 373–377, ISSN 0001-0782

Hsieh, F. (2004). Fault-tolerant Deadlock Avoidance Algorithm for Assembly Processes. *IEEE Transactions on Systems, Man and Cybernetics, Part A,* Vol.34, No.1, (January 2004), pp. 65-79, ISSN 1083-4427

Lawley, M. (1999). Deadlock Avoidance for Production Systems with Flexible Routing. *IEEE Transactions on Robotics and Automation*, Vol.15, No.3, (June 1999), pp. 497-510, ISSN 1042-296X

Lawley, M. (2002). Control of Deadlock and Blocking for Production Systems with Unreliable Resources. *International Journal of Production Research*, Vol.40, No.17, (November 2002), pp. 4563-4582, ISSN 0020-7543

Lawley, M. & Reveliotis, S. (2001). Deadlock Avoidance for Sequential Resource Allocation Systems: Hard and Easy Cases. *International Journal of Flexible Manufacturing Systems*, Vol.13, No.4, (October 2001), pp. 385-404, ISSN 0920-6299

Lawley, M.; Reveliotis, S. & Ferreira, P. (1998). Application and Evaluation of Banker's Algorithm for Deadlock-free Buffer Space Allocation in Flexible Manufacturing Systems. *International Journal of Flexible Manufacturing Systems*, Vol.10, No.1, (February 1998), pp. 73–100, ISSN 0920-6299

Lawley, M. & Sulistyono, W. (2002). Robust Supervisory Control Policies for Manufacturing Systems with Unreliable Resources. *IEEE Transactions on Robotics and Automation*, Vol.18, No.3, (June 2002), pp. 346-359, ISSN 1042-296X

Papadimitriou, C. (1982). *Combinatorial Optimization: Algorithms and Complexity*, Prentice-Hall, ISBN 0486402584, New Jersey, USA

Park, S. & Lim, J. (1999). Fault-tolerant Robust Supervisor for Discrete Event Systems with Model Uncertainty and Its Application to a Workcell. *IEEE Transactions on Robotics and Automation*, Vol.15, No.2, (April 1999), pp. 386–391, ISSN 1042-296X

Ramadge, P. & Wonham, W. (1987). Supervisory Control of a Class of Discrete Event Processes. *SIAM Journal on Control and Optimization*, Vol.25, No.1, (March 1985), pp. 206–230, ISSN 0363-0129

Reveliotis, S. (1999). Accommodating FMS Operational Contingencies through Routing Flexibility. *IEEE Transactions on Robotics and Automation*, Vol.15, No.1, (February 1999), pp. 3–19, ISSN 1042-296X

Reveliotis, S. (2000). Conflict Resolution in AGV Systems. *IIE Transactions*, Vol.32, No.7, (July 2000), pp. 647-659, ISSN 0740-817X

Wang, S.; Chew, S. & Lawley, M. (2008). Using Shared-Resource Capacity for Robust Control of Failure-Prone Manufacturing Systems. *IEEE Transactions on Systems, Man and Cybernetics, Part A*, Vol.38, No.3, (May 2008), pp. 605-627, ISSN 1083-4427

Wang, S.; Chew, S. & Lawley, M. (2009). Guidelines for Implementing Robust Supervisors in Flexible Manufacturing Systems. *International Journal of Production Research*, Vol.47, No.23, (December 2009), pp. 6499-6524, ISSN 0020-7543

10

Robustness and Security of H∞-Synchronizer in Chaotic Communication System

Takami Matsuo, Yusuke Totoki and Haruo Suemitsu
Oita University, Dannoharu, Oita
Japan

1. Introduction

In recent years, a large amount of work on chaos-based cryptosystems has been published (Kocarev (2001); Millérioux et al. (2008)). A general methodology for designing chaotic and hyperchaotic cryptosystems has been developed using the control systems theory (Grassi et al. (1999); Liao et al. (1999); Yang et al. (1997a;b)). The chaotic communication system is closely related to the concept of chaos synchronization. An overview of chaotic secure communication systems can be found in (Yang (2004)). He classified the continuous-time chaotic secure communication systems into four generations. In the third generation, the combination of the classical cryptographic technique and chaotic synchronization is used to enhance the degree of security. Specifically, Yang *et al.* proposed a new chaos-based secure communication scheme in an attempt to thwart the attacks (Yang et al. (1997a;b)). They have combined both conventional cryptographic method and synchronization of chaotic systems. Their cryptographic method consists of an encryption function (the multi-shift cipher), a decryption function (the inverse of the encryption function), a chaotic encrypter that generates the key signal for the encryption function, and a decrypter that estimates the key signal. The approach has a limitation since the cryptosystem design may fail if different chaotic circuits are utilized. So far, this generation has the highest security in all the chaotic communication systems had been proposed and has not yet been broken. From the control theoretic perspective, the transmitter and the receiver in the chaotic communication system can be considered as the nonlinear plant and its observer, respectively. Grassi *et al.* proposed a nonlinear-observer-based decrypter to reconstruct the state of the encrypter (Grassi et al. (1999); Liao et al. (1999)). They extended the Chua's oscillator to the observer-based decrypter. The cryptosystem does not require initial conditions of the encrypter and the decrypter belonging to the same basin of attraction. If we can design a decrypter without the knowledge of the parameters of the encrypter, the chaos-based secure communication systems are not secure, because the parameters of the encrypter is selected as static secret keys in the cryptosystem. Parameter identification and adaptive synchronization methods may be effective for intruders in building reconstruction mechanisms, even when a synchronizing system is not available. Therefore, it is important for secure issues to investigate whether adaptive identifiers without the system information of encrypter can be constructed or not.

We have recently designed an observer-based chaotic communication system combining the cryptosystems proposed by Grassi *et al.* (Grassi et al. (1999)) and by Liao *et al.* (Liao et al. (1999)) that allows us to assign the relative degree and the zeros of its encrypter system (Matsuo et al. (2004)). Specifically, we constructed three cryptosystems based on a Chua's circuit by assigning its relative degree and zeros. The cryptosystem consists of an encryption function (the multi-shift cipher), a decryption function (the inverse of the encryption function), a chaotic encrypter that generates the key signal for the encryption function, and a decrypter that estimates the key signal. The proposed cryptosystem allows us to assign the relative degree and the zeros of the encrypter dynamics by selecting an output vector that generates a transmitted signal as partial states of the encrypter. As in (Fradkov et al. (1997; 2000)), we can design an adaptive decrypter for minimum-phase systems with its relative degree 1. Therefore, the encrypter dynamics should be design such that its relative degree is more than two and its zeros are unstable so as to fail to synchronize the cryptosystem adaptively. At the same time, the designed cryptosystem should be robust with respect to uncertainties of the transmission lines such as a time delay, and noises. Suykens $et\ al.$ (Suykens et al. (1997a;b)) presented a nonlinear H_∞ synchronization method for chaotic Lur'e systems based on the dissipativity of nonlinear systems to minimize the influence of the exogenous input such as the message signal and channel noises.

However, many proposed systems with robustness against parameter uncertainties and signal uncertainties are difficult to implement in practice with a reasonable degree of security. The basic difference between the conventional cryptography and the chaos cryptography is that the conventional encryption is defined discrete sets and the chaos encryption is defined on continuous sets. This makes the keyspace behavior of chaotic systems vary different that of conventional systems. Due to the continuous-value property, keys in chaotic cryptosystems form a key basin around the actual secret key.

When one key is very close to the real one, it could decrypt part or all of the ciphertext (Alvarez et al. (2006)). To avoid brute-force attacks, a secret parameter should be sensitive enough to guarantee the so-called avalanche property: even when the smallest change occurs in the parameter, the ciphertext will change dramatically (Alvarez et al. (2006)).

Various attacks such as the nonlinear forecasting, the return map, the adaptive parameter estimation, the error function attack (EFA), and inverse computation based on the chosen cipher attack, are proposed to recover messages from the chaotic ciphers (Zhou (2005)). Short (Parke et al. (2001); Short (1994; 1996)) and Guojie $et\ al.$ (Guojie et al. (2003)) have proposed the attack strategies against chaotic communication systems. Short analyzed only the encrypter by using the nonlinear forecasting method that belongs to ciphertext-only attack when the attacker does not know the structure of the encryption system. They discussed the secure property of chaos communication based on chaotic parameter modulation from the chosen-ciphertext attack under the Kerckhoff principle (Guojie et al. (2003)). Guojie $et\ al.$ discussed the secure property of chaos communication based on chaotic parameter modulation from the chosen-ciphertext attack under the Kerckhoff principle. We proposed chaotic communication systems using the adaptive control and robust control technologies (Matsuo et al. (2004; 2008)).

Wang $et\ al.$ (Wang et al. (2004)) presented the error function attack to evaluate system security as an efficient cryptanalysis tool based on the public-structure and known-plaintext cryptanalysis. By defining the EFA function, an eavesdropper can scan the whole keyspace to find out the proper key that satisfies the EFA function with zero value. Since keys that are not identical with but are very close to the real one can be used to synchronize the two systems very well, a key basin around the actual secret key is formed. Once the eavesdropper knows the key basin, the correct key can be easily obtained through some optimization algorithms. To evaluate the security performance, Wang $et\ al.$ also defined the key basin width by the distance between two trial keys located on the two sides of the key basin. The narrower than the whole keyspace the key basin width is, the higher the security of the cryptosysytem is. However, a systematic approach to get the key basin width is lacking. The brute-force-like calculations are needed to draw the shape of the EFA function. Thus, a considerable computing time is needed to get the key basin width. If the EFA function has numerous minima and a needle-like basin, the security level of the cryptosystem is high. In this case, the evolutionary optimization techniques such as the particle swarm optimization cannot find the secret key using the EFA function (Nomura et al. (2011)). Anstett *et al.* proposed a general framework based on identifiability for the cryptanalysis of chaotic cryptosystems (Anstett et al. (2006)). They also pointed out that cryptosystems involving polynomial nonlinearities are weak against a known plaintext attack.

In this chapter, we propose an H_∞ synchronizer in order to improve the robustness of chaotic communication systems with respect to delays in the transmission line based on the standard linear H_∞ control theory. To begin with, we derive an error system between the encrypter and the decrypter and reduce the design problem of the cryptosystem to the stabilization problem of a generalized plant in the robust control theory. Next, we give a synchronizer parameterization and an H_∞ synchronizer based on the robust control theory. Furthermore, the decrypter dynamics is designed via the linear controller parameterization to make the decrypter robust against disturbances in transmission line and/or sensitive to modeling errors of the decrypter. We present two design requirements on the robustness and the security. We need to design the free parameter such that both the requirements are satisfied. Since we cannot get this solution simultaneously, we design the dynamical compensator so as to satisfy the robustness requirement and then check the sensitivity to the key parameter mismatches whether the parameters in encrypter may play the role of the secret key or not, numerically. Finally, the proposed system is compared with that proposed by Grassi et al. using MATLAB simulations.

The following notation is used (Doyle et al. (1989)) :

$\mathcal{F}_l(G, Q)$: lower linear fractional transformation

$$\left[\begin{array}{c|c} A & B \\ \hline C & D \end{array} \right] := C(sI - A)^{-1}B + D$$

2. Observer-based chaotic communication system with free dynamics

Grassi *et al.* (Grassi et al. (1999)) proposed a nonlinear-observer-based cryptosystem that is an extension of the cryptosystem proposed by Yang *et al.* (Yang et al. (1997b)). The cryptographic method consists of an encryption function (the multi-shift cipher), a decryption function (the inverse of the encryption function), a chaotic encrypter that generates the key signal for the encryption function, and a decrypter that estimates the key signal. The transmitted signal through a public channel contains the nonlinear function that is equivalent to that of the encrypter. We add a dynamic compensator in the transmitted signal to the observer-based chaotic communication system proposed by Grassi *et al.* Figure 1 shows the relationship among the encrypter, the observer-based decrypter and the adaptive decrypter where we use the adaptive decrypter as a tool for ciphertext-only attacks.

The cryptosystem consists of an encryption function (the multi-shift cipher), a decryption function (the inverse of the encryption function), a chaotic encrypter that generates the key signal for the encryption function, and a decrypter that estimates the key signal.

- **Part 1 : dynamic encrypter**
  The chaotic encrypter is described by the following equations:

$$\dot{x} = Ax + b_2 f(x) + b_2 e_n \tag{1}$$

$$v = P(s)x \tag{2}$$

$$y = v + e_n + f(x) \tag{3}$$

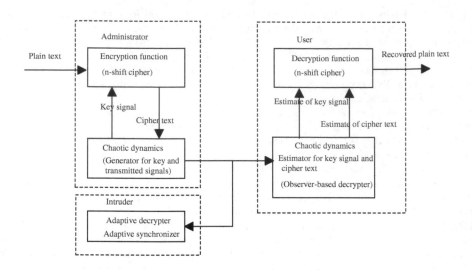

Fig. 1. Chaotic cryptosystem configuration.

where y is the transmitted signal that includes the nonlinear function, $P(s)$ is a transfer function that lets a decrypter synchronize the encrypter, and $s = \frac{d}{dt}$. We call this transfer function $P(s)$ a synchronizer.

- **Part 2 : encryption function**
  Given a plaintext signal $p(t)$, the ciphertext $e_n(t)$ is given by

$$e_n(t) = e_n(p(t), K(t)) \tag{4}$$

where $K(t)$ is a stream key signal that is generated by the encrypter dynamics and is given by the following equation:

$$K(t) = k^T x. \tag{5}$$

The signal e_n is a generic encryption function that makes use of the key signal and we choose a encryption function as the following n-shift cipher:

$$e_n(p(t), K(t)) = q(\cdots q(q(p(t), K(t)), K(t)), \cdots), K(t))$$

$$q(x, k) = \begin{cases} (x+k) + 2h, & -2h \leq (x+k) \leq -h \\ (x+k), & -h < (x+k) < h \\ (x+k) - 2h & h \leq (x+k) \leq 2h \end{cases}$$

- **Part 3 : dynamic decrypter with free dynamics**
  Given the encrypter, the decrypter used by an authorized user is the following observer:

$$\dot{\hat{x}} = A\hat{x} + b_2 e_y \tag{6}$$

$$\hat{v} = P(s)\hat{x} \tag{7}$$

$$e_y = y - \hat{v} = P(s)(x - \hat{x}) + e_n + f(x) \tag{8}$$

$$\hat{e}_n = y - (\hat{v} + f(\hat{x})) \tag{9}$$

where $\hat{e}_n$ is a recovered signal of the plain text.

- **Part 4 : decryption function**
  Using the estimated signals $\hat{K}(t)$ and $\hat{e}_n(t)$ by the decrypter, the estimate of the plaintext $\hat{p}(t)$ can be recovered by the following equations:

$$\hat{p}(t) = d(\hat{e}_n(t), \hat{K}(t)) \tag{10}$$

$$\hat{K}(t) = k^T \hat{x} \tag{11}$$

where $\hat{K}$ is an estimate of the stream key signal and d is the decryption function given by

$$\hat{p}(t) = q(\cdots q(q(q(\hat{e}_n(t), -\hat{K}(t)), -\hat{K}(t)), \cdots), -\hat{K}(t)).$$

3. Design of H_∞-synchronizer

3.1 Error equations and generalized system

If the transmitted signal is disturbed by an additional disturbance $w(t)$, the signal is rewritten by

$$\tilde{y}(t) = v(t) + e_n(t) + f(x(t)) + w(t) \tag{12}$$

When some of parameters of the dynamic encrypter are unknown, the dynamic decrypter constructed by a receiver based on the information of the encrypter has parametric uncertainties. The decrypter used by any receivers including intruders is given by

$$\dot{\hat{x}} = \tilde{A}\hat{x} + \tilde{b}_2 e_y \tag{13}$$

$$\hat{v} = \tilde{P}(s)\hat{x} \tag{14}$$

$$\hat{e}_n = \tilde{y} - (\hat{v} + \tilde{f}(\hat{x})) \tag{15}$$

Denoting the uncertainties of $\tilde{A}, \tilde{b}_2$ in the encrypter dynamics as Δ, the perturbed nonlinear function of $f(x)$ as $\tilde{f}(x)$, and the perturbation of the H_∞ synchronizer as $\tilde{P}(*)$, we assume that the decrypter with the uncertainties is given by

$$\dot{\hat{x}} = A\hat{x} + b_1\Delta + b_2 e_y \tag{16}$$

$$\hat{v} = \tilde{P}(s)\hat{x}, \; e_y = \tilde{y} - \hat{v} \tag{17}$$

$$\hat{e}_n = e_y - \tilde{f}(\hat{x}) = \tilde{y} - (\hat{v} + \tilde{f}(\hat{x})). \tag{18}$$

A decrypter used by an authorized user satisfies $\Delta(t) = 0, f(\cdot) = \tilde{f}(\cdot), P(s) = \tilde{P}(s)$ since he knows all parameters of the encrypter. On the other hand, a decrypter used by an intruder has uncertainties in the encrypter dynamics, the nonlinear function, and the synchronizer. In this chapter, we assume that the intruder knows the H_∞ synchronizer, $P(s) = \tilde{P}(s)$ but does not know the values of A, b_2, i.e. $\Delta(t) \neq 0$, and the nonlinear function, i.e. $f(\cdot) \neq \tilde{f}(\cdot)$. Defining the estimation error of the decrypter as $e(t) = \hat{x}(t) - x(t)$, we have the following error system:

$$\dot{e}(t) = Ae(t) + b_1\Delta(t) + b_2 w(t) - b_2\xi(t) \tag{19}$$

$$\xi(t) = P(s)e \tag{20}$$

We assign the estimation error of the key signal e_K or that of cipher text $\tilde{e}_n$ to the controlled output as follows:

$$e_K(t) = \hat{K}(t) = k^T e(t)$$
$$\tilde{e}_n = \hat{e}_n - e_n = \tilde{y} - \hat{v} - \tilde{f}(\hat{x}) - e_n$$
$$= -\xi + (f(x) - \tilde{f}(\hat{x})) + w$$

If $\lim_{t \to \infty} w(t) = 0, \lim_{t \to \infty}(f(x) - \tilde{f}(\hat{x})) = 0$ and $\lim_{t \to \infty} e(t) = 0$, then the plaintext can be recovered by the decrypter ,$\lim_{t \to \infty}(e_n(t) - \hat{e}_n(t)) = 0$.
Since $f(\cdot) = \tilde{f}(\cdot)$ for authorized users, we have

$$|\tilde{e}_n| \le |\xi| + |f(x) - f(\hat{x})| + |w|$$
$$\le |P(s)e| + \gamma \|e\| + |w|.$$

Thus, if $\lim_{t \to \infty} w(t) = 0$ and $\lim_{t \to \infty} e(t) = 0$, then we attain the recover the plaintext, *i.e.* $\lim_{t \to \infty}(e_n(t) - \hat{e}_n(t)) = 0$.
For each controlled output, the generalized plant in Fig. 2 is defined as:

- When the controlled output is e_K, the generalize plant is

$$G_1(s) = \left[\begin{array}{c|cc} A & [b_1 \quad b_2] & -b_2 \\ \hline k^T & 0 & 0 \\ I & 0 & 0 \end{array} \right] \tag{21}$$

- When the controlled output is the upper bound of $|\tilde{e}_n|$, the generalize plant is

$$G_2(s) = \left[\begin{array}{c|cc} A & [b_1 \quad b_2] & -b_2 \\ \hline k^T & [0 \quad 1] & -1 \\ I & 0 & 0 \end{array} \right]. \tag{22}$$

3.2 Synchronizer parameterization

To design the synchronizer based on the static output-feedback-based controller, we rewrite the generalized plant as in Fig.2. Since we can select the input of the synchronizer as arbitrary scalar signal, the signal in Eq.(2) is chosen as $v(t) = P(s)x(t) = P_o(s)c^T x(t)$, where c is an arbitrary vector.
We call a stabilizing compensator $P_o(s)$ for the generalized plant $G(s)$ the synchronizer of the chaotic cryptosystem. The design problem of the synchronizer is summarized as follows:

Given a generalized plant $G(s)$ as in Fig. 2, parameterize all synchronizer $P(s)$ that internally stabilize $G(s)$.

We consider the n-th order generalized plant in Fig.3, where (A, B_2) is stabilizable and (A, C_2) is detectable;

$$G_o(s) = \left[\begin{array}{cc} G_{11} & G_{12} \\ G_{21} & G_{22} \end{array} \right] = \left[\begin{array}{c|cc} A & B_1 & B_2 \\ \hline C_1 & D_{11} & D_{12} \\ C_2 & D_{21} & 0 \end{array} \right] \tag{23}$$

and the p-th order dynamic stabilizing compensator,

$$P_o(s) = \left[\begin{array}{c|c} A_c & B_c \\ \hline C_c & D_c \end{array} \right]. \tag{24}$$

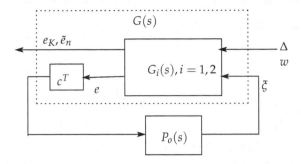

Fig. 2. Generalized plant and synchronizer in the chaotic communication system.

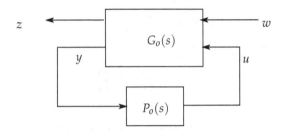

Fig. 3. Generalized plant and controller in the robust control theory.

For any choice of K_0, we can obtain the parameterization of $K(s)$ as follows (Matsuo et al. (1998)):

$$P_o(s) = \mathcal{F}_l(\tilde{P}_o(s), Q(s)) \tag{25}$$

$$\tilde{P}_o(s) = \left[\begin{array}{c|cc} A_K + H_0 C_2 + B_2 F_0 & -H_0 & B_2 \\ \hline F_0 & K_0 & I \\ -C_2 & I & 0 \end{array}\right] \tag{26}$$

$$Q(s) = \left[\begin{array}{c|c} A_{c22} & B_{c2} \\ \hline C_{c2} & D_{c2} \end{array}\right]$$

$$A_K = A + B_2 K_0 C_2$$

where

$$A_{c22} : \text{stable}$$
$$F_0 \text{ s.t. } A_K + B_2 F_0 \text{ is stable}$$
$$H_0 \text{ s.t. } A_K + H_0 C_2 \text{ is stable.}$$

Since $P_o(s)$ is a stabilizing compensator for each $Q(s) \in RH_\infty$, (25) is one of the parameterization of stabilizing compensators. This LFT form is equal to the Youla parameterization when the static output feedback gain, K_0, is selected as zero. When the generalized plant can be stabilized by a static output feedback gain, *i.e.* there exists an output feedback gain K_0 such that A_K is stable, we can set $H_0 = 0$, $F_0 = 0$. In this case, the parameterization of all stabilizing compensators is as follows (Matsuo et al. (1998)):

$$P_o(s) = \mathcal{F}_l(\tilde{P}_o(s), Q(s)) \tag{27}$$
$$= K_0 + Q(s)(I + C_2(sI - A_K)^{-1}B_2Q(s))^{-1} \tag{28}$$

where

$$\tilde{P}_o(s) = \left[\begin{array}{c|cc} A_K & 0 & B_2 \\ \hline 0 & K_0 & I \\ -C_2 & I & 0 \end{array}\right]. \tag{29}$$

In Fig. 2, since C_2 is replace to c^T, where c^T can be selected as an arbitrary vector, there exists a scalar k_0 such that $A_k = A - b_2 k_0 c^T$ is stable, as long as (A, b_2) is stabilizable. In this case, we can set $H_0 = 0$, $F_0 = 0$. The parameterization of all synchronizers in Fig. 2 is obtained as follows (Matsuo et al. (1998)):

$$P_o(s) = \mathcal{F}_l(\tilde{P}_o(s), Q(s)) \tag{30}$$

where $Q(s) \in RH_\infty$ and

$$\tilde{P}_o(s) = \left[\begin{array}{c|cc} A_k & 0 & -b_2 \\ \hline 0 & k_0 & 1 \\ -c^T & 1 & 0 \end{array}\right]. \tag{31}$$

We call this parameterization a synchronizer parameterization. By selecting $P_o(s)$ as constant gain k_0 i.e. $Q(s) = 0$, the proposed cryptosystem is equivalent to that proposed by Grassi *et al.*

3.3 Design problem of H_∞ synchronizer
The input-output relation of the generalized plant $G(s) = G_1(s)$ or $G_2(s)$ from the exogenous input $[\Delta \ w]$ to the controlled output z is given by

$$z = \mathcal{F}_l(G(s), P(s)) \left[\Delta(s) \ w(s)\right]^T \tag{32}$$
$$= \left[T_1(s) \ T_2(s)\right] \left[\Delta(s) \ w(s)\right]^T \tag{33}$$

The free dynamics $Q(s)$ is designed to make the decrypter robust against the disturbances in the transmission line of sensitive to the modeling errors of the decrypter by intruders. We present two design specifications:

1. **Robustness requirement:** The proposed decrypter can recover the plain text by the transmitted signals when the generalized plant with the synchronizer is internally stable. Moreover, the H_∞ synchronizer has an additional synchronization property with respect to plant uncertainties. To recover plain texts, the decrypter should be robust with respect to time delay uncertainties in the transmission line. Design the free parameter $Q(s)$ such that for a given γ_2,

$$\|T_2(s)\| < \gamma_2. \tag{34}$$

2. **Security requirement:** To attain the secure cryptosystem, the decrypter of the intruder should not synchronize the encrypter. Therefore, The free parameter $Q(s)$ is designed to

the error system sensitive to Δ. Design the free parameter $Q(s)$ such that for a given γ_1,

$$\underline{\sigma}\{T_1(j\omega)\} > \gamma_1, \text{ for } \omega \in [0,\infty). \tag{35}$$

However, since the generalized plant does not have a direct term from the uncertainty Δ to the transmitted signal $\tilde{y}$, (35) cannot be hold for all $\omega \in [0,\infty)$. Therefore, to satisfy the security requirement, we change the transmitted signal $\tilde{y}$ and the feedback term in the decrypter e_y as

$$\tilde{y}(t) = v(t) + e_n(t) + f(x(t)) + w(t) + c^T A b_2$$
$$e_y = \tilde{y} - \hat{v} - c^T \tilde{A}\tilde{b}_2$$

In this case, the estimation error of the cipher text includes the direct term from the uncertainty to the transmitted signal as follows:

$$\tilde{e}'_n = \xi + (f(x) - \tilde{f}(\hat{x})) + w + \Delta'$$

In particular, when there is a perturbation in the nonlinear function, $f(x) \neq \tilde{f}(\hat{x})$ generates the direct term from the uncertainty to the transmitted signal.

We need to design the free parameter such that both the requirements are satisfied. Since we cannot get this solution, we design the dynamical compensator so as to satisfy the robustness requirement, and then check the security requirement whether the error system is sensitive to the modeling errors of the decrypter, *i.e.* the designed cryptosystem is secure against to attacks by intruders.

4. Simulations

We design a robust cryptosystem via Chua's circuits as in Yang *et al.* (Yang et al. (1997b)) and in Fradkov *et al.* (Fradkov et al. (2000)), and carry out simulations using MATLAB/Simulink.

4.1 Encrypter based on Chua's circuit
The chaotic encrypter based on the Chua's circuit is given by

$$\dot{x} = Ax + b_2 f(x_1) + b_2 e_n \tag{36}$$

$$y = P(s)x + e_n + f(x) \tag{37}$$

$$f(x_1) = G_b x_1 + \frac{1}{2}(G_a - G_b)(|x_1 + 1| - |x_1 - 1|)$$

$$A = \begin{bmatrix} -p_1 & p_1 & 0 \\ 1 & -1 & 1 \\ 0 & -p_2 & -p_3 \end{bmatrix}$$

$$b_2 = \begin{bmatrix} -p_1 \\ 0 \\ 0 \end{bmatrix}, x = \begin{bmatrix} x_1 \\ x_2 \\ x_3 \end{bmatrix}$$

We select the parameters in the Chua's circuit given by Liao *et al.* (Liao et al. (1999)) as $p_1 = 10, p_2 = 13.14, p_3 = 0.07727, G_a = -1.28$, and $G_b = -0.69$. The initial conditions are given by

$$x_1(0) = 1.1, x_2(0) = 0, x_3(0) = 0$$
$$\hat{x}_1(0) = 0, \hat{x}_2(0) = 0, \hat{x}_3(0) = 0$$

The encryption function is 30-shift cipher, the parameter h is equal to 1 and the key signal $K(t)$ is the second state variable x_2, *i.e.*

$$K(t) = \begin{bmatrix} 0 & 1 & 0 \end{bmatrix} x(t).$$

Moreover, we select $c^T = -\begin{bmatrix} 0 & 1 & 1 \end{bmatrix}$.
MATLAB has a built-in music file, `handel.mat`, with a short segment of Handel's *Messiah*. We use it as the plaintext signal.

4.2 Grassi-type system
In the encrypter presented by Grassi *et al.* (Grassi et al. (1999)), the dynamic synchronizer is simplified as $P_o(s) = k_0 = 0.8$.

4.3 Design of H_∞-synchronizer
The generalized plant $G_1(s)$ in designing the H_∞ synchronizer is shown in Fig. 4. The weighting function $W(s)$ in the exogenous signal is selected as $W(s) = 10 \times \frac{2.1Ls}{Ls+1}$, $L = 1 \times 10^{-3}$ and $\gamma = 0.75$ so as to stabilize the error system with time delay uncertainties. The H_∞ synchronizer is obtained by using MATLAB LMI toolbox as follows:

$$P(s) = \begin{bmatrix} a_k & b_k \\ \hline c_k & d_k \end{bmatrix}$$

$$a_k = 10^5 \begin{bmatrix} -0.8762 & 1.9816 & -0.3890 & 0.0685 \\ 2.0890 & -4.7937 & 0.9380 & -0.1581 \\ -0.4425 & 1.0122 & -0.2074 & 0.0331 \\ -2.2132 & 5.3464 & -1.0531 & -0.0258 \end{bmatrix},$$

$$b_k = 10^5 \begin{bmatrix} 2.2024 & -0.0009 & 0.0114 \\ -5.3148 & 0.0046 & 0.0005 \\ 1.1245 & 0.0083 & 0.0008 \\ 5.8935 & 0.0186 & -0.1098 \end{bmatrix},$$

$$c_k = 10^3 \begin{bmatrix} -0.0549 & 0.2164 & -0.4198 & -5.4334 \end{bmatrix},$$

$$d_k = \begin{bmatrix} 0 & 0 & 0 \end{bmatrix}.$$

4.4 Nominal performance of H_∞-synchronizer
Figs. 5,6, and 7 show the responses of the Grassi-type decrypter and the H_∞-type decrypter of the nominal system. Fig 5 shows the plaintext and recovered signal for each decrypter. Fig 6 shows the transmitted signal and the estimation error of decrypter for each decrypter. Fig 7 shows the cipher text and the percentage error of the recovered signal for each decrypter. The nominal system means that the communication system has neither time delay nor parameter mismatches between the encrypter and the decrypter. The speed of response of the H_∞-type decrypter is faster than that of the Grassi-type.

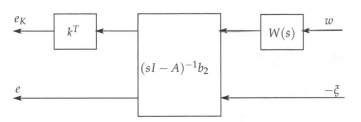

Fig. 4. Generalized plant $G_1(s)$.

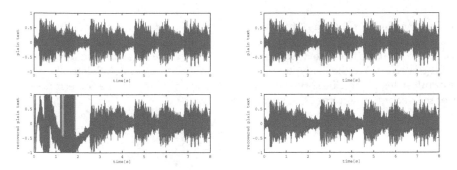

Fig. 5. The plaintext and the recovered plaintext in the nominal transmission line. Above left : the plaintext for the Grassi-type decrypter. Above right : the plaintext for the H_∞-synchronizer. Below left : the recovered plaintext by the Grassi-type decrypter. Below right : the recovered plaintext by the H_∞-synchronizer.

4.5 Robustness of H_∞-synchronizer against time delay in transmission line

Figs. 6 and 7 show the responses of the Grassi-type decrypter and the H_∞-type decrypter for the generalized plant $G_1(s)$ in the presence of the time delay $L = 0.1$ in the transmission line, respectively. The responses of the H_∞-type decrypter for the generalized plant $G_2(s)$ in the presence of the time delay $L = 0.1$ in the transmission line is almost same as that for the generalized plant $G_1(s)$. The H_∞-type decrypter has a better robust performance to the time delay than the Grassi-type.

4.6 Security performance of H_∞-synchronizer

We assume that intruders have parameter mismatches in the decrypter. In this simulation, we consider the following parameter mismatches:

$$\hat{v} = P(s)\hat{x}, \; \hat{e}_n = y - (\hat{v} + \tilde{f}(\hat{x}))$$

$$\tilde{A} = \begin{bmatrix} -p_1 & p_1 & 0 \\ 1 & -1 & 1 \\ 0 & -\tilde{p}_2 & -p_3 \end{bmatrix}$$

$$\tilde{f}(x_1) = \tilde{G}_b x_1 + \frac{1}{2}(\tilde{G}_a - \tilde{G}_b)(|x_1 + 1| - |x_1 - 1|)$$

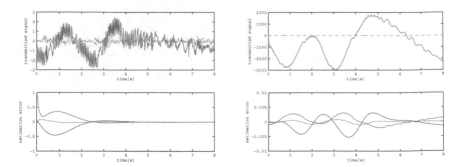

Fig. 6. The transmitted signal and the estimation error of decrypter in the nominal transmission line. Above left : the transmitted signal(solid line) and the plain text(dotted line) of the Grassi-type decrypter. Above right : the transmitted signal(solid line) and the plain text(dotted line) of the decrypter with the H_∞-synchronizer . Below left : the estimation errors of full states of the Grassi-type decrypter. Below right : the estimation errors of full states of the decrypter with the H_∞-synchronizer.

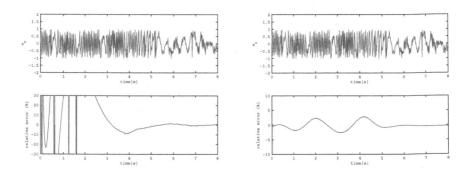

Fig. 7. The cipher text and the percentage error of the recovered signal in the nominal transmission line. Above left : the ciphertext in the Grassi-type decrypter. Above right : the ciphertext in the decrypter with the H_∞-synchronizer. Below left : the percentage error of the recovered signal of the Grassi-type decrypter. Below right : the percentage error of the recovered signal of the decrypter with the H_∞-synchronizer.

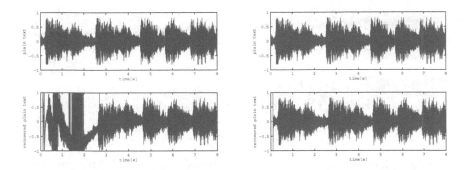

Fig. 8. The plaintext and the recovered plaintext in the transmission line with delay time. Above left : the plaintext for the Grassi-type decrypter. Above right : the plaintext for the H_∞-synchronizer. Below left : the recovered plaintext by the Grassi-type decrypter. Below right : the recovered plaintext by the H_∞-synchronizer.

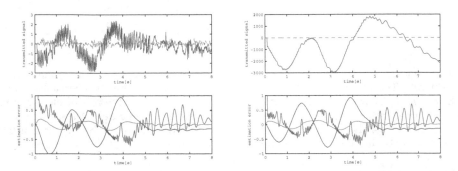

Fig. 9. The transmitted signal and the estimation error of the decrypter in the transmission line with delay time Above left : the transmitted signal(solid line) and the plain text(dotted line) of the Grassi-type decrypter. Above right : the transmitted signal(solid line) and the plain text(dotted line) of the decrypter with the H_∞-synchronizer . Below left : the estimation errors of full states of the Grassi-type decrypter. Below right : the estimation errors of full states of the decrypter with the H_∞-synchronizer.

In this simulation, we select the candidates of the static secret keys as the parameters p_2, G_a, G_b, and $P(s)$. Intruder A has the following parameter mismatch:

$$\tilde{p}_2 = 13.15, p_2 = 13.14$$
$$\tilde{G}_a = G_a = -1.28, \tilde{G}_b = G_b = -0.69$$
$$\tilde{P}(s) = P(s).$$

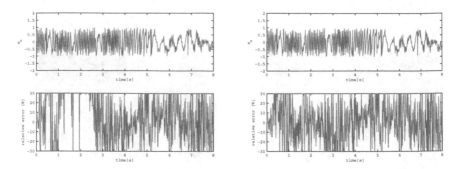

Fig. 10. The cipher text and the percentage error of the recovered signal in the transmission line with delay time. Above left : the ciphertext in the Grassi-type decrypter. Above right : the ciphertext in the decrypter with the H_∞-synchronizer. Below left : the percentage error of the recovered signal of the Grassi-type decrypter. Below right :the percentage error of the recovered signal of the decrypter with the H_∞-synchronizer.

Intruder B has the following parameter mismatches:

$$\tilde{p}_2 = p_2 = 13.14,$$
$$\tilde{G}_a = -1.3, \tilde{G}_b = -0.65$$
$$\tilde{P}(s) = P(s).$$

Figs. 11,12, and 13 show the responses of the H_∞-type decrypter used by the intruders A and B, respectively. The proposed synchronizer is sensitive to the parameter mismatches caused by Intruder A. The parameters in the dynamic encrypter may play the role of the secret key. However, Intruder A can identify the recovered wav file as the Handel's *Messiah* in spite of noisy sound. Fig. 14 shows the EFA function of the proposed H_∞-type decrypter. Since the width of the key basin in EFA function is not so narrow, the cryptosystem is not so secure.

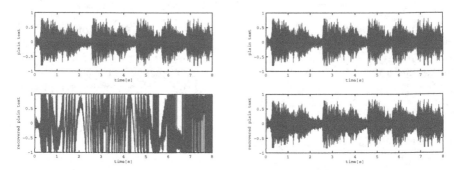

Fig. 11. The plaintext and the recovered plaintext by the intruders A and B. Above left : the plaintext. Above right : the plaintext. Below left : the recovered plaintext by Intruder A. Below right : the recovered plaintext by Intruder B.

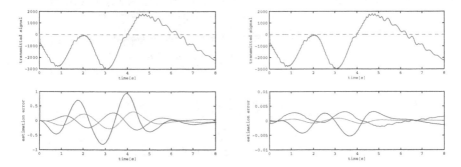

Fig. 12. The transmitted signals and the estimation errors of the intruders' decrypters. Above left : the transmitted signal(solid line) and the plain text(dotted line). Above right : the transmitted signal(solid line) and the plain text(dotted line). Below left : the estimation errors of full states by Intruder A. Below right : the estimation errors of full states by Intruder B.

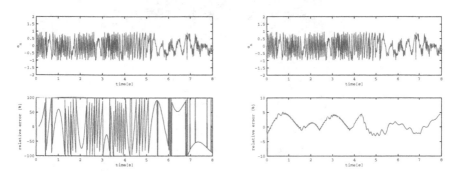

Fig. 13. The cipher text and the percentage error of the recovered signal in the transmission line with delay time. Above left : the ciphertext. Above right : the ciphertext. Below left : the percentage error of the recovered signal by Intruder A. Below right : the percentage error of the recovered signal by Intruder B.

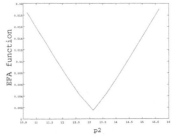

Fig. 14. The key basin of p_2 in EFA function for H_∞ synchronizer.

To improve the security of the H_∞ synchronizer, we select the secret key as a element of $P(s)$. Intruder C has the following parameter mismatch in the H_∞ synchronizer:

$$\tilde{p}_2 = p_2 = 13.14$$
$$\tilde{G}_a = G_a = -1.28, \tilde{G}_b = G_b = -0.69$$
$$\tilde{P}(s) = \left[\begin{array}{c|c} \tilde{a}_k & b_k \\ \hline c_k & d_k \end{array}\right]$$
$$\tilde{a}_k(1,1) = a_k(1,1) + 450$$

The parameter mismatch of the element $a_k(1,1)$ is about 0.51%, because $a_k(1,1) = -0.8762 \times 10^5$.

Figs. 15,16, and 17 show the responses of the H_∞-type decrypter used by Intruder C. In this case, the decrypter with the parameter mismatch causes instability. The parameters in the H_∞ synchronizer $\tilde{P}(s)$ may play the role of the secret key.

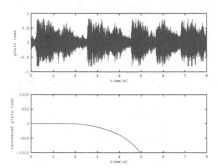

Fig. 15. The plaintext (top) and the recovered plaintext by Intruder C (bottom).

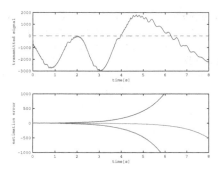

Fig. 16. The transmitted signal (top) and the estimation error of decrypter by Intruder C (bottom).

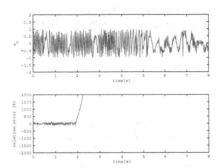

Fig. 17. The cipher text (top) and the percentage error of the recovered signal by Intruder C (bottom).

5. Conclusion

In this chapter, we added an observer-based chaotic communication system proposed by Grassi *et al.* to a dynamical compensator in its transmitted signal to improve the robustness of the cryptosystem with respect to delays in the transmission line. The proposed chaotic system has a good robust performance with respect to the time delay in the transmission line. Moreover, we checked the security in a point of parameters mismatch by an intruder.

6. References

Anstett,F.; Millerioux,G. & Bloch,G. (2006). Chaotic Cryptosystems : Cryptanalysis and Identifiability, *IEEE Trans. Circuits Syst. I*, Vol.53, No.12, pp.2673–2680

Alvarez,G. & Li, S. (2006). Some Basic Cryptographic Requirements for Chaos-Based Cryptosystems, *Int. J. of Bifurcation and Chaos*, Vol.16, No.8, pp.2129-2151

Cuomo,K.M. & Oppenheim,A.V. (1993). Synchronization of Lorenz-Based Chaotic Circuits with Applications to Communications, *IEEE Trans. Circuits Syst. I*, Vol.40, pp.626-633

Dedieu,H. & Ogorzalek,M.J. (1997). Identifiability and Identification of Chaotic Systems Based on Adaptive Synchronization, *IEEE Trans. Circuits Syst. I*, Vol.44, pp.948-962

Doyle,J.C.; Glover,K.; Khargonekar,P.P. & Francis,B. A. (1989). State-Space Solutions to Standard H_2 and H_∞ Control Problems, *IEEE Trans. Automat. Contr.*, Vol.34, No.8, pp.831-846

Fradkov,A.L. & Markov,A.Y. (1997). Adaptive Synchronization of Chaotic Systems Based on Speed Gradient Method and Passification, *IEEE Trans. Circuits Syst. I*, Vol.44, No.10, pp.905–912.

Fradkov,A.L., Nijmeijer,H., & Markov,A.Y. (2000). Adaptive Observer-Based Synchronization for Communication, *Int. J. of Bifurcation and Chaos*, Vol.10. No.12, pp.2807-2813

Grassi,G. & Mascolo,S. (1999). A System Theory Approach for Designing Cryptosystems Based on Hyperchaos, *IEEE Trans. Circuits Syst. I*, Vol.46, No.9, pp.1135-1138

Guojie,H. Zhengjin,F., & Ruiling,M. (2003). Chosen Cipher Attack on Chaos Communication Based on Chaotic Synchronization, *IEEE Trans. Circuits Syst. I*, Vol.50, No.2, pp.275-279

Kocarev,L. (2001). Chaos-Based Cryptography: a Brief Overview, *IEEE Circuits and Systems Magazine*, Vol.1, No.3, pp.6-21

Liao,T.L. & Huang,N.S. (1999). An Observer-Based Approach for Chaotic Synchronization with Applications to Secure Communications, *IEEE Trans. Circuits Syst. I*, Vol.46, No.9, pp.1144-1149

Matsuo,T. & Nakano,K. (1998). Robust Stabilization of Closed-Loop Systems by PID+Q Controller, *Int. J. of Control*, Vol.70, No.4, pp.631-650

Matsuo,T., Suemitsu,H., & Nakano,K. (2004). Zeros and Relative Degree Assignments of Adaptive Chaotic Communication Systems, *Int.J. of Bifurcation and Chaos*, Vol.14, No.12, pp.4233-4247

Matsuo,T.; Toshimitsu,Y.; & Suemitsu,H. (2008). H_∞-Synchronizer for Chaotic Communication Systems, *Int.J. of Bifurcation and Chaos* Vol.18, No.4, pp.1175-1187

Millérioux,G.; Amigó,J. M. & Daafouz,J. (2008). A Connection between Chaotic and Conventional Cryptography, *IEEE Trans. on CAS–I*, Vol.55, No.6, pp.1695-1703

Nomura,T.; Irie,T.; Suemitsu,H. & Matsuo,T. (2011). Stochastic Security Testing for Chaotic Communication Systems against Error Function Attack, *IEEJ Trans. on Electrical and Electronic Engineering*, Vol.6, No.5, in press

Parker,A.T. & Short,K.M. (2001). Reconstructing the keystream from a chaotic encryption scheme, *IEEE Trans. on CAS–I*, Vol.48, No.5 pp.624-630

Short,K.M. (1994). Steps toward unmasking secure communications, *Int. J. Bifurcation and Chaos* Vol.4, No.44, pp.959-977

Short,K.M. (1996). Unmasking a modulated chaotic communications scheme, *Int. J. Bifurcation and Chaos*, Vol.6-, No.2, pp.367-375

Suykens,J.A.K.; Vandewalle,J. & Chua, L.O. (1997a). Nonlinear H_∞ Synchronization of Chaotic Lur'e Systems, *Int.J. of Bifurcation and Chaos*, Vol.7, No.6, pp.1323-1335

Suykens, J.A.K.; Curran, P.F.; Vandewalle, J. & Chua, L.O. (1997b). Robust Nonlinear H_∞ Synchronization of Chaotic Lur'e Systems, *IEEE Trans. Circuits Syst. I*, Vol.44, No.10, pp.891-904

Wang,X; Zhan,M.; Lai,C.-H. & Gang,H. (2004). Error Function Attack of Chaos Synchronization Based on Encryption Schemes, *Chaos*, Vol.14, No.1, pp.128-137

Yang,T. & Chua,L.O. (1997a). Impulsive Control and Synchronization of Nonlinear Dynamical Systems and Application to Secure Communication, *Int. J. of Bifurcation and Chaos*, Vol.7, No.3, pp.645-664

Yang,T.; Wu,C.W. & Chua,L.O. (1997b). Cryptography Based on Chaotic Systems, *IEEE Trans. Circuits Syst. I*, Vol.44, pp.469-472

Yang,T. (2004). A Sruvey of Chaotic Secure Communication Systems, *Int.J. of Comput. Cogn.*, Vol.2, No,2, pp.81-130

Zhou,J.; Pei,W.; Huang,J.; Song,A. & He,Z. (2005). Differential-like Chosen Cipher Attack on A Spatiotemporally Chaotic Cryptosystem, nlin.CD/0506026

Permissions

The contributors of this book come from diverse backgrounds, making this book a truly international effort. This book will bring forth new frontiers with its revolutionizing research information and detailed analysis of the nascent developments around the world.

We would like to thank Andrzej Bartoszewicz, for lending his expertise to make the book truly unique. He has played a crucial role in the development of this book. Without his invaluable contribution this book wouldn't have been possible. He has made vital efforts to compile up to date information on the varied aspects of this subject to make this book a valuable addition to the collection of many professionals and students.

This book was conceptualized with the vision of imparting up-to-date information and advanced data in this field. To ensure the same, a matchless editorial board was set up. Every individual on the board went through rigorous rounds of assessment to prove their worth. After which they invested a large part of their time researching and compiling the most relevant data for our readers. Conferences and sessions were held from time to time between the editorial board and the contributing authors to present the data in the most comprehensible form. The editorial team has worked tirelessly to provide valuable and valid information to help people across the globe.

Every chapter published in this book has been scrutinized by our experts. Their significance has been extensively debated. The topics covered herein carry significant findings which will fuel the growth of the discipline. They may even be implemented as practical applications or may be referred to as a beginning point for another development. Chapters in this book were first published by InTech; hereby published with permission under the Creative Commons Attribution License or equivalent.

The editorial board has been involved in producing this book since its inception. They have spent rigorous hours researching and exploring the diverse topics which have resulted in the successful publishing of this book. They have passed on their knowledge of decades through this book. To expedite this challenging task, the publisher supported the team at every step. A small team of assistant editors was also appointed to further simplify the editing procedure and attain best results for the readers.

Our editorial team has been hand-picked from every corner of the world. Their multi-ethnicity adds dynamic inputs to the discussions which result in innovative outcomes. These outcomes are then further discussed with the researchers and contributors who give their valuable feedback and opinion regarding the same. The feedback is then collaborated with the researches and they are edited in a comprehensive manner to aid the understanding of the subject.

Apart from the editorial board, the designing team has also invested a significant amount of their time in understanding the subject and creating the most relevant covers. They scrutinized every image to scout for the most suitable representation of the subject and create an appropriate cover for the book.

The publishing team has been involved in this book since its early stages. They were actively engaged in every process, be it collecting the data, connecting with the contributors or procuring relevant information. The team has been an ardent support to the editorial, designing and production team. Their endless efforts to recruit the best for this project, has resulted in the accomplishment of this book. They are a veteran in the field of academics and their pool of knowledge is as vast as their experience in printing. Their expertise and guidance has proved useful at every step. Their uncompromising quality standards have made this book an exceptional effort. Their encouragement from time to time has been an inspiration for everyone.

The publisher and the editorial board hope that this book will prove to be a valuable piece of knowledge for researchers, students, practitioners and scholars across the globe.

List of Contributors

Nelson Aros Oñate
Departamento de Ingeniería Eléctrica, Facultad de Ingeniería, Universidad de La Frontera, Temuco, Chile

Graciela Suarez Segali
Departamento de Ingeniería Química, Facultad de Ingeniería, Universidad Nacional de San Juan, San Juan, Argentina

V. Pavan Kumar Malladi
Department of Chemical Engineering, National Institute of Technology Calicut, Kozhikode, India

Nitin Kaistha
Department of Chemical Engineering, Indian Institute of Technology Kanpur, Kanpur, India

Kiyanoosh Razzaghi and Farhad Shahraki
Department of Chemical Engineering, University of Sistan and Baluchestan, Zahedan, Iran

Chen He
State Power Economic Research Institute, State Grid Corporation of China, China

Bai Hong
China Electric Power Research Institute, China

Toru Eguchi, Takaaki Sekiai, Naohiro Kusumi, Akihiro Yamada, Satoru Shimizu and Masayuki Fukai
Hitachi Ltd., Japan

Wojciech Grega
Department of Automatics, AGH University of Science and Technology, Poland

Tetsuo Shiotsuki
Tokyo Denki University, Japan

Armando A. Rodriguez
Electrical Engineering, Ira A. Fulton School of Engineering, Arizona State University, USA

Jeffrey J. Dickeson
Electrical Engineering, Ira A. Fulton School of Engineering, Arizona State University, USA

John M. Anderies
School of Human Evolution and Social Change, School of Sustainability, Arizona State University, USA

Oguzhan Cifdaloz
ASELSAN, Inc. Microelectronics, Guidance and Electro-Optics Division, Turkey
Arizona State University, USA

Shengyong Wang, Song Foh Chew and Mark Lawley
University of Akron, Southern Illinois University Edwardsville, and Purdue University, USA

Takami Matsuo, Yusuke Totoki and Haruo Suemitsu
Oita University, Dannoharu, Oita, Japan

Printed in the USA
CPSIA information can be obtained
at www.ICGtesting.com
JSHW011424221024
72173JS00004B/668